THE DISCIPLINE
OF
LEISURE

SOCIAL IDENTITIES

General Editors: Shirley Ardener, Tamara Dragadze and Jonathan Webber

Based on a prominent Oxford University seminar founded over two decades ago by the social anthropologist Edwin Ardener, this series focuses on the ethnic, historical, religious, and other elements of culture that give rise to a social sense of belonging, enabling individuals and groups to find meaning both in their own social identities and in what differentiates them from others. Each volume is based on one specific theme that brings together contemporary material from a variety of cultures.

Volume 1
Changing Sex and Bending Gender
Alison Shaw and Shirley Ardener

Volume 2
Medical Identities: Healing, Well-Being and Personhood
Kent Maynard

Volume 3
**Professional Identities: Policy and Practice
in Business and Bureaucracy**
Shirley Ardener and Fiona Moore

Volume 4
**The Discipline of Leisure:
Embodying Cultures of 'Recreation'**
Simon Coleman and Tamara Kohn

Volume 5
**Where Humans and Spirits Meet: The Politics of Rituals
and Identified Spirits in Zanzibar**
Kjersti Larsen

THE DISCIPLINE OF LEISURE

EMBODYING CULTURES OF 'RECREATION'

Edited by
Simon Coleman and Tamara Kohn

Berghahn Books
New York • Oxford

First published in 2007 by
Berghahn Books
www.berghahnbooks.com

Tα-P

Publication of this work was assisted by a publication
grant from the University of Melbourne.

Library of Congress Cataloging-in-Publication Data
The discipline of leisure : embodying cultures of 'recreation' / edited by Simon
Coleman and Tamara Kohn.
      p. cm. -- (Social identities)
  Includes bibliographical references and index.
  ISBN 978-1-84545-372-5 (hardback : alk. paper)
  1. Leisure--Social aspects. 2. Recreation--Social aspects. I. Coleman, Simon,
1963- II. Kohn, Tamara.

  GV14.45.D57 2007
  306.4'812--dc22

                          2007043685

British Library Cataloguing in Publication Data

A catalogue record for this book is available from the British Library

Printed in the United States on acid-free paper.

ISBN: 978-1-84545-372-5 (hardback)

CONTENTS

1 The Discipline of Leisure: Taking Play Seriously   1
Simon Coleman and Tamara Kohn

PART I: **SURVEYING THE SELF**

2 Bob, Hospital Bodybuilder: The Integrity of the Body,
the Transitiveness of 'Work' and 'Leisure'   23
Nigel Rapport

3 Of Metaphors and Muscles: Protestant 'Play' in the Disciplining
of the Self   39
Simon Coleman

PART II: **TEMPORALITIES OF LEISURE**

4 An Adventure Tourist Experience   57
Maurice J. Kane and Hazel Tucker

5 Reframing Place, Time and Experience: Leisure and
Illusion in Mallorca   73
Jacqueline Waldren

PART III: ENACTING NATIONALITY

6 Animal and Human Bodies in the Landscapes of
English Foxhunting   91
Garry Marvin

7 Playing Like Canadians: Improvising Nation and Identity
through Sport   109
Noel Dyck

8 A Relaxed State of Affairs?: On Leisure, Tourism, and
Cuban Identity   127
Thomas F. Carter

PART IV: TRANSCENDING THE NATION

9 Staged Discipline as Leisure: Notes on Colonial Sociability in Cairo   149
Petra Kuppinger

10 Bowing onto the Mat: Discourses of Change through Martial Arts
Practice   171
Tamara Kohn

Notes on Contributors   187

Index   189

1

THE DISCIPLINE OF LEISURE: TAKING PLAY SERIOUSLY

Simon Coleman and Tamara Kohn

Playing for Real

A few years ago, one of us came upon on a small article in the Sunday magazine of a British newspaper.[1] The title of the piece was 'Go See a Night of Leisure' and it referred to a forthcoming debate at the Victoria and Albert Museum on what makes British people relax. The debate was to be presented by Tom Hodgkinson, editor of a journal splendidly called *The Idler*, and what really caught the attention was a distinction Hodgkinson wanted to make between two ways of having a good time: *pleasure*, he claimed, involved drugs and drink (and, we might assume, rock and roll); *leisure*, on the other hand, he saw as a more disciplined, sanctioned form of fun – no drugs, and precious little drink.

The title of our book suggests that Hodgkinson may have been on to something. Pleasure and leisure, despite being virtual homonyms, can reveal worlds of difference in their experience and implementation. The former is a state of mind or body that has been achieved, however briefly; but the latter suggests more of a *temporal* state, a *potentiality* for action of whatever sort. In addition, they often relate to the world(s) of work in radically dissimilar ways: while we presumably hope that pleasure can occasionally be obtained from our labours, moments of leisure snatched from the working day are often likely to induce feelings of guilt. However, this volume is dedicated to exploring some of the blurred boundaries and ambiguities that emerge when we bring leisure and work together in our ethnographic purview. We accept that the two are often separated in ideologically charged ways, but we wish to juxtapose such ideologies with practices that tell a rather different story. In the process, we hope to uncover ethnographic areas that have been of increasing interest to anthropology in recent years, but which remain – for reasons we shall discuss – relatively unexamined compared to other aspects of social and cultural life, and certainly in relation to their public prominence. While much has been written about changing practices of work in post-industrial contexts and the impact such economic transformations have had on identity, constructions of locality and understandings of space and time, we believe that more ethnographic research is needed on contemporary leisure as a site of production as well as consumption, a form of remaking the self and of associated frameworks of sociality.

The close focus afforded by an ethnographic perspective is particularly well-suited to exploring the ambiguities inherent in the interplays between leisure and other activities. It is also an ideal methodological tool for examining the meanings and experiences of embodiment and a central concern of this book will be the body as a site of identity formation and disciplined 'recreation' of the self. Indeed, much of our ethnographic focus is on sport and related activities rather than on, say, the arts. Most contributors use accounts of sporting or sports-related activity as ethnographic lenses through which to explore how selves can be remade in physical activities that simultaneously deflect and reflect the rigours of modernity, providing both apparent escape from, and pathways back to, anxieties about the effective deployment and deportment of the body. Furthermore, not only does sport complicate our ideas of escape and discipline, it also forces us to look at how different leisure activities may relate to each other in patterns of distinction or complementarity. For instance, as we shall see below, Kohn's aikido practitioners seek the pub as a refuge from the mat, whereas Rapport's bodybuilder finds that even away from the gym there is little escape from the rigours of the various disciplines to which he subordinates his body. Both cases explore the meanings of sporting activity for informants in the context of other aspects of their lives, and this strategy is surely one of the strengths of an ethnographic approach.

We see sport as a genre of leisure, therefore, and one that highlights issues of disciplining the body in powerful ways. Our approach necessarily overlaps with considerations of play, and in particular the extent to which it can or cannot be said to exclude instrumentality in its expression (see e.g. Lindquist 2001). We examine the objectification of the body in communities of practice that often transcend particular localities and temporalities, resulting in negotiations over correct etiquette and the meanings of tradition. Forms of bodily transformation are analysed not only as means of enacting (and contesting) identities, but also as complex mediators between contemporary ideologies of freedom, choice and (self-)control. In the rest of this introduction, we discuss the specific contributions of our authors before moving to a more general consideration of the benefits to be gained from an exploration of the disciplinary dimensions of leisure, and in particular sport.

The Volume

The chapters of our volume range geographically from Cairo to Sweden, North America to New Zealand; one (Kuppinger's) is predominantly historical, and others are mixed or contemporary; some share individual informants' voices and others analyse communal experiences of practice, but all are based on contexts of so-called modernity or encounters with it. Numerous resonances across case studies exist, but we have arranged papers to suggest forms of internal dialogue within the text.

The first two, by Rapport and Coleman respectively, examine the complexities of self-realisation through disciplining the body, not least through the physical experience, or metaphorical appropriation, of bodybuilding. In this section of the volume we are invited to compare secular and sacred takes on these themes. Rapport's chapter is based on a case study of 'Bob', a porter in a Scottish hospital. As Bob speaks to Rapport and reflects upon his time in and outside of the hospital, it becomes clear that the boundaries between the hospital and the outside world, and between the work environment and the time and space of recreation and 'leisure' beyond it, are routinely permeated by Bob's actions and intentions. Bob's body can be seen as a project of his personal development, a manifestation of his being and becoming, as he encounters the challenges and disciplines of all aspects of his life; but his project also entails its own limits, as Bob is engaged in self-monitoring of bodily progress and even damage.

Coleman, meanwhile, explores some of the implications of the term 'muscular Christianity', as used from the nineteenth century until the present. He notes how the term and its associated ideologies of patriotism and morality have been exported from the U.K. to the U.S. and beyond, and blended with various forms of mission, millenarianism and positive thinking. This broader historical survey is complemented by an ethnographic exploration of sporting practices and narratives as they are manifested within 'Health and Wealth' congregations in the U.S. and Sweden. Sport is shown to feed into a very wide range of disciplinary practices, both through its material technologies of the body and through the metaphors it helps to construct in articulating charismatic Protestant discourses of self-surveillance. If Rapport's point is that Bob's body moves between the institutional spheres of his life, providing them with a degree of 'integrity', Coleman explores some of the ways in which evangelicals deploy sporting metaphors to *assert* the resonances between their religion and other aspects of life, so that the permeation of institutions becomes a performative – and performed – claim about the ubiquitous relevance and effectiveness of faith.

Part II moves into areas more readily associated with tourism, but again the two chapters contrast significantly along a significant dimension: that of the temporalities associated with leisure. Kane and Tucker explore the experiences of recreational tourists on an adventure white-water kayaking tour, tracing the development of a 'short-lived society' of people engaged in 'serious leisure', involving kayaking on New Zealand's helicopter-only accessed rivers. Such tours affirm physical ability, dedication and discipline, even as the experience of being a 'tourist' far from home is simultaneously constructed as freedom and play. Waldren's piece frames place, time and experience rather differently, examining long-term expatriate appropriations of Mallorca (through art, yoga, sex, and so on) alongside more conventional touristic visits. Behind the apparently idyllic physical landscape of the island lies a more complex social landscape, in which providers and consumers of leisure compete to make their practices, visions and ideologies effectively transform one another. Expatriates have established lifestyles that transcend locality and temporalities, fostering transnational identities and cultural diversities, while 'locals' re-design landscapes, tradition and heritage in the hopes of attracting the leisured to experience the location and objectification of the body in an idyllic setting.

The spatial framework of leisure becomes the nation, albeit configured in radically different ways, in Part III, as we encounter contributions that involve the production and performance of charged landscapes through bodily (including visual) practices. Marvin explores a sport that has been banned in England and Wales since the time of his writing: fox-hunting with hounds and horses.[2] He is interested less in the fact that animals are killed and more in *how* these deaths are brought about, how the contest is enacted. The participants in foxhunting regard it as a 'country sport' but also pay close attention to its ritual and ceremonial nature, and central to the event is a contest between humans and foxes mediated through relationships with other animals – hounds and horses – as well as through an engagement with the challenges of the landscape. Numerous forms of disciplining are occurring here: of animals by humans, humans by animals, in the contest of a performance space, the English countryside, that is reenacted and reproduced as it is traversed by human and non-human participants.

While the politics of fox-hunting involves the internal defence of what is seen as a form of quintessential Englishness against the worst excesses of liberal, urban (post)modernity, we encounter a rather different discourse of engaging with nationality in Dyck's contribution relating to sport and the disciplining of immigrant identities in Canada. Dyck shows us further ambiguities associated with play. On the one hand he describes a positive view of sport that sees it as an effective vehicle for fostering the social and cultural integration of immigrants and their children in community athletic activities; on the other, there is revealed a decidedly more problematic view of the ideological nexus between immigration, ideas of integration and sport, since the expectation that immigrants can and should join in the sporting activities preferred by other Canadians may be held with an intensity that readily transgresses the line between hospitality and the demand for assimilation. Thus the bodies of immigrant children comprise contested territory between sports-minded Canadians and immigrant parents, and we are reminded again of the role of sport in the construction of personhood.

Marvin's piece involves the (relatively) disciplined traversing of a (relatively) unpredictable territory; Dyck's contribution explores the encounter between national identities; these themes of space and identity are taken up in different ways by Carter's analysis of leisure, tourism and sport spectatorship in Cuba. As in Dyck's chapter, the role of the state is of explicit importance here, but it is one of a very different complexion to that of Canada. Carter compares the 'selling' of Cuba to foreign tourists with the experiences of Cuban baseball fans in the *Estadio Latinoamericano*, the national baseball stadium, and in the process he re-explores the the complexities of leisure being predicated upon notions of conspicuous consumption and capitalist production. Such an aim echoes Waldren's analysis of the 'selling' of Mallorca. Carter's analysis can also be compared with Springwood's work (e.g. 2002) on Japanese objectification of the U.S. through images and practices of baseball. However, as an explicitly modernist critique of Western capitalism, Cuban socialism orders time, space, and production in rather different patterns to those evident in Japan or Mallorca. With international tourism so important to the country's currency earnings, the contradictions between socialist ideology, capitalist leisure, foreigners' active consumption and locals' relaxation are striking. These contradictions come to the fore in the simple pursuit of attending a baseball game. Thousands of Cubans are juxtaposed with a handful of foreigner tourists, and the spatial, social and ideological separation between these two groups becomes evident, framed within the space and time of the game.

Finally, the two chapters in Part IV explore the choreography of explicitly transnational encounters, but our juxtapositioning of the two again reveals a vast gulf in the ideologies and aims that are put on display. Kuppinger's account of social life in colonial Cairo seems to take us far from a focus on sport, but it retains our interest in the embodiment of discipline through juxtapositions of labour with leisure. Kuppinger shows how such activities as dinner parties, afternoon teas and horse races were meticulously planned and orchestrated by colonisers, chosen in order to create, maintain and enhance social distinctions. In addition to recreating colonial social hierarchies, the events also served the purpose of illustrating in 'elegant' and subtle manners colonial dominance over the colonised, particularly in face-to-face interactions where local workers were made to wear costumes/uniforms and compelled to act out scripts written in minute detail by the colonizer. Kohn, by contrast, illustrates how a disciplined practice, that of the Japanese martial art of aikido, can be opened out to a potentially global constituency. Aikido places of practice now exist in locations across the globe, and over the past forty years they have generated thousands of highly trained aikido practitioners and instructors who teach the art to students, who in turn describe their engagement in many ways. Aikidoists' stories of personal discovery suggest that the workplace and home are often conceived of as tangential and relatively stagnant in 'personal development' terms when compared to the place of aikido practice; 'the mat'. On the mat, time that is supposedly free for leisure becomes filled with committed work on disciplining the body. As with Zarrilli's account of the Indian martial art of *kalarippayatu* (1995), we see how optation shades into discipline in ways that have an impact on identity within, but also beyond, the time devoted to the activity itself.

These chapters could of course have been juxtaposed in different ways, highlighting other cross-cutting themes. For instance, we can look again at the complex connections between obligation and optionality. Kohn shows how aikido training is initially chosen by freewill but then becomes more laborious as further commitment is required; but such commitment does not come from an explicit chain of command, since it emerges more subtly as self-understanding is more and more constructed, apparently produced, through aikido. Rapport's friend, Bob the bodybuilder, meanwhile, depends for his ambiguous state precisely on the ability to suspend himself between at least two disciplinary apparatuses, the hospital and the gym. Incidentally it seems a tragic irony that he ends up being incarcerated in an even more total institution, that of a prison. But the important point here is that both martial arts specialists and bodybuilders appear to need leisure *from* their leisure, further options for relaxation in relation to a chosen activity that is also a form of obligation; aikido enthusiasts chat in the pub – perhaps the superfluity of words spoken over the beer makes up for the relative silences on the mat; Bob indulges himself physically in ways that are sometimes as exaggerated as the disciplines of weightlifting itself (see Harré 1989).

Embodiment of course recurs in numerous ways throughout the volume. Recall that Terence Turner (1994: 36) claims that Foucault's body has no flesh since it is begotten out of discourse by power. Whether or not Turner is fully correct, one cannot accuse our contributors of a similar sin of omission: we have bodybuilders, children's bodies, martial arts bodies, and, excusing the pun, dogsbodies in abundance (though Marvin's point is partly that the latter are *hound*s, and not just normal canines). Kohn's aikido practitioners ostensibly work on a mat but their aches and exercises permeate into a wider social and work world; things are 'taken away' from the mat, as principles of movement inform other parts of one's life, thus becoming reinforced through their easy and often wordless diffusion into new spheres. Coleman's piece similarly juxtaposes ritual, sport and the everyday life of evangelicals in exploring the resonances and mutual reinforcements between these three embodied (as well as highly 'narrativised') activities. In Rapport's chapter, Bob's built-up body appears to retain its integrity and the signs of his project of personal development across the boundaries that usually divide the gym, the hospital and the outside world. If in Kohn's and Coleman's cases body work leads into a new kind of sociality, a potentially transnational corps of practitioners who maintain nested identities reaching from the personal to the global, in Bob's case his project leads rather more often into forms of social separation. He struggles rather ambivalently to remove himself from being encompassed by institutions and relationships, into a situation where bodybuilding gives him access to a home that compasses 'elsewhere'. Rapport therefore shows how Bob is constantly on the move between institutional and/or discursive fixities.

This sense that chapters give of forms of disciplined physicality that permeate different social contexts recalls Thomas Csordas's more overtly phenomenological approach to embodiment. Discussing American Catholic charismatics, Csordas (1997: 68ff) writes of the dangers of confining analysis of what he calls processes of self-objectification to events of ritual performance. The charismatic habitus inhabits space, projects the self into the world, as part of the ritualisation of life. Bodily performances in church bleed over into spheres of everyday life, producing a kind of dialectic between performance events and non-ritual interaction, and in their different ways Coleman, Rapport and Kohn reveal a similar sort of process.

Evident in some chapters are forms of deterritorialisation. In Rapport's case this largely means that Bob's body is the vehicle for a sense of self that implies personal capacities that transcend, even challenge, the assumptions, spaces and values of any given institution. In Kohn's chapter locality itself is transformed through a mat that gives access to a global community of practice – in her view, locality becomes resituated not in a place but in the body. Her depiction of aikido again recalls Zarrilli's (1995) tracing of the emergence of *kalarippayatu* into public spaces suitable for a transnational, self-defence paradigm that is also a Foucauldian technology of the body. But aikido, *kalarippayatu* and even bodybuilding contrast rather beautifully with Garry Marvin's example of bodies – which admittedly belong to various species – moving through the English landscape. Marvin's bodies are in motion, but they are constrained by forms of etiquette that produce not only a locally but also a nationally resonant notion of landscape. A farmer can kill a fox with a gun, but that is not sport and it is not really disciplined; when humans and their domesticated animals loudly and ostentatiously chase a wild but tricksterish fox around the countryside they are not merely performing sport, they are also surely appropriating landscape and territory – beating a certain kind of bounds. The political tensions over such appropriation of land are revealed through the contrast between the need for riders to be considerate when traversing others' land and the total freedom of the wild fox, who is given license to guide the hunt until its extinction or disappearance. More broadly, England itself is subject to an 'alternative' form of mapping, that of the Hunt counties, which create forms of physical as well as social belonging in the landscape.

Foxhunting provides a fascinating overlay of play and formal etiquette on to agricultural land that is otherwise (at other times) the location for hard work in the production of food. The Mallorca described by Waldren similarly provides a context for work and play to inhabit the same stage, not least as time and space come to have different meanings for locals and foreigners: what seems like an obligatory responsibility for one group (such as picking fruit) is a selected pastime for another. In an admittedly distant way, both of these cases point to a process described by Rojek (1989: 5) in the organisation of 'modern' leisure: the conversion of old work-spaces into new leisure spaces, though of course foxhunting itself has been practised for centuries.

Our points about space and place can be compared with Bale's cultural geographical approach to landscape, sport and modernity (2002), and more particularly his thesis that sports have emerged as highly rationalised representations of the modern, possessing the potential to eliminate regional differences as a result of creating rule-bound, ordered, enclosed and predictably segmented forms of landscape. For Bale (ibid.: 8), the spatial character of the globally applied rules of sport facilitates 'body-trading' (Shilling 1993: 20), encouraging 'sameness' wherever it might be. The placelessness thus produced provides a curious parallel with Augé's (1995) notion of 'non-places' as contexts of seemingly neutral social exchange, but in this volume we see how part of the interest of sports arenas lies in the intensification of the gaze they produce, as evident in Carter's chapter on Cuba and his description of how baseball fans create an enclosed society of the spectacle. The seeming 'neutrality' and fixity of a sporting arena such as that provided for baseball allows for focus on the movements of the players (and, in some cases, spectators) themselves in a way that may also be mediated by television. Indeed, Carter points early on in his chapter to possible resonances between the sporting and the sexual gaze in the cauldron of the stadium.

Incidentally, the theme of the transferability or otherwise of the location of action may remind British readers of annual discussions in the media of the continued viability of grass as a surface for play at Wimbledon Tennis Club – discussions that in effect invoke contrasts between lived-in place and generic space. Unlike clay or concrete, grass provides a growing, unpredictable medium for the tennis ball, a stubbornly indisciplined provider of randomness in 'bounce' that embodies the particularities of court, time and weather. 'Wimbledon' as globally renowned tournament can therefore retain its self-consciously eccentric Englishness in part through expressing an indexical relationship to a particular sporting arena, just as foxhunters may celebrate locality through the deployment of arenas of action that are known yet unpredictable.

If the spatial construction of arenas of practice provides varying interchanges between fixity and movement, placelessness and uniqueness, so there is a more general balance to be struck between freedom and constraint in the experience of sports – especially those that include an element of danger.[3] Thus Tucker and Kane describe the negotiations that kayaking provokes between extreme adventure and package tourism. As revealed in participants' narratives, kayaking is valued in part because of the perilous situations it produces, but such peril is itself framed – and tamed – through the self-disciplined activities of the skilled practitioner.[4] In foxhunting, the danger is not only to the fox: just as etiquette covers the niceties of social intercourse so the skills of the riders ensure safe passage over testing terrain. Both activities reveal as well the importance of unpredictability of outcome in these cases to the cultivation of a sense of freedom. In contrast, other chapters are more concerned to trace subtexts of control that are combined with ambiguous forms of social 'integration'. Dyck's contribution examines how involvement with sport may be marshalled to bring together the often problematic identities of 'Canadian' and 'immigrant'. In the phrase 'playing like Canadians' we can see how the mimetic can easily seem to shade into the performative, as 'playing' turns ideally (in the views of some) into 'becoming', even though Dyck provides important nuance to his argument by indicating the syncretic and improvisational possibilities afforded by sport – possibilities that reach far beyond stark dichotomies of sport as *either* promoting *or* resisting integration.

Dyck's chapter describes the results of movement from non-Western into Western contexts, while Kuppinger provides an historical account of the opposite process, as forms of 'integration' are shown to reinforce the colonial project in Egypt. However, in both cases we see how disciplined physical performances on the part of a 'dangerous' group (immigrants and Egyptian locals respectively) can be interpreted by the politically dominant as signifiers of their own security. The perceived perils here are not produced by sporting participation per se, but are rather the result of political and cultural 'dislocation'. Kuppinger's piece is of course not predominantly about sport, but it *is* about the controlled deployment of bodies and the disciplinary (in the Foucauldian sense) dimensions of forms of 'doing' and 'viewing'. As Kuppinger points out, whereas other chapters of the volume examine circumstances where individuals discipline themselves in order to enhance their leisure, in the case of colonial servants we see how people were forced, largely against their own will, into rigorously prescribed movements for the sake of others' recreation.

Disciplinary Dimensions

Our book, then, is about the ambiguities that exist in the theoretical and ethnographic spaces that exist between leisure and work. The 'discipline *of* leisure' can suggest at least three different meanings, and the contributions to this volume, at various points, can be seen to be invoking and analysing each one:

1. Most obviously, there is the assertion – frequently made in existing literatures – that leisure is a site of release, a form of freedom that is seen to require discipline in order to keep it under control, or at least boundaries that can contain it and give it meaning.

2. We also show, however, that forms of leisure such as sport entail their own forms of discipline and practice, and so should not be seen purely as the objects or mere expressions of broader economic and political forces.

3. Finally, we advocate the need for more attention to be paid to leisure by our own discipline, indicating that the anthropology of leisure is a productive path for researchers to follow.

(1) Leisure as Release

By far the most scholarly attention has so far been paid to the first of our 'dimensions'. Varieties of this argument often rely on the assertion of an inherent opposition between work and leisure, but only in certain contexts. Thus Victor Turner (1982; see also Dumazedier 1968; cf. Rojek 1989: 1) asserts that in societies where 'work' is less specialised, less associated with physical and temporal alienation from the domestic or kinship sphere, sharp demarcations between work and leisure simply do not exist. However, in industrial capitalism leisure time becomes associated with 'freedom from a whole heap of institutional obligations prescribed by the basic forms of ... technological and bureaucratic organization' and 'freedom to enter, even to generate new symbolic worlds of entertainment, sports, games, diversions of all kinds' (Turner 1982: 36–37). In effect, the genres of industrial leisure – theatre, poetry, film, art, religion, sport – are all said to gain significance out of self-conscious opposition to work. While they may certainly involve hard training, they provide vital compensation through optionality and spontaneity – what Elias and Dunning (1986; see Dunning and Rojek 1992: ii) called the 'quest for excitement', which was also subjected to a 'civilising' process. Turner's perspective not only provides a restatement of classic arguments associated more widely with notions of structure and anti-structure, but also a reassertion of the idea of modernity as constituted by separate spheres of action: leisure exists as non-work and non-utility (effortful, perhaps, but inherently enjoyable), in societies no longer governed by the inevitability of common obligation and engagement.

Yet, Turner himself notes (1982: 37) that work and leisure must inevitably interact even in the West, and that modes of work organisation can 'affect' leisure pursuits. There is now a wealth of writing that is precisely concerned with the 'penetration' of leisure by its – supposed – opposite. Of course, such work has its counterparts in older writings: there are for instance Simmel's analyses of the restlessness of modern subjectivity in the new industrial cities, or Veblen's discussions of the emergence of conspicuous consumption by the 'leisure class'. In more recent work, the emergence throughout the nineteenth century of new technologies and reductions in working hours has been seen as 'productive' of leisure as well as goods, alongside middle-class concerns that urban workers in the new cities required 'rational' recreation (Ladd and Mathison 1999: 213).[5] Games such as cricket and football were thus domesticated in Britain, forming part of the codified and choreographed public performances that constituted much of life in the Victorian nation state.[6]

Mangan (1988: 2) follows Hobsbawm's (1983: 298) assertion that sport could replace religion in the late nineteenth century as a means of promoting (often national, even nationalistic) cohesion, but one that also expressed and helped to constitute class divisions. Sport might thus provide catharsis – a potent combination of Turner's freedom *from* and *to* – but also civilisation of the body, much as Victorian school rooms educated increasing numbers of pupils even as they became means of physical confinement and mutual surveillance (Markus 1993). Sandiford's account of Victorian cricket notes that the hedonistic, 'pleasurable' diversions of the early industrial period, such as drinking and gambling, 'were seen by fun-hating factory owners and respectable religious bodies and individuals as distracting from the serious business of industrial labour or spiritual sobriety' (1994: 5).

Thus, as team games and other athletic pursuits were expanded, requiring disciplined preparation as well as play, providing spectacle as well as participation, efforts to control sports indicated their moral and cultural importance within public life. Indeed, evangelicals came to use cricket as a propaganda weapon after 1880 (ibid.: 36). At the end of the nineteenth century in Britain, the Rev. Thomas Waugh's *The Cricket Field of a Christian Life* presented the pitch as a kind of cosmological playground, with the Christian team battling (and batting) against Satan's devious and immoral bowlers.[7] More broadly, Clarke and Critcher (1985) conclude that British leisure was monitored by an institutional apparatus comprising magistrates, clergy, police, mill owners and poor law commissioners. Government fomented but also took control of the leisure explosion of the 1880s (there are echoes here of the state intervention described by Dyck and Carter in this volume), producing the public parks, libraries, municipal museums and baths that are still part of contemporary British urban landscapes. So for Clarke and Critcher leisure was made in the image of Victorian capitalism and of course has continued to expand in subsequent decades, as disposable incomes and 'free' time have increased, and tourism has become one of the largest industries in the world. Moreover, such state intervention has been echoed in other countries. For instance, Löfgren (1999: 271–273) notes that when the Social Democrats came to power in Sweden in the early 1930s leisure became a symbol of modernity, a tool to foster a new and classless breed of mobile citizens who would discard antiquated (and presumably unhealthy) routines, forging a new unity through community gymnastics and sports.

These kinds of interventionist approaches, as Lithman (2000: 164ff) points out with regard to children's recreation, start to raise existential questions about what constitutes a proper 'person' and how he or she might be constituted through social institutions and influences. Dyck (2000: 5) locates such a question in a fruitful comparative context in his reference to formalised archery contests among the Waiwai of southern Guyana and northern Brazil (studied by Mentore 2000). It appears that in this context the determination of winners is less significant than the placement of the hunter at the centre of the social gaze, and we should not allow the West's obsession with winning to cloud our perception that our own forms of recreation also invoke powerful forms of mutual and self-surveillance.

Hargreaves (1982: 9–10) emphasises the socially coercive character of sport in the West through reference to Althusser, whose theory of reproduction views sport as a cultural apparatus of the state and a structure in which capitalist ideology becomes a 'lived condition'. In this view, modern sport is fundamentally constituted by and promotes ideologies of individual competitiveness, chauvinism, nationalism and sexism (see also Hargreaves 1989).[8] Or, as Lithman (2000: 165) puts it, the neo-Marxist argument is that sport does not offer compensation for frustrations of alienated labour in capitalist society, but instead seduces both athlete and spectator into relations more authoritarian than the economic sphere itself.

We might see the Althusserian view as highly reductive in its focus on what are perceived to be the essentials of sporting (and other leisure) activities, but it highlights significant ways in which bodily practices engage with wider systems of power and authority, thus opening up a theme central to all of the papers in this volume. The point is relevant to activities beyond the state, of course, not least since sport and colonialism have so often been conjoined, as the Other is disciplined along with the Self (here, the obvious parallel is with Kuppinger's chapter). A recent analysis is provided by Bale's (2002) discussion of body culture and colonial representation in Rwanda. His argument is that the taking of control of Rwanda by European powers occurred in the same period as several 'body cultural' developments in Europe, including the gymnastics movement, bodybuilding, and the development of modern sports. The colonial project and sport were thus 'naturally' linked through a discourse that displayed infatuation with achievement and victory – indeed, a discourse of modernity. Such discourse may be powerfully applied in contemporary contexts. For example, Billig's 'Banal Nationalism' (1995) suggests how the imagery of sports pages can 'flag' a nationalist sentiment and 'winning' fervour that can be easily amplified and mobilized in other (e.g. war-related) contexts. Views on the relations of practice and identity such as those above are remarkably similar to debates over religious conversion, for instance van der Veer's (1996) volume on 'Conversion to Modernities', which traces the ways in which the globalisation of Christianity (of the kind promoted by the Christians described in this book by Coleman) has brought with it much wider moves in the direction of transformed (if complexly constituted) 'modern' imaginations, publics and conceptions of the self.

It may be that an advantage of sport over religion as an agent of socialisation has been its seemingly more optative character. Certainly, sport raises the question of self-surveillance as a powerful tool of control and bodily self-production, so that the apparently voluntary character of the activity may in fact augment its disciplinary force, as the participant willingly submits to the rules and etiquette of the game. Nowhere is this possibility more evident than in a practice discussed by two of the chapters in this volume (see Rapport and Coleman respectively), that of bodybuilding. Rapport's contribution in particular evokes some of the issues discussed by Mansfield and McGinn in their discussion of discourses surrounding bodybuilding and what, following Foucault, they refer to as 'the biopolitical realm' (1993: 51). The panoptic anthropometric disciplining of the muscular body is in some ways a paradigm of the forms of modernity already referred to, bringing together the rationalised objectification of the self, the commodification of human flesh and a combination of hyper-individualism with a subjection of the self to the appraising gaze of (often unknown) others.

Yet, such descriptions of control and social (re-)production (either self-administered or openly managed by the state) need also to include an account of the possibility of degrees of resistance on the part of those subject to the moral and physical disciplines of sport and its administration. For instance, in their depiction of the powerful institutional apparatus surrounding British leisure practices over the past century, Clarke and Critcher (1985) are careful to note the ways in which Workers' Educational Associations and Working Men's Clubs could provide alternative appropriations of leisure to those of the middle, southern classes. In 1888, the Football League began promoting a game that was based in the North and the Midlands for a quarter of a century until it emerged more strongly in London. More broadly, Bourdieu (e.g. 1978; see also Hargreaves 1982: 12–13) has provided an account of the sport and the habitus that encompasses mutually contradictory, class-specific tastes: the instrumental orientation of 'working class' sport leads to a valorisation of games demanding strength and endurance, whereas more privileged classes are said to regard the body as an end in itself for reasons of appearance or health, and thus to participate in running and other movement with no other aim than physical exercise. The significant point here, as Hargreaves (1982: 13) points out, is the way the field of sporting practices becomes a site of struggle over the definition of the legitimate body and the appropriate use of the body in sport – amateur vs professional, participant vs spectator, élite vs mass, even the ascetic versus the hedonistic. This struggle is well illustrated in Brownell's ethnographic study of the ideological and political positions of sporting practice or 'body culture' in socialist China (1995). She demonstrates how sporting events act as cultural displays of the legitimate body, moulded and monitored by the State in its attempts to define itself in a global context, while being simultaneously contested at local and national levels around issues including gender and history (ibid.). Likewise, the rich ethnographic account by Alter on Indian wrestling demonstrates quite clearly that the sport is experienced as a 'way of life' that is chosen and self-defining, rooted in the honing of particular skills, as well as being a mind/body practice that produces the moral qualities around which ideas about nation and world and utopic futures are imagined (1992).

Many of these themes that are introduced in the works above (including control and resistance, physicality and the gaze, the colonial and the modern), are powerfully explored in Appadurai's account of the decolonisation of cricket in India (1995). Appadurai notes the important role that cricket plays in the contemporary nation state – an object of patronage by Indian business corporations, a beneficiary of media support from government, and a major national passion in the four decades since Indian independence in 1947 (ibid.: 38–39). Historically, cricket provides a prototypical example of the alliance between empire-building and disciplinary practices, as it was seen (ibid.: 25ff.) as a public form that could introduce upper-class English ideas of sportsmanship, self-control and manliness to Indian populations, counteracting perceived tendencies towards Oriental effeminacy. Again, the discussion of colonial discipline echoes that of Kuppinger. However, the more recent appropriation of the game in India has taken it in new directions. Here, we point to the part of Appadurai's argument that shows how the game provides a bodily hexis, tying 'even the most rustic boy … at the level of language and the body to the world of high-powered cricket spectacles' (ibid.: 37). The Victorian moral integument of cricket has been rendered less relevant, as cricket becomes a form of agonistic play that not only links (the male) gender, the nation, fantasy and bodily excitement, but also embodies a hijacking of a former English habitus (ibid.: 44–46).

Appadurai's example shows the complexities of a sport's relationship to ideological hegemony, and the seemingly contradictory orientations that can result. Cricket in India both excludes (e.g. male from female) and includes (involving membership of the national imaginary); it invokes a Victorian colonial past but also subverts it, consciously or not; it requires extensive training of the body and yet provides access to its performances through granting – requiring – extensive spectatorship in some cases. A sport such as cricket, heavy with moral and historical valencies, can invoke freedom and discipline simultaneously because of the richness and ambiguity of its associations.

An ethnographic parallel is provided by Zarrilli's analysis of *kalarippayatu* (see above) – a practice that has taken the opposite ethnographic journey to cricket by emerging in India and then branching outwards. Zarrilli notes that 'the martial arts are techniques of bodily practice that allow an individual to gain agency or power *within certain specific contexts*' (1995: 189; italics in original). He shows how *kalarippayatu* can be seen as a Foucauldian technology of the self that contains some of the ambiguities we are referring to (ibid.: 209), between serving as a pathway to self-realisation and leading instead to self-domination. Indeed, the processes we are describing lead us back to colonialism but also to some much wider theoretical perspectives on social reproduction. In line with Jean Comaroff's (1985) remarks on cultural mediations among the colonised Tshidi of the South Africa – Botswana borderland, we emphasise the interplay between human action and constraint, while also arguing that dominance and subordination can be invoked in multiple ways within the same sport. In this book, we see further variations on this theme, with both evangelical Christians (Coleman) and participants in fox hunts (Marvin) producing forms of resistance against wider norms precisely *through* movement that contains strong elements of self-discipline.

(2) Leisure as 'Possessive' of Agency

We have explored the notion that leisure is 'disciplined' by wider forces, and argued for a nuanced approach to the meanings and directions of such disciplining. However, we need also to mention some wider concerns with this theoretical position, and here we come – more briefly – to a second sense of 'the discipline of leisure'. For us, the 'of' might refer more to a possessive sense than one indicating the direction of control; in other words, we need also to look at the specific practices and norms of leisure activities in their own right, without always assuming that the only relevant aspect of their operation is that they are subordinate to wider forms of authority and even hegemony. In theoretical terms, we need not always analyse leisure as purely epiphenomenal or anti-structural in relation to work.

The study of activities such as sport may therefore lead us into examining local understandings and experiences of embodiment, emotion, skill and aesthetics in ways that take us away from assumptions that the only thing of interest relating to sport is its connections with more 'serious' realms of analysis. A number of the chapters in this volume – for instance Marvin on the look and emotion of horse riding, Tucker and Kane on the experience of danger, Kohn on the feeling of becoming a skilled martial artist – invoke such themes without losing sight of other dimensions or contexts. Our argument here is not that sport or leisure can be seen as 'autonomous' realms of action. Such a view would fall into the structure/anti-structure dichotomies mentioned earlier, as well as failing to acknowledge the vital point that ideas of choice, flexibility and satisfaction must be interpreted in relation to wider social and discursive formations (Rojek 1995: 1). However, we do assert that it diminishes the study of leisure to view it only through lenses of dominance and submission. Indeed, we should not have to justify the study of such activities by saying that, despite their frivolous exterior, they are 'really' about other, more weighty matters.

In providing a strong ethnographic focus, most of the chapters in this volume begin by exploring individual sensations and expressions, feelings and ideas, framing the activities that in turn fill participants' lives in a variety of emically critical ways. Detailed descriptions of leisure practice are potentially very rich sources of material that can as easily support theoretical arguments about individual agency and identity as they can about the shared political structures that the individual encounters in a larger societal context. Alter's book, *The Wrestler's Body* (1992), is a perfect example of an ethnography that illustrates the relationships that exist between the agency of the individual wrestling body and the 'somatic' ideals that shape that body. The chapters in this volume often celebrate the power of leisure for leisure's sake, providing rich descriptions of the passionate somatic experiences of individuals. Jackson suggests that the world is 'something we do not simply live and reproduce in passivity, but actually produce and transform through praxis, creating a sense that life is worth living' (2005: xxii). The reader will discover that it certainly is a cause for celebration when you are deep in the moment on a wild kayaking adventure (Kane and Tucker), when you are out on the hunt (Marvin), disciplining your body on the 'mat' (Kohn) or in the gym (Rapport), or enjoying the idyllic landscape of a village in Mallorca (Waldren). Exploring the ability that individuals have within those joyous moments and their reflections upon them to produce and transform the socio-cultural contexts in which they are situated is a worthy, or indeed a 'serious' focus in the study of leisure.

(3) Leisure and the Academy

Concerns over the seriousness or otherwise of leisure and sport have probably contributed to the length of time it has taken for these themes to gain a profile in the social sciences – indeed, for academic disciplines *studying* leisure to develop. We might draw on an argument derived from Bourdieu's analysis of cultural capital and assert that middle class scholars have seen the value of analyses of, for instance, art, but not of sport. MacClancy (1996: 1) refers, as we have, to the influence of the belief that sports are separate from more 'important' aspects of the social world such as work, politics and economics. Such a view is of course ironic, given that much contemporary writing has, if anything, subsumed sport and other forms of leisure within theories associated with wider hegemonies and dominant institutional formations. Even more recently, Dyck and Archetti (2003: 6) note the reluctance in anthropology itself to give sustained attention to the study of games and sport. In their view, these products of modernity produce an asymmetry between winners and losers and thus invoke values of competitive, industrial societies that are often perceived to be outside the purview of ethnology. In a parallel point, Dunning (1986: 3) argues that 'the founding fathers' of the social sciences did not highlight sport because it was not seen to form a universal property of social systems worldwide.

Whatever we think of the assumptions behind the past neglect of sport, we can assert that anthropology now does not confine itself to the study of non-industrial societies; that the themes it raises in relation to embodiment, play, excitement and surveillance have universal resonance; and that we can hardly as a discipline avoid the study of competition. Moreover, as we explore in this volume, sport itself is a major global export, with such activities as football/soccer permeating even some of the 'remotest' of places. Migration and globalisation have, in effect, replaced overt processes of colonialism as vehicles for such transfers.

We do not claim to have covered all aspects of leisure in this introduction or in the book as a whole. Nor do we argue that anthropologists are the only social scientists equipped to study leisure – far from it. However, contributors aim to show the richness of sport and other forms of recreation as objects of study, and moreover as objects that need not be viewed through predictable and rigid theoretical lenses that oppose structure and anti-structure, work and leisure, obligation and optation. If 'all the world's a pitch' rather than a stage, we need to extend our ethnography into places where we can literally inhabit, and observe, fields of play.

Notes

1. *Observer Magazine* 18 November, 2001: 6.
2. The ban has been in place since February 2005.
3. Compare Lindquist's (2001: 15) discussion of two philosophical views of play: one, emerging from Aristotle and Plato, seeing play as rule-governed and civilising activity; the other, with origins in pre-Socratic thought and filtered through Schopenhauer and Nietzsche, perceiving it as a chaotic indetermination of forces, a manifestation of free will and potential creativity.
4. Studies of the relationship between chosen involvement in dangerous leisure activity and pleasure have been usefully reviewed in Lyng's social psychological analysis of voluntary risk taking or 'edgework' (1990). Drawing from studies of extreme sports enthusiasts, he demonstrates how the practice of highly skilled but dangerous leisure activity enhances feelings of self-determination, competence and at least an illusion of control in a potentially chaotic situation.
5. Behind such discussions flits the spirit of Max Weber, who highlighted the complex interplay between inner and outer signs of transcendence in the attempted mastery of both the self and the modern world.
6. Cashmore (1990: 79) discusses Elias's term 'sportization' – a description of the process by which precise and explicit rules governing contests came into being in the nineteenth century, to ensure equal chances for competitors.
7. Sandiford notes that Waugh adopted the Victorian habit of glorifying the bat as opposed to the ball, while also supporting the popular view that soccer led to too many emotional excesses.
8. Hargreaves (1982: 15) goes on to explore how the Gramscian concept of hegemony directs us to consider how sport is involved in the mediation of certain ideas and apparatuses, some of which become linked class interests and dominant groups, including mode of production, state, education, media, family, ethnic groups, sexual patterns and other cultural practices.

References

Alter, J. 1992. *The Wrestler's Body: Identity and Ideology in North India*, Berkeley: University of California Press.

Appadurai, A. 1995. 'Playing with Modernity: The Decolonization of Indian Cricket' in C. Breckenridge (ed.) *Consuming Modernity: Public Culture in a South Asian World*. Minneapolis/London: University of Minnesota Press, pp. 23–47.

Augé, M. 1995. *Non-Places: Introduction to an Anthropology of Supermodernity*. London: Verso.

Bale, J. 2002. *Imagined Olympians: Body Culture and Colonial Represnetation in Rwanda*. Minneapolis: University of Minnesota Press.

Billig, M. 1995. *Banal Nationalism*, London and New Delhi: Sage Publications.

Bourdieu, P. 1978. 'Sport and Social Class.' *Social Science Information* 17(6): 819–40.

Brownell, S. 1995. *Training the Body for China: Sports in the Moral Order of the People's Republic*, Chicago: The University of Chicago Press.

Cashmore, E. 1990. *Making Sense of Sports*, London: Routledge.

Clarke, J. and C. Critcher 1985. *The Devil Makes Work: Leisure in Capitalist Britain.* London: Macmillan.

Comaroff, J. 1985. *Body of Power, Spirit of Resistance: The Culture and History of a South African People.* Chicago: The University of Chicago Press.

Csordas, T. 1997. *Language, Charisma, and Creativity: The Ritual Life of a Religious Movement.* Berkeley: University of California Press.

Dumazedier, J. 1968. 'Leisure' in D. Sills (ed.) *Encyclopedia of the Social Sciences.* New York: Macmillan and Free Press, pp.248–53.

Dunning, E. 1986. 'Preface' in N. Elias and E. Dunning (eds) *Quest for Excitement: Sport and Leisure in the Civilising Process.* Oxford: Blackwell, pp.1–18.

Dunning, E. and C. Rojek 1992. 'Introduction: Sociological Approaches to the Study of Sport and Leisure' in E. Dunning and C. Rojek (eds) *Sport and Leisure in the Civilizing Process: Critique and Counter-Critique.* London: Macmillan, pp.xi–xix.

Dyck, N. ed. 2000. *Games, Sports and Cultures.* Oxford: Berg.

Dyck, N. and E. Archetti 2003. 'Embodied Identities: Reshaping Social Life Through Sport and Dance' in N. Dyck and E. Archetti (eds) *Sport, Dance and Embodied Identities.* Oxford: Berg, pp.1–19.

Elias, N. and E. Dunning 1986 (eds) *Quest for Excitement: Sport and Leisure in the Civilizing Process.* Oxford: Blackwell.

Hargreaves, J. 1982. 'Theorising Sport: An Introduction' in *Sport, Culture and Ideology* (ed.) J. Hargreaves. London: Routledge and Kegan Paul, pp.1–29.

Hargreaves, J. 1989. 'The Promise and Problems of Women's Leisure and Sport' in C. Rojek (ed.) *Leisure for Leisure: Critical Essays.* London: Macmillan, pp.130–49.

Harré, R. 1989. 'Perfections and Imperfections of Form: Cults of the Body and their Aesthetic Underpinnings.' *International Journal of Moral and Social Studies* 4: 183–94.

Hobsbawm, E.J. 1983. 'Mass-Producing Traditions: Europe, 1870–1914', in E.J. Hobsbawm, E.J. and T. Ranger (eds) *The Invention of Tradition.* Cambridge: Cambridge University Press, pp. 263–307.

Jackson, M. 2005. *Existential Anthropology: Events, Exigencies and Effects,* Oxford: Berghahn Books.

Ladd, T. and J. Mathison 1999. *Muscular Christianity: Evangelical Protestants and the Development of American Sport.* Grand Rapids, Mi: Baker Books.

Lindquist, G. 2001. 'Elusive Play and its Relations to Power.' *Focaal: European Journal of Anthropology* 37: 13–23.

Lithman, Y. 2000. 'Reflections on the Social and Cultural Dimensions of Children's élite Sport in Sweden' in N. Dyck (ed.) *Games, Sports and Cultures.* Oxford: Berg, pp. 163–81.

Löfgren, O. 1999. *On Holiday: A History of Vacationing.* Berkeley: University of California Press.

Lyng, S. 1990. 'Edgework: A Social Pyschological Analysis of Voluntary Risk Taking.' *The American Journal of Sociology* 95(4): 851–86.

MacClancy, J. 1996. 'Sport, Identity and Ethnicity' in J. MacClancy (ed.) *Sport, Identity and Ethnicity.* Oxford: Berg, pp.1–20.

Mangan, J. 1988. *Pleasure, Profit, Proselytism: British Culture and Sport at Home and Abroad.* London: Frank Cass.

Mansfield, A. and B. McGinn 1993. 'Pumping Irony: The Muscular and the Feminine' in S. Scott and D. Morgan (eds) *Body Matters: Essays on the Sociology of the Body.* London: The Falmer Press, pp.49–68.

Markus, T. 1993. *Buildings and Power: Freedom and Control in the Origin of Modern Building Types*. London: Routledge.

Mentore, G. 2001. 'Society, Body and Style: An Archery Contest in an Amerindian Society' in N. Dyck (ed.) 2000 *Games, Sports and Cultures*. Oxford: Berg, 65–80.

Rojek, C. ed. 1989. *Leisure for Leisure: Critical Essays*. London: Macmillan.

Rojek, C. 1995. *Decentring Leisure: Rethinking Leisure Theory* London: Sage.

Sandiford, K.A. 1994. *Cricket and the Victorians* Aldershot: Scolar Press.

Shilling, C. 1993. *The Body and Social Theory*. London: Sage.

Springwood, C. 2002. 'Farming, Dreaming, and Playing in Iowa. Japanese Mythopoetics and Agrarian Utopia' S. Coleman and M. Crang (eds) *Tourism: Between Place and Performance*. Oxford: Berghahn, pp.176–90.

Turner, T. 1994. 'Bodies and Anti-bodies: Flesh and Fetish in Contemporary Social Theory' in T. Csordas (ed.) *Embodiment and Experience: The Existential Ground of Culture and Self*. Cambridge: Cambridge University Press, pp. 27–47.

Turner, V. 1982. *From Ritual to Theatre: The Human Seriousness of Play*. New York: Paj.

van der Veer, P. (ed.) 1996. *Conversion to Modernities: The Globalization of Christianity*. London: Routledge.

Zarrilli, P. 1995. 'Repositioning the Body, Practice, Power, and Self in an Indian Martial Art' in Carol A. Breckenridge, (ed.) *Consuming Modernity: Public Culture in a South Asian World*. Minneapolis/London: University of Minnesota Press, pp.183–215.

PART I

SURVEYING THE SELF

2

BOB, HOSPITAL BODYBUILDER: THE INTEGRITY OF THE BODY, THE TRANSITIVENESS OF 'WORK' AND 'LEISURE'

Nigel Rapport

Introduction: Case-Study and Implications

Bob carries himself distinctively as he bestrides the corridors, offices and wards of Constance Hospital. His porter's uniform of blue fabric trousers and yellow polo-shirt (with name tag on the left breast) are tightly stretched across a bodybuilder's frame, in particular chest and neck. Bob has well-developed *trapezius* and *latissimus dorsi* muscles, as well as pectorals and *deltoids*. And he holds them with a certain tightness and expansiveness through the day. With his blonde hair in crew-cut style, his glasses magnifying a slight squint in his eye, and a slight stoop in his posture, Bob – 'B. HUME, SUPPORT SERVICES' – is a readily identifiable figure at Constance.

Constance Hospital, Easterneuk, is a major teaching hospital, furnished with a wide range of medical specialisms, in a large town in the east of Scotland. State-funded, it caters to an increasingly large catchment area, dealing with all manner of medical need from physical to psychological, surgery to therapy, accident-and-emergency to long-term care. Constance has thousands of employees, among whom are more than one hundred and thirty porters. Porters are not medically trained; hence, in a setting geared to the privileging of medical know-how and skill, the ministering and the administration of medical expertise, porters occupy a lowly position. 'You might think porters are a small cog in a large machine', I was told by a portering sub-manager during my induction to the job, 'but don't think you're nothing just because people say you are. People might say you're "just a porter" but it's not true; no part of the hospital could run without you (the same with domestics)'.[1] In practice, much exchange is orchestrated hierarchically, with porters and domestics engaged in routine practices regarded as less precious then those of clerks, carpenters, laboratory technicians, nurses, doctors (students, surgeons and consultants) and administrators. Porters are involved in tasks calling for physical stamina, even strength, more than any other criteria. They ferry patients (and sometimes visitors) across the hospital, in wheelchairs, beds and trolleys; they deliver mail within the hospital; they carry body parts and samples of bodily substances between different parts of the hospital complex; they transport dead bodies from hospital ward to mortuary; and they act as security personnel, policing the boundaries between hospital and outside world. (Interestingly, the English word 'porter' has a dual etymology deriving from the Latin word *portiarius*, a door-keeper, gate-keeper or janitor, and also from the Latin *portare*, to carry.) In this chapter, by focusing on an individual case-study, I shall explore the ways in which this institutional structure is animated and lived – comes alive – in the context of a particular person's life. Bob Hume might be employed as a porter at Constance Hospital, but he is also a bodybuilder. And it is as a bodybuilder, I shall argue, that he fills out his porter's uniform and occupies the plant, fulfilling his portering duties. In the process he calls into question any plain differentiating between work and leisure.

Elsewhere, Tamara Kohn (1995) has urged an expanded appreciation of what, as anthropologists, we might apprehend as 'communicative events': to include, for instance, daydreams and dreams. In elaborating on how Bob Hume speaks and acts, reflects upon his time in the hospital as well as outside it, and also embodies that reflexivity, I shall consider the ways and extents to which what is communicated is that the nature of the hospital as a hierarchical institution, deploying categories of social distinction, comes to be obviated by Bob's acts of will. Certainly, I shall hope to show how the boundaries between the hospital and the outside world, as between the work environment and the time and space of recreation and 'leisure' beyond it, are routinely permeated by Bob's actions and intentions. What, in contrast, might be said to retain an integrity is Bob's body. It is the project of his personal development and investment – a kind of 'capital' to build up and spend, in Shirley Ardener's phrasing (2002: personal communication) – the means and also the manifestation of his being and becoming.

The wider implications of the case-study concern a refocusing of social-scientific attention: less on bodies-in-institutions than on bodies-in-between. Stretching the metaphor, here is the body per se as porter: carrying the energy and agency by which institutions are animated, gate-keeper to the meanings and identities which institutions come to host.

Meeting Bob Hume

I first met Bob Hume during the two-week period of 'shadowing' another, more experienced porter – accompanying him on his round of tasks – which followed my morning of induction into the job. Bob and I had taken a trolley down to a ward to collect a patient for an ambulance trip to another institution and were now waiting while the nurses (behind closed curtains) transferred the patient to the trolley from his bed. 'Don't work too hard at this job', Bob began. 'The others in the buckie [the porters' lodge] don't so why should you? And when you've done a job, go for a walk; don't go back to the buckie straight away … But it's not a bad job, like, not too hard'. A domestic cleaner, languidly pushing a broom, hears Bob's talk and wanders over to us: 'New porter?', she says to Bob, and half to me. I smile and nod. 'How many have they taken on?' 'Six', Bob explains, 'but one has already gone to St. Winifred's [another Easterneuk hospital], and few of the others will stay; three, maybe, there's always a fast turnover'. 'Will you stay?', the domestic asks me directly. 'Probably', I mumble, smile, and look away. She's been here 16 years, the domestic explains to both of us, and she still gets lost in the laboratory block sometimes; all the corridors look the same! 'That's shite', says Bob to her in reply. 'It's really not so hard to get round, Nigel. Don't listen to her. And you don't get lost, it's just talk: she never really got lost. How long did you say you'd been here!?'. Bob grins and the domestic does too, while still insisting that she does lose herself by the 'labs'.

Collecting our patient, Bob and I leave the ward. 'The lab. block is really not hard', Bob continues. 'I've been working here about a year, though only a few months of that as a front-door porter; so I don't know my way around as well as I could, but it's still only occasionally that you get lost'. I ask him what he did before he was on the front-door. 'I used to be on security, at the reception desk. If there was violence, or an incident where someone got unruly, they'd call me. But it was a good number, and not much happened. A few incidents: visitors or patients getting violent. Just 'cos of drink usually … Now never take a patient onto Pipe Street', Bob changes tack as we pass the entrance to that part of the hospital where the extensive heating and ventilation pipe systems run, 'That's an instant sacking!'. I tell Bob I have heard about Pipe Street from Pat, the portering manager who ran my induction course: he said I was to report it immediately if ever I saw vermin there. 'Vermin!', Bob is aghast, 'In Pipe Street?! Huh! Pat is full of shite'.

I have taken time over this first exchange with Bob because it introduces nicely a number of themes that Bob would dwell on in our later interactions, as well as the forthright manner of his delivery. Bob would maintain his own point of view; also he would distance himself from the workaday banter of the hospital employees, which could not be taken at face value as the truth; he would get away with not working hard if he could; and he would disparage both the portering management and the rest of the porters as was necessary to maintain his own interests and his distance from them.

For instance, it was not long after the above conversation that Bob confided in me that while most were okay, there were 'some c***s here among the porters' – anywhere, he supposed. In part this was for my benefit; if I, a university professor, was deigning to spend some time among a less reliable and a less sophisticated set, then, he wanted me to know, he was too, in a way. In seeing me perusing the tabloid newspapers which are the porters' daily fare, in their rest room, Bob advised me: 'Don't read that, Nigel. The Sun and [The Daily] Record are all crap'. These seem to me complex utterances. In part Bob wanted to assure me that he recognised the gulf between my usual social milieu and this, and that he too partook of something of the former (he had his education and his middle-class associates); he also wanted me to remain unsullied, perhaps, as a reminder to him – a tangible link – of his more proper existence elsewhere.

However, this was also part of Bob's routine speaking persona when engaging with porters at large. Almost in a challenging way, and even when surrounded by a roomful, Bob would distinguish himself:

NIGEL: Are you coming on the porters' night out, Bob?

BOB: No. It's not my thing. I don't like quite a number of them even when they're sober! Drunk and I'd probably want to strangle them!

And Bob would be disparaging:

Porters are all a bunch of fucking drunks. That's the main qualification for the job! 'How much do you drink?' 'As much as my belly will take! More again, after I'm sick!' [he laughs]. You could write a book about this lot, Nigel; it would sell millions. The things you could say! I could feed you the information … They're drunken, sexist, dirty, skiving …

I think Bob enjoyed the uncertainty his fellows must have felt regarding how much of an insider Bob saw himself as being, or wanted to be. My feeling is that the routine stance he set himself was on the edge. Such as when he impugned the physicality of the porter's trade and denied the need for it to be, in Constance Hospital, almost exclusively male:

But the porters are so sexist [i.e. exclusively male sex]. And I don't know why. There is nothing porters do that women could not. In fact, no job that men do is impossible for women to do – or only those few using extreme strength.

If anyone was to think portering was hard physical graft, I understand Bob to be implying, they should consider the extremities that bodybuilding treats.

Bob summed up for me his feelings towards the rest of the porters one day like this:

I don't like many of the porters in the hospital, Nigel. After work I don't want to see them. I mean, if I saw them downtown and they were in trouble, of course I'd help: I'd wade in, no question. 'Cos they're my workmates. But they also drive me mad. They are so limited. And their conversation is so boring. Haven't you noticed? It's a three-way conversation with them: betting, drinking, shagging women. That's all they talk about, all the time. And, you know, if you came back in five years you'd find the same people having exactly the same conversations!

Not that Bob's distancing himself from the portering staff entailed seeing himself as any closer to, or openly sympathetic of, the management, it should be made clear. 'Managerial scum' was his comment on discovering that the dates he requested for his annual leave had not been granted. It was a regular refrain that Management were 'messing him about', and that the way they allocated him jobs and shifts 'was not right'. One day I found Bob in the porters' lodge in a distracted mood, wearing civilian clothes; inspecting next week's schedule he has found that he has been given yet more nights. 'Where is Fred McCrae [the shop steward]?', he demands of the portering charge-hand, 'And who's his replacement shop steward if he's away?'. Bob finally agrees with the charge-hand that he should go 'upstairs' now and talk to Davy Gallagher, the relevant sub-manager, about it personally. Some days later he tells me what happened: how he 'got aggressive' when he went to complain about his shifts, actually seeing Sue McBride, the manager, and how she later complained to Davy Gallagher [the sub-manager] that she had felt scared when faced by him; physically intimidated. 'And since that day', Bob concluded with a satisfied grin, 'they've both given me a wide berth. I may work here but they leave me alone! They both learnt that they can't just take me for granted!'

Bob and Bodybuilding

What gave Bob this otherness to his hospital persona – the reason neither Management nor porters could 'take him for granted' – I would argue, was that his sense of self, and a confident public identity which Bob intended in many ways to be larger than life, derived from his longstanding practice as a bodybuilder. Distant from the porters and their world it was his body, its changing capacities and proclivities, to which he was close; performing the bodybuilder in the hospital he distanced himself from the porters' limitations and the management's inefficiencies (not to mention the patients' pathologies), and kept himself pure, unsullied. His muscle was 'moral', in Simon Coleman's phrasing: working on his body was a life-project of ethical fulfilment.

Conversation between him and me soon routinely turned to bodybuilding; it was visibly apparent the time and energy that Bob devoted to the practice, while – at least between the ages of fourteen and twenty-nine – it had also been a major preoccupation of mine. Bob first introduced his bodybuilding to me in this way:

BOB: I'm an oddity, Nigel. Most porters have no hobbies outside work; they just work and booze. But I don't drink. I used to, but not any more, not for eight years or so ... And I'm just back to working my legs. 'Cos I injured them two years ago; I had my cartilage scraped – there's none there now – and my bones were getting stuck in one position. I couldn't bend my knee. So I had an operation. In fact, I had my first work-out last night! Yeah! And now it feels strange, bouncy, when I walk.

NIGEL: You better take it easy at first, you know.

BOB: I'm certainly gonna begin slowly; I'd never be one to rush things you know, and risk more injury. It's just crazy doing that ... So I just began with some leg-raise machine ... But you know my weight has gone down to fourteen-four![2]

NIGEL: What was it?

BOB: Fifteen-two.[3] So I wanna start putting it on again ... I do a nine-week protein blitz, then rest the body for three weeks and get the system back to normal. I'm about to start a blitz again now.

NIGEL: What d'you take?

BOB: Vitamin and protein supplements. '*Centrum*' [I look blank]. Not heard of it? I'm surprised. It's like 'HMB'. Heard of that? [I nod weakly] But it's cheaper 'cos it's not so effective.

NIGEL: What does it cost?

BOB: Eighteen quid, and that lasts me about a month ... But you gotta take supplements if you wanna get bigger; eating will not do it by itself. And I eat an enormous amount too and do all my own cooking. [I look quizzical] Oh Yes; I can't trust anyone else to do it. Or expect them to!

NIGEL: How about steroids?

BOB: No. I wouldn't know where to get them. And I'd be worried about side-effects. Like, they say they can make you go deaf.

What becomes clear, however, as Bob and I talk more regularly is that the above represents what might be called the strong or confident or proud position – the strong thesis – of Bob's bodybuilding habit, and that actually its terms are the subject of a struggle in his life. What will it take to maintain himself at the extreme? His training, his diet, his weight, his loosenings or lapses of control over these facets of his bodily regimen, are frequently aired.

There is, for instance, the question of sleep, also of being in bed as against being in the gym training. On the one hand, Bob insists he can cope with two or three hours' sleep and does not mind early shifts at the hospital or a few hours of sleep between shifts; and this can go on for a number of days before he starts noticing a lack of ability to concentrate. Recently, he recalls, he finished a weekend shift and went straight on to a party and felt fine, even though it meant some seventy-two hours without proper sleep. When he goes training, meanwhile, 'he really trains'; usually it means a session from five p.m. till ten-thirty. On the other hand, Bob muses how he loves his bed and is just too lazy. He can go to bed at about midnight after an evening shift and then sleep for sixteen hours, waking up around eight a.m., having a sandwich and a drink, and then going back to bed to sleep. This can mean that he misses the work-outs that he intended for himself; it also entails Bob elaborating on what happens when he misses sleep: his 'inability to concentrate' means that he feels physically exhausted and shaky, and 'his head shuts down'.

The same is true as regards diet. He wants to put on weight and knows how important intake of the right foods is towards this end; he has, for instance, three carefully prepared breakfasts ('the best meal'): a drink of raw eggs, then Weetabix, and then cooked eggs. After this morning's meal he went out and did a new circuit, training new muscle groups, before his afternoon hospital shift, and it felt very good; tomorrow morning when he wakes up he will feel really stiff, properly sore. 'Everything is a mental attitude', Bob explains, putting his hands up besides his eyes (like blinkers) and taking them forwards as if tracing a straight course ahead: 'losing, gaining weight, all of it; if you train without the right attitude you just get injured'. But then, accepting chocolate from another porter in the buckie, after a brief struggle with his conscience, Bob also admits that he's weak: and while other people might not be able to see him putting on weight where it should not be, on his belly and his sides, he can. Moreover, his knee has recently given out again which means no more weight-training for a while; his weight has dipped further, to fourteen stones and two pounds.

In the course of Bob's struggles with himself it seems at times that he sees through the discourse or mantra of bodybuilding to a real body of his, underneath, which has its own rhythms:

> I like being fourteen-two, Nigel. I was taking in too much protein, and the body can only absorb so much. After that it becomes fat. You know my body-fat percentage was thirty percent [he grins and shakes his head incredulously]! I was carrying it all in my back.

And again, while insisting that he would 'never dream' of taking drugs – 'does not do steroids', 'would never put a needle' into himself, 'would NEVER mess with needles' – Bob also recognises that everything is a steroid of some sort, all these supplements which bodybuilders use are: 'even *Centrum!*'.

Fixing his focus on his body, its tendencies and his work on it, Bob removes himself cognitively and socially from encompassment by the institution of the hospital, its personnel and relationships. But what this leads him into, it now appears, is a struggle which Bob does not always win, nor one he seems routinely to want to. There are times when he appears pleased about the laziness he can accord the rest of the porters, their hobby-less state, for the resort, the fall-back position it affords him – eager, for instance, for chocolate. Bob's body seems to represent a middle way and an integrity which distinguishes him from all institutional discourse: that of the bodybuilders and their gym as well as the porters and the hospital.

For it is also the case that bodybuilding involves Bob in other sets of relations with which he can seem equally ambivalent:

> I was told last year that I had great middle *deltoids* and that they could be championship material, but since then my weights and my motivation have gone right down! Isn't that weird? You'd think it would be the opposite ... But I've been in here [at the gym] four times in the past two months. I just can't motivate myself, Nigel. But I know that if I don't train properly, eat properly, take supplements, and the rest, I'll not grow and the whole thing won't be worth doing.

This exchange took place while Bob and I were working-out at his regular gym; it is perhaps time to bring Bob's relations outside the hospital into clearer focus.

Bodily Relations

He is very independent, Bob tells me, and has lived in his own house since he was sixteen. Now he is thirty-three, and it's a complicated arrangement but –'until she kicks me out!' – he lives with his girlfriend and looks after not his own two kids (whom he has hardly seen for six years) but her kids' kids; she has a girl and a boy and they each have a boy. His girlfriend is a bit older than him – mid-forties – and works as a child counsellor. In fact, he and she are really like chalk and cheese. Take diet, for instance: he eats more in a day than she does in a week – literally. She can get by on a packet of crisps, a day; seven in a week! She eats nothing at all. If she's eating her occasional steak or chicken he'll eat with her but otherwise, even if she's just eating eggs or some such rubbish (since, you can't put on weight just with eggs), he'll eat separately.

Watching Bob and his girlfriend, Moira, together it is clear that their difference in eating habits is a regular part of their joint discourse. When Bob talks about Moira's diet, moreover, it is not with distaste; more amazement, even pride. Because, she doesn't starve herself, he assures me, and she isn't dieting, and she has a great body – not too thin; it's just that she has never needed to eat, since she was small. Occasionally, these days, she feels a bit funny – the ageing process – and then he advises her that she must take vitamin supplements too, like him.

On the other hand, Moira is not too keen on him putting on a lot more muscle either; she says it's like cuddling a rock. She says the paraphernalia of bodybuilding competitions – the suntan lotion and the rest; pectoral muscles being tensed – makes her feel like vomiting. Bob thinks, however, that she'll come around. After all, he employs a personal trainer – you have to if you are a serious lifter – and would like to compete at National Juniors level, even though what he's most into is shape: bodybuilding as distinct from weightlifting.

When I first met Bob he worked out at a gym called 'Healthy Bodies', he told me. There were some very big guys there but he had the nicest shape. But there were also coming to be too many distractions there – women in leotards – so he decided to change gyms. After all, he never found it hard to settle into a new place or make friends, and 'The Braehead Leisure Centre' was no 'fitness club' with posers and what have you, but only for those seriously into weights. He was one of the smallest and one of the weakest guys who trained there, some of whom (whose photographs adorned the walls) had won bodybuilding championships. Of the ten lads he trained with he was certainly in the lower five. The best, indeed, was a young lad – only small, eleven stone or so at first, then moved up to thirteen – who could be a champ. He lifted championship weights – benching one hundred and forty kilos,[4] squatting one hundred and thirty – and might break the Scottish record one day, even the British one …

Some months after Bob first told me about his young friend, the possible champ, I heard about him again. But now Bob added that after moving up from eleven stone to thirteen:

> he then went up to fifteen stone. And he said he was one big scab, just full of puss. And that if you pressed him he would explode: all the puss would escape. Now I've not seen him for an age … He might be dead! Aye, he'll be dead.

What I take this to signify is Bob displaying the same kind of internal struggle concerning the relationships that surround his bodybuilding as we found in the case of his bodily regimen, as well as in the case of the porters. His girlfriend – chalk to his cheese – might well throw him out; he is smaller and weaker than most he trains with, but does he want to become like them anyway, if winning championships entails endangering the body with drugs, risking injury, infection, life itself? He is told he is championship material but bodyshape is what he most works for – although this is something, too, that his girlfriend claims not to appreciate.

In other words, relationships to do with his bodybuilding, and concerning people beyond the hospital – girlfriend, personal trainer, training buddies – who might seem to provide an alternative to hospital institutionalism and its personnel, appear, on closer inspection to be no more central to Bob's life; or rather they provide no more fixed a focal point. What perhaps they do afford is a counterweight, a place for Bob to go for social and emotional support, but not a place in which Bob needs to stay. In the same way, then, that Bob points up the contradictions in the dietary regimen of bodybuilding to which he episodically submits himself – everything is really a drug, a steroid, even *Centrum* – he also sees through the relationships in which bodybuilding involves him and points out their shortcomings.

Let me finish an ethnographic account of Bob's bodybuilding, then, by coming full circle and returning to two incidents in the milieu of the hospital. Having decried most of his porter colleagues for having no hobbies outside work beyond boozing, it was interesting to see Bob return a compliment one day; after being greeted by one of the charge-hands by the welcome shout of 'Here's Steroids!', Bob retorted that the charge-hand's nickname was 'Mighty Mouse' because he too worked out – in fact, Bob joked with me, it was the charge-hand who got him his steroids in the first place! And again, having laughingly and repeatedly insisted to a nurse that he knew that her son planned to get married – however well she might claim to know her son and his plans and deny Bob's charge – Bob explained to me he was just 'winding her up' because her son was someone he loved to tease. Her son worked at the Reception at Bob's gym – a big lad himself – and Bob could not wait to hear how she went home and her son was forced to deny it: '"That Bastard, Bob", he'll go!!'. What Bob most liked to be, I would conclude, was not a bodybuilder as such, far less a hospital porter, but a bodybuilder-in-the-hospital: 'Bob, Hospital Bodybuilder'.

Discussion: Irony and the Importance of Elsewhere

I was in my late twenties when I began to find bodybuilding tedious; establishing myself in new gyms as I moved between towns and jobs, keeping up the same levels of accomplishment – never mind improvement – felt increasingly more like work than recreation. Bob professed not to mind moving between gyms and groups of lifters and re-establishing himself, but at thirty-three he too seemed to be finding the required effort and motivation harder to come by. Evidently, looking at his body, he had put in the time in the past, and he was still massively muscled; when we worked-out together in his gym our circuits were too different – in particular exercises (in muscle groups exercised) and in weights lifted – for me really to serve as his partner and 'spotter'. However, what I have argued is that not only did Bob use bodybuilding as means to distance himself, cognitively and socially, from the hospital and the rest of the porters, but also that Bob was pleased, on occasion, to know himself as 'Steroids' in the hospital: as the hospital's bodybuilder; even though at the same time he knew that he slept rather than worked-out, ate chocolate and put down fat deposits on his back. Bob's bodybuilding seemed intimately connected with a multiplying of identities and milieux, and a juggling and translocation among them.

In his poem, 'The Importance of Elsewhere', Philip Larkin describes his alienation from the milieux in England in which he lives (1990: 104; also see Rapport 2000). It is not that he finds himself a stranger, as he does, say, in Ireland. In fact, quite the opposite; he is able to accommodate himself to visiting Ireland because there he is 'separate' and things should feel strange: 'since it was not home, Strangeness made sense'. But living in England he has no such excuse for his loneliness and alone-ness; these are meant to be his 'customs and establishments'. 'Here', Larkin concludes, 'no elsewhere underwrites my existence'.

Erving Goffman has written famously about the characteristics of what he termed 'total institutions': social environments, from prisons to boarding schools to hospitals, where a number of individuals 'together lead an enclosed, formally administered round of life' (1961: 11). On arrival in the institution, individuals find their senses of self 'mortified': 'the boundary that the individual places between his being and the environment is invaded and the embodiment of self profaned' (ibid.: 32). Their conceptions of self no longer supported by everyday social arrangements, individuals-in-the-institution embark upon new and radically altered, alienating, moral careers: ones of curtailment and dispossession, disfigurement and violation. Encompassed by the institution, their time and interests captured by the institutional regimen provided them, they find every aspect of their lives overwritten. More recently, of course, Michel Foucault (1977) has generalised upon these insights and seen bodies 'totally imprinted by history' everywhere. Not only the inmates (the prisoners, school-children and patients) but also the employees of total institutions (the warders, teachers and medics) find themselves mortified and alienated. And more than this, since, according to Foucault, identity and sense of self is itself the product of discourse, there is never a time when 'the laws of individual desire, the forms of individual language, the rules of individual actions, and the play of individual mythical and imaginative discourses' are not overwritten and over-determined in this way (1972: 22).

The indiscriminateness of Foucault's notions, whereby the 'governmentality' (1977) of discourse is responsible for all identity, individual or other, seemingly free or constrained, supposedly gratifying or alienating, is a far cry from Goffman's (1961) more humanistic vision wherein institutions are something one can imagine individuals entering and leaving. In one respect, however, Foucault's connecting up of life within the institutional milieu to that beyond it is useful for this discussion. For my own argument (and clear overlaps exist with Tamara Kohn's account of aikido practitioners) would be that what we see Bob effecting through his bodybuilding is a measure of control over his identity and a maintaining of a sense of integrity concerning his bodily self whether in the hospital or out, as well as in negotiating the transition between. As 'hospital bodybuilder' Bob compassed or contained a sense of elsewhere within himself, and as such was never contained, alienated or overwritten by the locale in which he found himself – hospital, gym or wherever. He moved between the work of the hospital and the 'leisure' of the gym, between the 'work' of the gym and the 'leisure' of the hospital, and between the work of a bodily regimen and the leisure of luxuriating his body in chocolate and sleep. He could be said to be at home in keeping on the move between institutional or discursive fixities (cf. Rapport and Dawson 1998). '[N]either here nor there', Bob's home was 'both here and there – an amalgam, a pastiche, a performance' (Bammer 1992: ix). What I want to reiterate, however, is that this amalgam, pastiche, and transitive performance which Bob practised – which, indeed, Bob embodied since it was his body that is the focus of so much of his attention in the construction of his identity – was his project not his alienation. Bob eluded the control of the institution – eluded the singularity of discourse and setting as such – through a bodily focus by which he came to contain multitudes ('elsewheres') within himself: weightlifter, porter, luxurist.

Finally, for someone practising the transitive performance of keeping on the move between institutional fixities, regimens and relationships, it should not be surprising that the particular roles which Bob juggled were themselves regularly swopped. Before I met him Bob had been a builder (on the continent as well as around Scotland), a heavy drinker, a voluntary worker for adults with learning difficulties, and a staunch Episcopalian. Part-way through my time as a porter, Bob lost his job and found himself in jail (for the attempted theft of hospital property). In playing such extremes, the integrity of his body was his 'bank' as well as his capital, one could say: his store of identity and the thing he could put store by in his role-migrations.

'Irony' I have described (2003a: 42ff) as an intrinsic part of the human condition. It compasses a certain cognitive detachment or displacement, a casting doubt on the necessity, truthfulness and entirety of the normative, commonsensical and institutional. Hayden White refers to irony as 'trans-ideological' (1973: 38). Included in its definition is the ontological premise that human beings are never cognitively imprisoned by pre-ordained and pre-determining schemata of cultural classification and social structuration; they can everywhere appreciate the malleability and the mutability of social rules and realities, and the contingency and ambiguity of cultural truths. The cognitive displacement of irony, I would maintain, is a universal human capacity and resort. To adapt Simon Coleman and John Elsner (1998), Bob exhibits an irony in his engagement with the 'canonical' forms, the institutional and discursive fixities, of both portering and bodybuilding practice which comes close to parody; his ironic performances make the forms 'cipher[s] for the cultivation of powerful personal … experiences' (ibid.: 60) and their transitiveness expressive, above all, of Bob's 'experimental whims' (ibid.: 61).

Conclusion: Portering 'Work' and 'Leisure'

Despite his protestations to the contrary, Bob's having a hobby, a leisure pursuit that afforded him cognitive distance from workmates and place of work, was not something peculiar or special to him. Among the porters of Constance Hospital it may even have been something of a norm (see Rapport 2003b). A number of younger porters were involved in rock bands; some others sold cut-price videos, cds and tapes, cigarettes and whiskey; for a great many, watching and playing football was the most important thing in the week, for others it was the time spent drinking in the pubs and clubs of Easterneuk – the local watering-hole, 'The Hilltop', being only one hundred metres from the hospital door. For other porters again, I would say, time in the hospital was passed by it being itself turned into a pursuit of 'leisure': of practical jokes, of bantering or 'good crack', of smoking and eating, of wasting time.

Even the exaggerations of his recreational identity find a resonance among other porters. In another place (Rapport 1995) I have explored the connections between exaggeration and identity: the clarity and definiteness that may be derived from stereotyping, from typifying the world as comprised of absolute contrasts (cf. Douglas 1966: 4). Rom Harre (1989) has also examined what he terms 'the Exaggeration Principle' – '"If this big is good, huge is better"' – at play in modern 'cults' of identity from bodybuilding to dieting, dog-breeding, car-customising, and sunglasses- and handbag-wearing. As an identity-accessory, he argues, exaggerations of size are metonyms for potency. Here, then, is Bob Hume bestriding Constance Hospital, exaggerating his muscle mass and tone, his alienness, his health, strength and self-discipline; also his sloth, his machismo and his lack of sexism, his impatience with other porters and his ability to joke along with them. But here, too, are other porters, with exaggerated masculinity, aggressiveness, bravado, mateyness, derring-do and devil-may-care attitudes. To be a porter among porters in Constance Hospital is, it may be argued, in many regards to adopt workaday personae and to occupy work spaces in ways that flagrantly breach and disavow the disciplines of proportion, sobriety, institutionalism, hierarchy, health and sickness that the administration would induce (see Rapport 2004).

We have heard how, for Bob Hume, there was a slippage, a flexibility, regarding the status of hospital and gym as either 'work' or 'leisure'. Albeit that the hospital was where he got paid – and to assure himself of his wages he could not decide to sleep through his shift-time as he could his time for work-outs – his attitude to the hospital as it related to the gym was variable. He both escaped from the hospital as work-place to the recreational space of the gym, and he escaped from the rigours of the gym to the relaxation of the hospital; he also escaped from working on his body to luxuriating in it. Finally, I would say, this too was not Bob's special preserve. 'Work' and 'leisure' among the porters of Constance Hospital pertained not to certain fixed times or locations nor to certain circumscribed practices; rather, they were attitudes, frames of mind, by which times, locations and practices were approached – and juggled (cf. Dawson 2002). Other porters might not be serious bodybuilders like Bob, but in their singing, their drinking, their footballing, their entrepreneurialism and their sedition – their 'disciplined' practising of these – they provided themselves with elsewheres whereby their lives and their bodies were imprinted by their intentions, and where 'work' and 'leisure' significantly pertained to their own constructions of routine and recreation, and their own ironic jugglings of identity.

Acknowledgements

The research on which this essay was based was funded by the Leverhulme Trust (grant no. XCHL48), under the aegis of their 'Nations and Regions' programme, and part of the 'Constitutional Change and Identity' project convened by Professor David McCrone of Edinburgh University.

I am grateful to audiences in Washington and in Oxford for help with drafts of the essay, and in particular to the generous commentaries of Simon Coleman, Tamara Kohn and Shirley Ardener.

Notes

1. With the permission of the hospital authorities (the Chief Executive and the Dean, to whom I wrote), the portering charge-hands and union (to whom the hospital authorities then spoke), I undertook the day-to-day shiftwork of a porter over a period of nine months (followed by three months of broader interviewing). I hoped as far as possible to insinuate myself into a porter's life-world at Constance Hospital (and, to a lesser extent, outside the hospital too) by doing as and what other porters did. My fieldwork practice was not to tape-record informants but yet to aim for a detailed accounting of interactions I witnessed. As soon as possible after an interaction's end I would discreetly transcribe key words onto paper, for a full writing-up in my journal later.
2. 'Fourteen, four': i.e. fourteen stones and four pounds, or two hundred pounds total.
3. 'Fifteen, two': i.e. two hundred and twelve pounds.
4. 'One hundred and forty kilos': i.e. three hundred and eight pounds.

References

Bammer, A. 1992. 'Editorial', *New Formations* (special edition: 'The Question of "Home"') 2, no. 2: 1–24.

Coleman, S. and J. Elsner 1988. 'Performing Pilgrimage: Walsingham and the Ritual Construction of Irony', in *Performance, Ritual, Media*, (ed.) F. Hughes-Freeland. London: Routledge, pp. 46–65.

Dawson, A. 2002. 'Leisure and Change in a Post-Mining Mining Town', in *British Subjects: An Anthropology of Britain*, (ed.) N. Rapport, Oxford: Berg, pp. 107–20.

Douglas, M. 1966. *Purity and Danger*, London: Routledge and Kegan Paul.

Foucault, M. 1972. *The Archaeology of Knowledge*, New York: Harper.

———— 1977. *Discipline and Punish*, New York: Pantheon.

Goffman, E. 1961. *Asylums*, Hammondsworth: Penguin.

Harre, R. 1989. 'Perfections and Imperfections of Form: Cults of the Body and their Aesthetic Underpinnings', *International Journal or Moral and Social Studies* 4, no. 3: 183–94.

Kohn, T. 1995. 'She came out of the Field and into my Home: Reflections, Dreams and a Search for Consciousness in Anthropological Method', in *Questions of Consciousness*, (eds) A.P. Cohen and N. Rapport, London: Routledge, pp. 41–59.

Larkin, P. 1990. *Collected Poems*, London: Faber/Marvell.

Rapport, N. 1995. 'Migrant Selves and Stereotypes: Personal Context in a Postmodern World', in *Mapping the Subject: Geographies of Cultural Transformation*, (eds) S. Pile and N. Thrift, London: Routledge, pp. 267–82.

_____ 2000. 'Writing on the Body: The Poetic Life-Story of Philip Larkin', *Anthropology and Medicine* 7, no. 1: 39–62.

_____ 2003a. *I am Dynamite: An Alternative Anthropology of Power*, London: Routledge.

_____ 2003b. 'The computer as a focus of inattention: Five scenarios concerning hospital porters', in *New Technologies at Work*, (eds) C. Garsten and H. Wulff, Oxford: Berg, pp. 25–44.

_____ 2004. 'From the Porter's Point of View: Participant-Observation by the Interpretive Anthropologist in the Hospital', in *New Qualitative Methodologies in Health and Social Care*, (ed.) F. Rapport, London: Routledge, pp. 99–122.

Rapport, N. and A. Dawson. 1998. 'Home and Movement: A Polemic', in *Migrants of Identity: Perceptions of Home in a World of Movement*, (eds) N. Rapport and A. Dawson, Oxford: Berg, pp. 3–38.

White, H.V. 1973. *Metahistory: the Historical Imagination in 19th Century Europe*, Baltimore: Johns Hopkins University Press.

3

OF METAPHORS AND MUSCLES: PROTESTANT 'PLAY' IN THE DISCIPLINING OF THE SELF

Simon Coleman

My first encounter with a muscular Christian took place when I was still finishing my undergraduate degree. I had just decided that my doctoral work would focus on conservative Protestantism when I heard that Jim, a fellow student of anthropology, had recently 'converted'. I confess I was somewhat sceptical as I went up the steps to Jim's room in college to see for myself. I was used to thinking of him as a friendly, if physically-imposing, presence, more renowned for his prowess on the rugby field – and in the bar – than for his academic abilities.

I found Jim squeezed, as usual, into a chair that was several sizes too small for him. Next to him was a cup of tea, and next to that was a Bible. Jim and I had never had much in common (my rugby prowess had always been limited, and his interest in anthropology appeared to be equally negligible). However, when he heard of my intentions to study evangelicalism, Jim's amiability took on a more focussed air. I realized pretty soon that he was taking the opportunity to tell me the story of his conversion, indeed to 'witness' to me. In the hour or so I spent in his room, I noticed that Jim did not utter a single profanity, something of a record up to that time. I also remember him telling a story of his 'old' self, who had committed a faintly obscene act in mixed company – an act that he now deeply regretted.

Jim's verbal testimony was impressive enough, but I was even more struck by the subsequent change in his life as a whole. He emerged with a respectable degree, went on to do graduate work (in theology, as far as I recall), and represented university teams in an increasingly successful rugby career that was occasionally covered in the national press.

What was the connection, if any, between Jim's sport and his faith? From Jim's point of view, God was behind both, and there was a 'purpose' behind the abilities he had been 'given' on the field. Using a more secular argument, we might ask whether both revived at the same time from a new sense of mental and physical discipline, inculcated by his personal reformation. In truth, I do not know the answers to these questions in Jim's case, but what I want to emphasise here are the ambiguous parallels, the potential resonances, between Jim's faith and his sporting life. I do know that he saw rugby as both a temptation and an opportunity for a Christian, a form of play that might become something of an unhealthy obsession, but might also provide him with a special opportunity to witness to his faith. Rugby was therefore more than a game, it provided a means – if used correctly – through which to effect change in his own life and in those of others.

These potentialities are hardly new in the lives of conservative Protestants, but I think we can go further than merely seeing sport as a 'calling' for the believer. I want to explore the complex relations of mutual reinforcement – and sometimes of repulsion – that have occurred between conservative Protestant religious forms and sport. Organised sport and evangelicalism experienced an important heyday in the middle to late nineteenth century in the West, at a time when both were responding to, but were also to some extent constituted by, new forms of work, leisure, rationality and urbanism (Mangan 1988). Since then, both have maintained ambiguous relationships to the 'serious' worlds of work and industry, and have often been regarded as 'mere' leisure-time pursuits in the context of secular modernity. Yet, both have flourished within modernity and maintained much more nuanced relations with each other and with other spheres of life than might be predicted by either secularisation theory or assumptions concerning the progressive rationalisation of the world.

Of course, the implications of Weber's Protestant Ethic have most frequently been explored in relation to pinpointing possible connections between emergent capitalism and religious ideology.[1] Here, I provide an analysis of other Protestant methods of disciplining the soul and the self, using the term 'muscular Christianity' as a (shifting) motif throughout the chapter. The term was probably first used in a critical review of a nineteenth-century novel (Charles Kingsley's *Two Years Ago*, originally published in 1857), but it was taken up by Kingsley's friend, the Christian socialist Thomas Hughes and author of *Tom Brown's Schooldays*, in order to link sporting practices with forms of ethical and moral training that evoked both masculinity and patriotism.[2] Kingsley and Hughes emphasised the need for harmony between body and soul, and in common with Herbert Spencer considered athletic training could encourage virtues of self-control, virility and fair play (Sandiford 1994: 35).[3] As we shall see, the term and its associated ideology were exported to the U.S. and beyond, where they were blended with various forms of mission, millenarianism and positive thinking.

The discussion of the history of 'muscular' forms of Christianity that the first part of this chapter provides is complemented by a more contemporary, ethnographic exploration of sporting practices and narratives, as they are manifested within a (U.S.-influenced) conservative Protestant ministry in Sweden. The aim here is to see some of the parallels over time but also a few of the shifts in the appropriation of sporting themes that might have occurred in more recent years. Sport at the ministry is shown to feed into a wide range of disciplinary practices through its material technologies of the body as well as through the metaphors it helps to construct in articulating charismatic Protestant discourses of self-surveillance. Furthermore, it is argued that bodily and even linguistic habits developed through religious and sporting practices leach into each other and into everyday practices, thus rendering the division between leisure and work, sacred and secular, highly problematic.[4] Sport is also shown to play a religio-political role, allowing religionists to deploy an apparently secular rhetoric in gaining a potential bridge to the non-religious world.

In 'playing' with sport, however, conservative Protestantism runs a risk that is particular to its own concerns: at what point do parallels and metaphors between the two become too literal in form, so that translation between spheres becomes a dangerous, even blasphemous, activity? We shall see how the forms of religion I describe sometimes display an ambivalent relationship to sport as metaphor and practice: it provides a bridge to the secular, and yet the traffic can of course proceed both ways. This last point was certainly one realised by my friend Jim as he combined his rugby with his faith. Yet, in terms of his personal biography and within his Christian witness to me, the two aspects of his life could hardly be separated.

From Sin to Spectacle: Peanut and Jelly or Oil and Water?

I have taken the subtitle for this section from a quote by the famous American footballer, Deion Sanders, who has asserted that sports and religion go together like peanut butter and jelly (the English equivalent might be jam and clotted cream). This contemporary view is disputed by the very writers who report Sanders' words, Higgs and Braswell, who suggest instead much more negative metaphor of oil and water (2004: 12–14). Such debates have a long history. More broadly, Christian attitudes to the body – both positive and negative – have varied greatly over the last two millennia, but the significance of corporeality to conceptualizing the Christian self and its relationship to divinity has remained. Biblical references range from the act of earthly creation (the Word made flesh, John 1: 14), to the Pauline body as 'temple' of the Holy Spirit, to the more corporate and sacramental sense of common participation in the body of Christ through the Eucharist. The body of the believer was used powerfully to make theological points by the desert ascetics of the Early Church, who combined flight from society with an attempt precisely to escape from the demands of physicality. Higgs and Braswell (2004: 213–214) note the argument that, for the Desert Fathers, asceticism did not travel far from the *ascesis*, the classical training of the athlete, and the Fathers themselves were regarded by their contemporary biographers as *athletae dei*, in effect killing the body in order to release the Spirit.[5]

Calvinism would intensify the Catholic mistrust of the flesh, while also displaying an intense dislike for distracting recreations and games. We see the body once more being used here as a somatic index of faith, with such austere acts as fasting signifying embodied spiritual commitment and suggesting the possibility of the outer flesh expressing the state of the interior soul (Griffith 2004: 15). Later, in the United States, ante-bellum forms of Protestantism would display a residually Puritan wariness towards unnecessary physical exercise.[6]

Nonetheless, some dissenting voices were evident. Methodism, rather more optimistic than Calvinism, led in some cases to the idea of using bodies for personal and social improvement rather than seeing them as impediment to the Christian life (Putney 2001: 52).[7] The notion of the body as repository of penitence and suffering thus began to be challenged by the search for a kind of spiritual and physical perfectionism (see also Griffith 2004: 4). In the United States, the middle of the nineteenth century also began to see some shifts in attitudes that are key to the subject of this chapter. Some churchmen were concerned about the apparent feminisation of a Protestant religion that seemed to attract the active engagement of rather more women than men, and so began to search for ways to engage the latter in Christian activities. More generally, in the newly expanding cities, increasingly full of immigrants with foreign faiths, means of reaching out to newly concentrated populations needed to be found. As Moore puts it, Protestant religious leaders started to realize that they had to give more attention to the way that people played – indeed, 'they had to pronounce the word 'leisure' without a grimace' (1994: 93).

The fascinating point here is the way evangelical forms combined with other strategies of creating lifestyles that were adapted to urbanism, in the process incorporating sport as both morally positive activity and edifying spectacle.[8] Ironically, some of the impulses came from the old country. Although it had been started in England, the Young Men's Christian Association was seen in America as a powerful means of providing a legitimate form of self-improving leisure, set apart from commercial entertainment and encouraging forms of sociality among fellow (male and Protestant) believers. The first American branches were formed in Boston and New York in the early 1850s (Moore 1994: 113). Thus the discipline of church attendance could be converted – or rather complemented – by the discipline of attending the gym, and the consciously masculine dimension of the new urban spaces created was evident. Translated to America and cultivated in such organisations as the YMCA, the idea of muscular Christianity combined inward-looking character development with the possibility of an outwardly-oriented evangelisation. Thus a number of factors were combining here: reform within the Protestant Church (the masculinisation of its image), the need to keep hold of the believer amid the temptations of urban life, and even the missionising, at times almost millenarian possibility of attracting the unsaved masses of the cities. According to Moore, sports in the YMCA became an explicitly spiritual exercise, albeit one that at least in its early days actually tended to attract a generally middle-class clientele. Robert J. McBurney, secretary of the New York YMCA, developed the 'Four-Fold Plan', advocating ministry to all areas of man's life, bodily, social, spiritual and intellectual. Robert Roberts, a devout Baptist who worked for the YMCA, coined the term 'body-building' (Putney 2001: 69). In time, both basketball and volleyball – both sports able to be played in covered, urban contexts, with the minimum of body contact, in between the football and baseball seasons – would also be developed under the auspices of the Association.

One of the first members of the Chicago 'Y' was Dwight Moody, a young businessman who was to become possibly the most celebrated American preacher in the latter half of the nineteenth century. Moody's championing of muscular Christianity was combined not only with his cultivation of business networks, but also with his adoption of consciously rational attempts to cultivate revival in urban spaces. Pragmatic use of physical activity complemented a general willingness to use any appropriate means to appeal to the loosely structured publics of the city. Sport as both metaphor and basis for authority was also famously deployed by Billy Sunday, who played baseball for the Chicago White Stockings (now the White Sox) in the 1880s before becoming a powerful, though rhetorically crude, evangelist.

If evangelical Christianity can be seen as helping to create a new form of Christian body, one more, intermittently influential, contribution has yet to be mentioned: the metaphysical, 'New Thought' Movement that flourished in the East of the U.S. from the latter half of the nineteenth century. Griffith (2004: 69) notes that the Movement's roots lay in a mixture of Swedenborgianism[9], mesmerism, spiritualism, holiness evangelism and, as it was sometimes called, 'mind cure'. The fundamental message of its practitioners was that the causes and cures of illness could be attributed to the mental and/or spiritual faculties of the person. Most famously, Mary Baker Eddy, the founder of Christian Science, subscribed to a version of mind cure, but her original mentor was Phineas P. Quimby, a New Hampshire healer who stressed that error, borne on another's words, might enter the porous body and – through multiple shifts and exchanges between matter and mind – cause sickness (ibid.: 72). Thus the body as well as the mind were to be subjected to constant monitoring in the search for the perfect state of being. Health could be attained ultimately by tuning the mind to Infinite Spirit, channelling cosmic energy into malleable physical matter (ibid.: 71). Such views, apart from their immediate influences, would contribute ultimately to some of the 'Health and Wealth' ideologies of the evangelical Christians whom we shall examine later (cf. Coleman 2000).

Throughout the twentieth century, while 'muscular Christianity'[10] in its original form tended to fade as a movement in Protestant circles (though retaining a hold in some of the more conservative churches), affinities between sport and the faith have continued to develop. After the years of conservative Protestant isolation leading up to the Second World War, sport began to be deployed to challenge the social and cultural peripherality of believers. For the opening night of Billy Graham's 1947 city revival in Charlotte, North Carolina, he invited the reigning American mile champion, Gil Dodds, on to the podium (Ladd and Mathison 1999: 96). While Dodds would go on to work for the parachurch organization Youth for Christ, numerous other organizations, including Sports Ambassadors, the Fellowship of Christian Athletes, Athletes in

Action, the International Sports Coalition and Sports Outreach America would similarly deploy sport as a means not only to bridge sacred and secular worlds, but also to transcend some of the denominational differences among more conservative Protestants. As Ladd and Mathison put it (ibid.: 215–16), in its more contemporary forms muscular Christianity has combined the pragmatic utility of sport as a means to Christian conversion with a more diffuse and meritocratic celebration of success. Thus they quote Brett Butler of the New York Mets: 'If Christ were a ballplayer, he'd be the best there was. He'd take out the guy at second base, then he'd say "I love you," pick him up, slap him on the butt and come back to the dugout' (ibid.: 217).

In recent decades, the provision of sporting facilities has become a significant part of the service provided by suburban megachurches, catering to Christian lifestyles that are much more confidently expressed than they were in the earlier decades of the century. So while the double-function of sport as both productive recreation and means of outreach has been retained, to it has been added a sense of it as a positive form of leisured consumption within the family. Such a position represents quite a transformation from the nineteenth-century emphasis on the disciplining and 'masculinisation' of the urban businessman and industrial worker.[11]

Despite such shifts, some common threads can be traced in the historical account I have provided. As Griffith notes: 'One link among such seemingly disparate American groups as seventeenth-century New England Puritans, Progressive Era New Thought physical culturalists, and late twentieth-century evangelical diet preachers is a general conviction about the devotional logic of physical discipline. Fit bodies signify fitter souls' (2004: 5–6). If the body has been seen as both agent of temptation and vehicle for grace, instrument of both pleasure and piety, its control and display (or conspicuous lack of display) have been deployed as means of practising theology through the body. Sport and physical recreation can therefore be shown to aid Protestant forms of self (and world) mastery. But they may also leave open the Foucauldian dilemma of how to understand the precise relationship between the metaphorical and the material in the disciplining of the self. In other words, to what extent can a fit or at least healthy body literally signify a soul that is pure? This is no idle question, since it has been at the heart of many debates within the conservative Protestant world for much of the last century.

With such questions in mind, we can turn to a contemporary Protestant movement and one of its ministries. Issues relating to the body have been central to both the fame and the notoriety of the so-called 'Health and Wealth' or Faith Movement, a charismatic branch of evangelicalism that has expanded greatly, particularly in urban contexts, within and beyond the United States from the 1970s on.[12] While combining classic elements of Pentecostal and Charismatic Christianity, the Movement has also taken on board elements of New Thought assertions of the connections between mind, spirit and matter. Indeed, it has been most marked by its espousal of the notion that the possession of Faith leads to prosperity in all areas of the believer's life, ranging from personal finances to social relationships and physical health. A fundamental way in which such prosperity is conceptualised relates to the idea that the world is constituted by two parallel realms, the 'natural' and the 'supernatural'. While the latter is seen as ultimately more 'real', the believer's task is to effect a form of exchange of agency, deploying the power derived from divine force to transform – gain success within – the mundane realm. As we shall see, such an orientation throws some of our questions concerning the relationship between metaphor and the material, as expressed in attitudes to the body and to sport, into particularly sharp relief. In the following, we focus on a ministry in which I have carried out fieldwork since the 1980s, and moreover one that has been heavily influenced – and retains strong ideological links with – its American counterparts.

Sport and the Spirit

I am in the corridor of the offices of the Word of Life ministry – a complex of congregation, Bible School and media business based in Uppsala, Sweden – looking at an exhibition of paintings produced by 'believing' artists. One picture particularly catches my eye (see also Coleman 2000). It is a picture of Jesus, long, dark hair trailing down, who stares directly ahead at the viewer. For anybody familiar with Victorian anxieties over the feminisation of Jesus the picture sends out a powerful message. This is a figure whose body positively ripples with muscles and pent-up energy – indeed, he looks so powerful that he appears to be breaking out of the canvas in order to join the viewer in the corridor. In a note accompanying the picture, the artist states that he was tired of seeing pictures of Jesus in a state of defeat (as for instance a crucifixion scene would imply), and so wanted to provide an alternative vision of the Saviour.

Of course, this is just a single image. But it does have intriguing aesthetic parallels with other aspects of Word of Life culture. Here for instance are the words of a visiting American preacher, describing a visit he paid to Jesus, and presenting to his Swedish audience in words something very similar to the image of Christ as bodybuilder:[13] 'And there Jesus stood … His hair came down to about here. And one thing that I noticed; it was that he had muscles! Isn't that great!' Indeed, a leading Faith preacher and frequent visitor to the group, Ray McCauley, is a former body-builder and Mr South Africa.[14]

Bodybuilding per se is not a constitutive part of Word of Life practices, but it is instructive to unpick some of the cultural logic of such representations of embodied power. Most obviously, there is a sense of the body as moving, dynamic, expressing a theology of positive faith (and indeed positive thinking) rather than penitence. If Jesus' body is strikingly muscled,[15] however, we should not assume that it has become so as a result of conventional physical training. Health and Wealth theology promotes a discourse of 'excess', not so much in relation to physical activity as in relation to 'the Word' – the biblical and other sacred language that is to be ingested by the believer through practices of reading and listening to sermons. As one Word of Life supporter stated to me in another context, 'An overdose of Jesus' love is exactly what we need', and what is significant here is less the notion of 'love' as the idea of an 'overdose', a sense that there might be no conventional limit to the benefits of spiritual sustenance. (One might recall Phineas Quimby's admonitions concerning the ingestion of language and gaining access to the infinite.) More generally, members talk often of the notion of assimilating language as a form of nourishing ingestion, a feeding of the spirit that can ultimately have physical effects. The point here is to express a sense of the verbal appropriating the physical, with results that are visible; or, to put it another way, we see here one way in which 'the supernatural' appears in ideological terms to reconstitute 'the natural'.[16]

Such themes take on extra significance in relation to the positioning of the Word of Life in the religious and cultural politics of Sweden.[17] The focus on the body per se is not problematic. Frykman (1987: 164ff) argues that around the turn of the nineteenth century bourgeois culture originally marked itself off from the peasantry and working-classes through the extensive control of body functions. As corporeal rituals symbolising a new, rational, progressive lifestyle were diffused nationally, 'domesticating' the lower orders, so ideas of order, hygiene, and efficiency became generalised. More broadly, when the Social Democrats came to power in the early 1930s leisure activities became symbols of modernity, meant to foster a classless breed of modern citizens, in healthy tanned bodies. The new welfare state attempted to forge unity through encouraging community gymnastics and sports (Löfgren 1999: 271–73). Even today, participation in sports and sports clubs remains high in Sweden, by international standards. Thus the body as symbol of social engagement is a common idea in Sweden, but a salient dimensions of the notion of Jesus with muscles is that it appears to replace a sense of the body built up through conventional, secular means with one that is constituted by explicitly spiritual forms of nourishment – flesh incorporating Word; furthermore, the discourse of individually-oriented excess that it expresses contrasts with the more culturally normative sense of disciplined and moderate body management. When we consider the ministry's reputation as a youth-oriented, aggressively evangelical, un-Swedish institution, it is no surprise that the Word of Life has often been accused by fellow Christians of a brash Americanism, a crass focus on religion as self-help rather than socially-oriented penitence (see Coleman 2000).

One implicit way in which the bodybuilding image resonates with forms of Faith ideology lies in the way it encourages, or at least visually expresses, the idea of monitoring the self through self-objectification and display. Members often talk of the need to present a positive image to others – through clothes and body language as well as expressions of faith – in accordance with the principle that negative thoughts, words and self-representations have negative effects. Perhaps even more than other sports, bodybuilding suggests precisely this idea of working on the self, and thus provides a suitable metaphor for the sense of constant striving for perfection. A curiously parallel practice is noted by Forstorp (1992: 96), who has studied another Faith congregation in Sweden, when he writes of being told by an informant that we are a mirror of what is inside us. In a ritualised echo of this sentiment (ibid.: 103), older children at the Faith school he examined are given as homework the task of saying Bible verses as they look at themselves (or one might say subject themselves to the evangelical gaze) in the mirror.

If such reflections of and on the body provide means of spiritual self-understanding, we can see how other sporting metaphors can reinforce the sense of striving and monitoring that is ideally constitutive of the charismatic life. In a recent article,[18] the chief pastor of the group, Ulf Ekman, constructs his message entirely out of adapting sporting biblical metaphors to a life of holiness. Ekman stresses that the author of Hebrews describes the Christian life thus: 'Your life is a race, and it is about running forward. If you have received Jesus as your Lord and Saviour … you still have a race to run. It is not about your salvation, for salvation is a gift; it is about what you do with what you have received, what you do with your salvation.' Among the theological ideas contained here is a key point: the sense that salvation is not enough, that it is rather the starting point for a Christian life in which there is no limit to what can be achieved – in working, social, political or religious life. Thus Ekman also refers to 1 Corinthians 9: 22–3 and claims that St Paul 'runs so that the Gospel may be preached to all people'. Referring to this vision of the believer as both mimetic of Paul and an athlete he adds that 'if you start panting after only a few feet, you need to go to a gym and start training so you can get back on the track again and finish the race … The Bible says that we are all to run!' In this view, the agent that is urging us 'to fight, train and do what sometimes hurts in order to win' is the Holy Spirit. As with the idea of Jesus as bodybuilder, inner training is ideally combined with outreach; the Christian life is one filled with power and movement but also a sense that one's achievements can be measured – in this case by winning whichever race is being run.

However, all we have examined so far are a picture and a form of biblical exegesis, both providing metaphorical expressions of Word of Life understandings of the power of both excess and display. So how might such images resonate with other understandings of bodily activity, and what might such resonances tell us about the ambiguities of the relationship between the material and the metaphorical amongst these charismatics?

We can begin to answer these questions by examining another normative statement by a Word of Life member, a teacher of sports at the Word of Life school called Rolf Stål.[19] Stål is writing in a pamphlet aimed at justifying the idea of Christian Schools in Sweden, but he takes the opportunity to examine the role of sports in the development of young members of the ministry. Some of what he says should by now be familiar: sport is seen as a way of providing role models for the young, as well as a pastime that prevents believers from being tempted by less salubrious pursuits. It is also seen as a way of reaching out to others, a secular bridge through which to engage people who might initially be attracted to physical activity rather than faith. What is particularly striking, however, is the way sport is effortlessly located within common charismatic tropes of spiritual practice and self-identity. Stål notes that in the congregation where he grew up sport was seen as a sin, but that in the Word of Life it is a part of the 'vision' for the group (59) since 'God wishes to use Sport!' Furthermore: 'As Christians we have been falsely accused of only stressing "spiritual" matters. In the Bible, and in our activities, there is a sound balance between spirit, soul and body', so that sports becomes a way of 'activating' pupils at the physical level. Thus Stål's final words are an admonition: 'Don't think small when it comes to sport!' Sport is thus presented as a signifier of a number of key themes: a generational shift, from older congregations to new; a means of regenerating an important dimension of the charismatic person; and an activity that – crucially – can partake of the aesthetic of constant expansion that marks the group.

If sport takes on a number of functions in such an account, it can also be shown to permeate and be juxtaposed with many activities within the ministry. In classic evangelical fashion, younger children are encouraged to combine sporting trips away with spiritual edification. Thus a summer camp held each year for ten-twelve year olds claims that 'During these camps many of the children decide to follow Jesus. It's the same with the sports camps arranged each winter.'[20] A significant element in taking the 'decision' is often the experience of being removed from family and exposed to concentrated teaching and peer pressure, but the result can be that the memory and experience of fundamental commitment is associated with the practice of sport and other physical activity, for instance in the oral narratives of their commitment to the faith that some younger members provided for me. Such juxtapositions also occur at the yearly, international conferences held in Uppsala. While adults attend the conferences, children are offered programmes combining music, theatre, youth services with 'Radical teaching about Jesus' and a full range of sports. Of interest here is the absolute lack of embarrassment in offering a panoply of activities that might have been anathema to earlier, more self-consciously pious generations of evangelicals – art and theatre join sport in a self-conscious appropriation of activities from the secular world.

Similarly striking combinations are evident elsewhere. Among the modules on offer at the 'Word of Life University' in the early 2000s, a course on Health Fitness could be found alongside others on Cultural Anthropology, American Foreign Policy, Oral Communication, Biblical Principles for Abundant Living and Signs and Wonders. The range of topics – merely a selection is given here – provides, in microcosm, an indication of the ideal skills required of a charismatic adapted to the new millennium: a reflexive attitude to culture within and beyond Sweden, an ability to use all the skills possible to convey one's message, but also an understanding that learning about the body is as relevant as understanding biblical principles.

My argument, however, is that sport can do more than combine easily with other Word of Life activities. My claim is that it can play a more dynamic, constitutive role in the creation of a broader charismatic aesthetic. By this I mean three basic things. First, that ideas and practices relating to the body and associated physical activities are assumed by believers to partake of the same fundamental principles that govern all aspects of the successful Christian life. In this chapter, we have seen three of these principles in action: the rhetoric of 'excess', the importance of self-monitoring and positive display (to the self and to others), and the sense of constant movement that should be part of the Christian life. Related to the first point is my second claim, that sporting metaphors and movements leach into, and are in turn influenced by, other activities. The ritual life of the ministry similarly valorises movement and expressions of bodily power in its services, which may involve dancing in the spirit and – on occasion in youth services I have attended – actual running around a hall. Becoming a member of the group involves not only an apparent ideological commitment to its principles, but also learning an embodied, kinesthetic mode of behaviour that may well be harder to shake off for ex-members than the group's theology precisely because it goes beyond words in its expression. We have already seen how the aesthetic of movement permeates narratives about sport, but consider the following account by an important functionary in the ministry, Svante Rumar:[21]

> When I was considering whether to assume the role of Dean for the Bible School, God gave me a picture. I saw a forest filled with runners carrying torches. Some runners amassed people around them and their little torches. Others ran toward a massive fire in the middle of the forest, into which they threw their torches, thereby creating an even greater fire, which warmed and lit up the entire forest in a way that the individual torches could not.
> I am so grateful today that I made the decision, together with many others, to throw my torch into the fire that God was igniting in this country, and that I can be a part of what He is doing and help strengthen the fire that has started to burn.

This is a very rich passage, and not all of its implications can be explored here. But note the imagery of running; of implicit measurement of others and of the self; and the sense of constant striving that is key to the religious aesthetic I have been describing. Rumar's 'vision' therefore takes on particular plausibility in Word of Life contexts because it is a verbal description of a practice that – metaphorically and literally – permeates so much of what it means to participate in the ministry. But it also contains a key ambiguity, which points to my third claim concerning the charismatic aesthetic I am describing. Can his 'vision' itself be taken as a literal event or a metaphorical account? He is telling a story, but it is after all a story given by God and therefore is likely to have a divine ontology, and moreover one that has a performative effect, prompting him not to start a fire in the forest, but to take an important job within the ministry. In fact, such ambiguity over whether metaphor might ultimately have a material referent is itself a common trope within the group. In a sense, we are back here to the charismatic sense that 'reality' comes in two forms, the natural and the supernatural. Metaphors suggest the possibility of the materialisation of divine intent in the world. So, for instance, is it appropriate to be a real bodybuilder as well as metaphorically? Not particularly, but at whatever age, as a Word of Life member one can expect health and other forms of prosperity in abundance. Charismatic commitment involves engaging rhetorically but also physically with principles of movement, monitoring of the self, and striving for a superabundance of the good. Referring to Catholic charismatics in America, Csordas (1997: 68) discusses the constitution and reconstitution of the self in ritual performance, but also warns of the dangers in confining analyses of 'self processes' to ritual alone, given the permeability of boundaries between ritual events and other spheres of life. Thus: 'To observe self-processes, or processes of self-objectification, is then not only to observe a striving for a sense of entity through performance but also to examine a series of shifting orientations among performance, experience, habitus, and everyday practice' (ibid.). My focus on the Word of Life has mostly not been about everyday experience per se, but I have attempted to show how Protestant charismatic practices of self-construction extend beyond conventional ritual forms, and that a significant set of parallel physical practices and metaphors are derived from sport. My point is that the charismatic technology of the body gains power precisely because it transcends the overtly ritual realm in exploring the agency and identity of the believer, demonstrating how different techniques of the body can derive from common aesthetic principles (cf. Dyck and Archetti 2003: 6).

Concluding Remarks

A Word of Life publication[22] tells the story of Kenneth Åsell, a shy child who took his revenge on teasing schoolmates by becoming a bodybuilder. Kenneth describes how the activity of bodybuilding – and even winning competitions – felt empty. However, his life changed in the late 1980s, when he was saved after meeting an American pastor who took Kenneth with him to a charismatic service.

One of the striking aspects of the story is that it is not a simple tale of replacing sport with spirituality. The pastor who helped to convert Kenneth was also a bodybuilder, and indeed their original encounter took place in a gym. Not only was the pastor a member of Power Team, a group of saved 'power sportsmen' who evangelise through performing around the world, but Kenneth continued his job as owner of a training centre, which is said to have become more successful after his conversion.

Kenneth's story, rather like that of Jim (although the two come from very different evangelical backgrounds) illustrates the ability of sport to be compatible with faith, indeed to provide an index of a life that is ideally full of grace, thus playing an important role in the monitoring of the believing self. In effect, we see how spiritual authority can be translated into physical prowess but also, potentially, vice versa. Indeed, Kenneth's story is actually a tale of how three aspects of his life – his faith, his body, his business – all respond to the same spiritual principles of growth, before being converted into a narrative that is a form of outreach to others. In this chapter, then, we have traced some of the shifts in the relationship between bodily practices and Christianity, especially conservative Protestantism, while retaining the claim that the body has provided a powerful index of religious commitment. Contemporary charismatic forms such as those displayed by the Word of Life may not present 'discipline' in the sense of a painful and penitential asceticism – far from it. And yet they do display a powerful form of self-regulation. The challenge for such believers is to retain the sense that the fundamental principles of the religious life operate in all spheres of existence, when to admit any doubt might be enough to cause those very principles to fail.

Notes

1. Though Victor Turner (1982: 37) notes that the Protestant Ethic affects leisure quite as much as work.
2. The critical review of Charles Kingsley's novel *Two Years Ago* appeared in the February 21, 1857 issue of *Saturday Review* (Ladd and Mathison 1999: 13–14). Kingsley's friend, Thomas Hughes, liked the term, attaching to it concepts of manliness, morality, and patriotism, sentiments that were at the root of his famous *Tom Brown's Schooldays* (1857) and *Tom Brown at Oxford* (1860). Hughes was also the author of *The Manliness of Christ.*
3. Interestingly, Sandiford (1994: 48) notes that muscular Christianity fed on emerging notions of social Darwinism. Spencer in due course began to fear that muscular Christianity was leading to violence, aggressive imperialism and war, and so became less of an advocate for it.
4. Here, there may be interesting comparisons with Kohn's argument (this volume) concerning aikido practitioners' ability to 'take things from the mat' into other areas of life.
5. Putney (2001: 51) points out further that the Church Fathers' discovery of Plato in the early Middle Ages intensified their aversion to carnal amusements.
6. To some extent, such attitudes fed into political forms of stereotyping, embodying assumptions concerning dissolute and undisciplined British aristocrats of the colonial period and, later, forming a critique of the 'southern gentlemen', who supposedly passed his time in gambling and other leisure pursuits.
7. Messenger (1999) discusses the subsequent establishment of Ocean Grove, New Jersey, founded in the nineteenth century as a Methodist utopian village that offered a safe holiday haven from the demands of the city and alternative seaside resorts such as Atlantic City.
8. Sandiford (1994) discusses the sports explosion that took place in Britain after 1850 and which sprang from improvement in standards of living, reductions in working hours and the development of more positive attitude towards 'manly' exercises.
9. Swedenborgianism was based on the writings of the Swedish philosopher and theologian Emanuel Swedenborg (1688–1772), who emphasised that humans live in a world of the spirit as well as of material reality.
10. Sinclair Lewis's famous novel *Elmer Gantry* (1927) was to satirise the idea of the corrupt preacher. Gantry was in fact fond of using sporting metaphors in his sermons.
11. Admittedly, one important element of the older 'penitential' attitude to the body has been retained, albeit translated into modern concerns. Griffith (2004) traces the long history

of Christian dieting movements in the United States, influenced by New Thought as well as more optimistic forms of evangelical Protestantism.

12. For a more detailed history and account, see Coleman 2000.

13. Swartling (ms).

14. One of McCauley's most famous congregants, Hansie Cronje, was captain of the South African cricket team for part of the 1990s, before being disgraced for match-fixing. Cronje wore a bracelet engraved with the initials WWJD 'What Would Jesus Do?' (*The Observer* 2 June 2002). He died in 2002 in a plane crash, having studied for a Master's degree in business.

15. Of course, not all representations of Jesus are heavily muscled, but he tends to be shown as young, vigorous, and free from the cross.

16. Numerous means exist to rationalise the unhealthy body, including the notion that the devil attacks those who are physically strong, or that healing/fitness has occurred 'in the supernatural' but not yet 'in the natural'.

17. Formed in the early 1980s, the group has been heavily criticised as a simple embodiment of a style of evangelicalism that has been seen by other church leaders as ill-suited to Swedish cultural and social ideals of mutual accommodation and cooperation among interest groups and church bodies. The congregation has around 2000 members, while the Bible School has over the years attracted thousands of students from Scandinavia and abroad to its courses, making it possibly the biggest such school in Europe. Many of those attracted to the ministry have come from other Protestant denominations.

18. *News Report* 2, 2004: 4–5. The article is called 'Press Toward the Goal for the Prize'.

19. The article (1989) is called 'Sport fulfils an important function' (all translations are mine) and appears in Ekman et al *Starta Kristna Skolor! En Rapport Från Livets Ords Kristna Skola* Uppsala: Livets Ords Förlag, pp. 59–61.

20. Word of Life Web site 13/07/99 (http://www.livetsord.se/).

21. *News Report* Issue 2, 2003, p.7.

22. *Magazinet* No. 7, September 1994.

References

Coleman, S. 2000. *The Globalisation of Charismatic Christianity: Spreading the Gospel of Success*, Cambridge: Cambridge University Press.

Csordas, T. 1997. *Language, Charisma, and Creativity: The Ritual Life of a Religious Movement*, Berkeley: University of California Press.

Dyck, N. and E. Archetti 2003 'Embodied Identities: Reshaping Social Life Through Sport and Dance' in *Sport, Dance and Embodied Identities*, (eds) N. Dyck and E.P. Archetti, Oxford: Berg, pp.1–19.

Forstorp, P.A. 1992. *Att Leva och Läsa Bibeln: Textpraktiker i Två Kristna Församlingar*, Linköping: Linköping University Press.

Frykman, J. 1987. 'Clean and Proper', in *Culture Builders: A Historical Anthropology of Middle-Class Life*, (eds) J. Frykman and O. Löfgren, New Brunswick, Rutgers University Press, pp. 157–220.

Griffith, R. 2004. *Born Again Bodies : Flesh and Spirit in American Christianity*, Berkeley: University of California Press.

Higgs, R. and M. Braswell 2004. *Unholy Alliance: The Sacred and Modern Sports*, Macon, Georgia: Mercer University Press.

Ladd, T. and J. Mathison 1999. *Muscular Christianity: Evangelical Protestants and the Development of American Sport,* Grand Rapids, Mi: Baker Books.

Löfgren, O. 1999. *On Holiday: A History of Vacationing,* Berkeley: University of California Press.

Mangan, J.A. 1988. *Pleasure, Profit, Proselytism: British Culture and Sport at Home and Abroad,* London: Frank Cass.

Messenger, T. 1999. *Holy Leisure: Recreation and Religion in God's Square Mile,* Minneapolis: University of Minnesota Press.

Moore, R. 1994. *Selling God: American Religion in the Marketplace of Culture,* Oxford: Oxford University Press.

Putney, C. 2001. *Muscular Christianity: Manhood and Sports in Protestant America, 1880–1920,* Cambridge: Harvard University Press.

Sandiford, K. 1994. *Cricket and the Victorians,* Aldershot: Scolar Press.

Stål, R. 1989. 'Idrotten fyller en Viktig Funktion' in *Starta Kristna Skolor! En Rapport Från Livets Ords Kristna Skola,* (eds) U. Ekman, M.-K. Nilsson and H. Gabre,Uppsala: Livets Ords Förlag, pp. 59–61

Turner, V. 1982. *From Ritual to Theatre: The Human Seriousness of Play,* New York: Paj.

PART II

TEMPORALITIES OF LEISURE

4

AN ADVENTURE TOURIST EXPERIENCE

Maurice J. Kane and Hazel Tucker

Introduction

I thought it went like a dream. I carved diagonally left to right across the top of the drop, railed on the lip and span into the flat water of the right hand eddy. Dreams, however, are rarely identical to reality. I had put more body power than style into the move, fought the water, it redirected my efforts shooting me back into the drop. I tried to turn, went nose vertical in the drop before cart-wheeling down stream. I was now tail vertical in the main flow, with fifteen meters till the hardest series of drops in this section. Pirouetting out of control to the left-hand side of the river, I flopped on to a semi-submerged rock and was upside down. The freezing water instantly produced a power roll that pulled me half out of my borrowed kayak, straight back on to the rock: flop, I had a wet head. I needed to slow down, pull myself back into my seat and probably change rolling sides. I didn't. I power rolled again, my spray skirt peeled open, and although I still had time to trust my skills, I bailed out.

The only thing worse than an 'ice block' head on a fast flowing glacier feed river is a totally wet body, especially five meters from the next drop, and with three hundred meters of serious rapids to follow. The water raced the kayak over the drop as I flailed to the left and was spattered on to a bus-sized boulder. I was being sucked down like in a movie, with my focus on two wet hands making imaginary grooves in the vertical granite. I was then in a washing machine tumbling in a tight ball under the boulder. I had never thought I'd drown kayaking, but now I was at the start of a rock sieve (where water squeezes through constrictions under large rocks). It was cold, black and the water was making a rag doll of my body, I could do nothing, and then I hit the tree. I had a burst of adrenaline, got a hold, reached along to the next broken branch stump, hoping I was going up out of the darkness, to air.

All of a sudden I was alive. I stood in knee-deep water ten metres from where my hand marks were still visible on the bus-sized boulder's right-hand end. My hangover was gone, the sun felt very warm on my face. I thought back to the sun in Northern India six months earlier, when a friend hadn't had the luck of a tree.

In one minute a new epic story had been born but one not often told. It was an epic, not an adventure, as the witnesses and those that know the rapid realise it should have had a different ending (Kane, Kayaking diary, 1995).

The leisure activity of white-water kayaking, especially in its practice as described above, can aptly be termed serious leisure. Serious in this sense is its potential physical danger ('ice-block' head), including extreme fear and 'rag-doll' submission to the power of water. Simultaneously, however, the participant can experience the high of success. It is these two opposing elements that together motivate participants in their leisure kayaking to gain, execute and retain specific skills. Such skills can become automatic reactions both in the physical practice of kayaking and in the social interaction surrounding the kayaking activity. Pierre Bourdieu (1984) has described such automatic actions as the 'feel for the game', or in one word, the participant's 'habitus'. Habitus is the knowledge, which can be unconscious or tacit, related to a specific 'field', and which produces both physical and social interaction within that field.

This chapter explores the combining of two leisure fields; 'serious' white-water kayaking and tourism. It examines how the participants on a white-water kayaking package tour negotiate the expectations, roles, images and narratives in this experience. At its extremes the negotiation is between, on the one hand, the potential physical danger of kayaking, and on the other hand, the package tourist experience, which is succinctly described by Bauman (1996: 29) as a world tamed and domesticated, where 'shocks come in a package deal with safety'. Indeed, Schmidt (1979) has previously described this form of packaged and guided tour as 'insulated adventure', where 'the tourist exchanges some of the freedom that would be available to him [her] in other traveller roles (and hence opportunities for adventurism) for the relatively problem-free situation provided by the guided tour' (ibid.: 446). For the participants on this tour, indeed, the organisation provided the 'tourism insulation' of stress-free access to kayaking adventures and thus the perception of safety and play. As they also undertook extreme white-water kayaking, however, the tour simultaneously presented the challenge and potential danger of the kayaking field.

The description that commenced this chapter was used with two intentions. Firstly it established the physical reality of the type of white-water kayaking that was the marketing focus of the package tour studied, although only a small section of its itinerary in practice. This marketing focus correlated with the potential to successfully experience extreme kayaking that is otherwise the reserve of the sports élite. In addition, the opening extract situated the first author within the 'field' of kayaking. The importance of this lies in the first author's ability to undertake ethnographic fieldwork on the tour with an informed understanding of the kayaking world. Having a personal history of the kayaking habitus allowed the fieldworker to actually be on the rivers with the kayakers and to join in the pre- and post river banter. The purpose of this chapter is to explore some of the complexities and tensions present in the 'kayaking tourist' identity. In doing so, it highlights the tour participants' negotiations of these contradictory roles, showing how the 'seriousness' of kayaking leisure is in apparent conflict with the freedom and play of being a 'tourist' far away from home.

The Tour and the Kayakers

The tour was conducted in the South Island of New Zealand over a two-week period in the summer of 2002. As an inclusive package tour it included all food, accommodation and equipment for the nine clients, all of whom consented to participate in the research. Their investment in this tour included a two thousand five hundred U.S. dollars tour tariff, which did not include a two thousand U.S. dollars airfare. Also on the tour was the first author in his research role, two kayaking guides leading the tour, plus two drivers who also did the cooking. Following a circular route from Christchurch, the largest South Island city, the tour travelled approximately fifteen hundred kilometres over two-thirds of the island. The time limit of the tour created a tension between the time spent white-water kayaking and the time spent travelling from river location to location, with only three locations stayed in for more than one night. The kayaking involved between two and eight hours on eleven of the fourteen days, on thirteen different rivers.

Tours such as this reflect the global growth in participation in kayaking over the last decades of the twentieth century. This increase was partly stimulated by travel/cultural discovery documentaries that, throughout the 1970s and 1980s, deployed adventure activities such as rafting and kayaking either to access remote areas or as the adventure challenge in stories of discovery. A further popularity boost came when white-water kayaking returned as a sport at the 1992 and 1996 Olympics. These factors stimulated the use of improved kayaking equipment, increased competitions, promotion and the recognition of kayaking as a sport, and established a professional élite group of kayakers. It was the international members of this élite group, visiting New Zealand for the world freestyle kayaking championships in 1999 and 2000, who promoted New Zealand as a kayaking destination on the world stage. Consequently, through adventure articles and videos New Zealand, and more specifically the West Coast of the South Island, became 'the hottest extreme kayaking destination on the planet' (Canard 2000: 15). In New Zealand, the most prestigious kayaking is on the West Coast's helicopter-accessed rivers (heli-kayaking), and indeed, these West Coast rivers were also a central focus and prominently marketed feature of the tour that forms the basis of this chapter. It should be re-emphasised, however, that only two of the fourteen tour days were scheduled to involve heli-kayaking.

The nine tour participants, two females and seven males, were all citizens of the United States of America. Seven were resident in the state of California, one in Georgia and one in Florida. They ranged in age from thirty-two years to fifty-five years. They had all attended some form of tertiary education, and their financial position would be described as middle class and higher. This structure of guided kayaking tour was not new to them, with four of the participants having been on over five such tours. Five participants had also been on a previous tour together, but they seldom kayaked together away from tour situations. There was a wide range of kayaking experience and skill levels. One participant had only been on one previous beginners' kayaking tour, while one had kayaked at a national level and been involved in kayaking for thirty-five years. All, however, shared a commitment to kayaking, which had provided the impetus to travel halfway round the world for this. It is this level of commitment to kayaking, and particularly to what is deemed prestigious in the kayaking world, that suggests that for these participants kayaking is a serious leisure (Stebbins 1982, 1992, 1996, 1999).

Interpreting Serious Leisure

Commitment, progression, belonging and the ethos of a defined culture are at the core of the concept of 'serious leisure', initially proposed by Stebbins in 1982. At this time Stebbins foresaw that with increased leisure involvement, an individual's identity-formation would be derived as much from leisure social worlds as from the dominant work-oriented social worlds. Leisure was contrasted to work and individuals could, depending on the social world they chose to focus on, create an identity that was oriented to the values of that social world. Stebbins defined categories and distinct qualities of serious leisure social worlds that created 'unique sets of special norms, values, beliefs, styles, moral principles, performance standards, and similar shared representations' (1999: 71). It is the uniqueness constructed around a particular leisure activity that provides the ability for participants to create a distinct identity and social stratification within their serious leisure social world. Research into recreational participation in climbing, rugby, skydiving, windsurfing and endurance racing has highlighted similar qualities and theories on identity, sub-culture and 'career stages' (Donnelly and Young 1988; Green and Chalip 1988; Celsi, Rose and Leigh 1993; Ewert, 1994; Wheaton, 2000; Kay and Laberge 2002a, 2002b). The latter of these by Kay and Laberge (2002a, 2002b) describe the participation and experience of a specific leisure recreation using the sociological ideas of Pierre Bourdieu.

Bourdieu's (1977, 1984, 1990, 1998) interest was in understanding and interpreting the practices of social interaction, with three of his most important ideas being 'fields', 'habitus' and different forms of 'capital'. For Bourdieu a 'field' is not a concept to group or define people such as serious leisure kayakers, it is a way of analysing their practices and interactions in terms of a 'way of thinking'. Central to how a 'field' functions and is defined are 'interests and stakes', or in other words, the participants' involvement and the level of this involvement. Within a field, participants compete for 'specific capital' to gain, retain and re-enforce their involvement. 'Specific capital' relates, as the name implies, to its specific field and may be of no interest or value in any other field. The establishment and evolution of specific capital is a dynamic process related to the essence of a field and within it the participants' 'way of thinking'. It is a way of thinking influenced by those with the most specific capital. In the case of the serious leisure kayaking field, the latter are the élite kayakers. On the researched tour, there were multiple fields or ways of thinking about the activities and experiences of the tour. With kayaking as the main focus, however, the participants' ability to compete for kayakings' specific capital was vital.

The ability to compete can be encapsulated in Bourdieu's idea of 'habitus', the participants' 'feel for the game'. In the practice of kayaking, for those with the most feel for the game, habitus is 'embodied and turned into second nature. Nothing is simultaneously freer and more constrained than the actions of the good player' [or kayaker] (Bourdieu 1990: 63). A participant's habitus is equally embodied in the social interaction within fields that develop around leisure activities, such as a kayaking social world. Habitus is a participant's 'system of disposition' but does 'not lead in a determinate way to a determinate action' (Bourdieu 2000: 149–50). Bourdieu's ideas allow us to interpret practice in a way that recognises the similarities in how we understand our experiences but also allows for new understandings as 'fields' are combined and 'ways of thinking' are negotiated against each other. This is exemplified in the present study through the combined fields of serious kayaking and tourism.

The Tour Experience

The flow of the experience of this tour was very similar to the experience of kayaking any single river. There was anticipation of the river/tour experience derived from guidebooks and promotional material, which was continually referred to for comparison in the initial stages. There was the initial coming together of the group that was going to share the experience, each member forming impressions of the others and asserting particular identities. At this initial stage, everyone shared, although to varying degrees according to previous experience, the leisure activity of kayaking, its social world and the kayaking 'way of thinking'. What every (paying) participant also had in common was their nationality, and the ability to pay for the tour. Later, the initial coming together was replaced with a focus on the new challenges this particular journey would present. River experiences vary but they usually present a combination of different channels to be explored, minor rapids as well as major tests of skill and commitment, plus sections of floating and enjoying the view. This tour had all these elements, with one distinct challenge and highlight in the West Coast heli-kayaking. Once the heli-kayaking was completed, this pivotal focus became a memory, a story to be created, moulded and re-created in its telling. The voicing of the participants' tour experiences will follow the flow of this typical river of experience, with three phases; initial identity formation, followed by a focus on the disciplining challenge of kayaking, and concluding with their creative experience stories. In all three stages, it is clear that the key point of the participants' negotiation of the experience concerned their being both leisure tourists and serious kayakers.

Just a Bunch of Kayakers

On the third day, Cara described the group to an enquiring outsider as being 'just a bunch of kayakers'. This reflects the dominance of kayaking in the identity formation within the group. Amongst the group, stories of previous kayaking experience were the currency of identity and status formation. Initially, kayaking conversations focused on personal preferences for a type of kayak, the effectiveness of paddles and the quality of particular kayaking clothing. As the first river was approached the environment was compared with elsewhere ('that looks a lot like northern California'), and the first glimpses of the river were greeted with 'it looks the same size ... colour ... flow as the (x) river'. All participants were keen to tell of their previous experiences, and those perceived to have the most experience, such as the guides, were often asked to comment on and affirm a participant's story. The point that the 'acceptable topic of conversation among tourists is their experience as tourists' has been observed in several tourist studies (Schmidt 1979: 461; Dann 1996; Pearce 1991; Ryan 1995; Selwyn 1996). It was through this discussion of kayaking experiences and also kayaking tour experiences that participants reaffirmed the supremacy of kayaking as the core of this tour, and stratified their intra group relationships.

There was limited discussion of other status signifiers, such as wealth, occupation or education. As Bruce expressed one evening, 'How did I do this trip with you for three days and not know what you do [your profession]?'. This is indicative of the notion of a 'short-lived society' (Foster 1986), where limited time and a packaged daily routine narrowly focuses social interaction. The tour structure and the tourist role may have concentrated social interaction, but it was the participants' commitment to kayaking, or in Stebbins' terms their 'serious leisure' (1982), that was directing social interaction and identity formation. Experience stories were valued in relation to their qualities in the field of kayaking. The relative lack of prestige given to Eric's experiences as a kayaking official at both the Barcelona and Atlanta Olympics highlights the complexity in this value system. It would appear that participation and stories of kayaking were of greater value than commitment to its administration as a sport. Eric's other global kayaking stories were often discussed and his knowledge sought. In contrast were Phil's experiences of a well-known river in Southern Carolina. As Phil recounted, 'I shouldn't have been there – a guy was taking me down. I went through a thing called "Hydro-electric" and in the book [guidebook] it says a swim here will probably be your last!' Phil had been tossed out of the kayak and swum this rapid twice and was viewed as both heroic for persevering but also lacking in skill. In the participants' kayaking field, participation must indicate skill and not just heroic commitment (Donnelly and Young 1988; Celsi et al. 1993; Wheaton 2000).

The ultimate validation of the participant's kayaking stories, in effect the 'symbolic capital' they were seeking to establish within the tour group, came in the practice of kayaking. On the initial rivers this symbolic capital was either transformed into specific capital or perceived as hollow, depending on skill level. There was an excitement about being on the water, and participants' discussion prior to a river trip speculated on each other's prospective failure or success, yet they did not talk afterwards about their own or each other's individual performances. Participants were disciplined in their practice by their potential to fail. They could not physically produce a kayaking practice that was beyond their 'habitus', their feel for the game. The result, if attempted, was usually failure, or success would be perceived as lucky rather than the result of skill. In this way the participants' identities were aligned to their embodied practice. Their competition for kayaking's 'specific capital', for identities and status as kayakers, could only be validated and established through displays of embodied practice that were valued within the field. The 'specific capital' gained indicates individuals' status level. High status bestows authority in kayaking knowledge, stories and opinions, while on the river infers leadership in route taking, skills display and, importantly, as reliable rescuers.

The participants' identity establishment and intra-group stratification dominated the first three days of the tour. This period was inwardly focused on the group, its serious leisure of kayaking and its way of thinking. Cara's description of the group displayed a second element that then became more prominent after these first three days, as participants sought to differentiate themselves from non-kayakers and to present identities as travelling kayakers rather than tourists. To distinguish themselves in the non-kayaking world, where their kayaking 'symbolic capital' could not be validated into specific capital, the participants had to rely on overt and physical identity markers. The vans loaded with kayaks presented a clear image. The participants understood that non-kayakers had a different way of thinking about their kayaking practice: 'Oh my work peers think I'm as nutty as a fruitcake' (Eric); 'I think they view it as a very dangerous sport and some wild streak in me' (Shane); 'Oh they think I'm insane' (Phil); 'Probably like a complete nut' (Robert). These descriptors linked kayaking to risk and danger, not to the practice of kayaking skills. Yet, the participants considered these descriptions positively as they differentiated and characterised their identity as distinct from others and with access to a different social world (Celsi et al. 1993; Kay and Laberge 2002a, 2002b). These adventurous social world and identity descriptors were also re-enforced by the distant, international travel aspect of this tour. As one participant said, 'anybody that's on this trip is adventurous ... but how many people go to New Zealand? No one I know!'

The overt presentation of kayaking also had the benefit of distinguishing the participants within the field of tourism. Rather than tourists, or even adventure tourists, in their way of thinking they were travelling kayakers. Rachael described the importance of kayaking and her way of thinking where being a tourist was only a means to further her kayaking: 'It's like now my life is being driven by, what big trip are we doing this year? What river are we going to do this year?' Like Rachael, all the participants' understanding of the tour and the identities they presented were oriented to a kayaking way of thinking. After the initial focus on confirming group identity and establishing individual kayaking capital within the group, attention became dominated by the challenge of the heli-kayaking trip.

The Disciplining Practice of Kayaking

In participants' kayaking history there was often an experience such as Eric's lucky escape or Rachael's revelation of kayaking's importance in shaping her future life. For Robert this discipline of kayaking and joy of its practice was all part of his first experience of the activity:

> I saw an article, and I'd actually built a kind of boat … did about a class three plus rapid without any life jackets or anything and just really enjoyed that. We got beat up pretty bad but! So I saw something in the paper about kayaking in Kernville [learn to kayak course] and thought I'd give it a shot and it was a weird experience because the second I got in and on my first real river I had this like vision … imagine the places to go doing something like this and imagine the people I'd meet … this is going to be part of my future. I knew right away that I love this sport.

Robert's vision of his ongoing love of kayaking came after experiencing the potential physical danger of kayaking and recognising the need for the discipline of learning skills if his imagined places and people were to be part of his future. The practice of kayaking always has this negative potential, even if on level water (for beginners) with only the risk of getting wet. The counterbalance is the joy of practice and the imagined joys of more exclusive or skilful experiences. All the participants had had some form of structured learning and in most cases this evolved out of negative experience. Shane's memory was typical:

> We realised we were pretty crappy boaters, so we decided to go take some lessons. We went down to Nantahala [Large kayak training/tour organisation in North Carolina]. We took the beginner, intermediate and advanced courses at Nantahala for three different years and that opened up the South East [of America].

Shane also followed a progression in his first international kayaking package tours with this organisation: 'I kind of worked my way up from the intermediate trip to the advanced trip down there [Costa Rica]'. As all other participants had taken previous kayaking tours with Nantahala, it was likely that some form of training was a prerequisite to advance to more prestigious and difficult tours. The participant's experience and understanding of kayaking had skills learning at its core, a discipline that extended to the experience of a kayaking tour. The influence of this discipline became progressively more apparent on the tour as the kayaking challenge increased and the pivotal heli-kayaking event approached.

In the first few days of the tour, as the participants (and guides) were establishing their kayaking capital, the trips had been relatively limited in challenges. The guides gathered two groups of mixed confidence and skill level around themselves and allowed each group to explore the rivers virtually unguided. The guides became increasingly directive, however, as the challenges and corresponding dangers on the rivers multiplied. Participants quickly adapted to this new disciplined experience although some of the more skilful participants did express dissatisfaction and requested more challenging options from the guides. They were looking for challenges where the potential dangers would be matched by their skill level and lead to the worthy joy of success. Bruce, the most skilled participant, described this in the following way:

> The challenge for me is that I always feel most excited after a rapid if I pick out the line I want to go and I can hit exactly that line. Because the risk is that water has a lot of force ... you predict to the best of your abilities, what it is going to do, and use the water in a way that you can get through the rapid doing the things you want to do.

The way the challenge was managed here was not uncalculated but was reflective of skills learned and a desire to test this learning. As the anticipation built up towards the West Coast trip, the guides offered more instruction, often initiated by them but also sought by all the participants, no matter what skill level. For some of the participants this came in response to their lack of confidence as the kayaking challenges increased. Cara was a skilled and experienced kayaker who had recently had a very challenging kayaking experience and now found the challenge was 'working up the courage to, to do it'. Meanwhile Robert admitted: 'I try to ride the fine line balancing skill and challenge, success and failure'.

The skill of kayaking is more then just getting down the river. Essentially it involves balancing three controllable variables, your kayak's speed, horizontal lean, and horizontal angle, in relation to the constantly variable water current. A tight fitting kayak, sitting with shoulders slightly forward and, as in many moving sports, a still head are among the first kayaking instructions taught. Demonstrations of skill usually display these features but those with the highest kayaking status display an effortless grace, feel and oneness with the water that disguise any effort or potential for danger.

The tour participants were clearly demonstrating their skill and 'feel for the game', not just in the field of kayaking but also in kayak tours. Indeed, part of their kayaking 'habitus' was their choice of a guided tour, matching their skills to the best opportunity to successfully experience prestigious kayaking. With their understanding of kayaking as a disciplined leisure activity or sport, the participants aligned themselves to the guides' discipline, for discipline brought success. As Allan reasoned, the guides would be 'irresponsible if they put us in a risk position'.

Risk, the negative potential outcome, was part of the field of kayaking and a major component in the prestige of the expectant pivotal tour experience. There was disappointment, however: 'It makes it relatively tame as adventure goes, to have somebody who can tell you for every rapid go right, go left, you know!' This comment reflected all the participants' disappointment with the first of the heli-kayak rivers, which was at very low water level and less challenging than rivers already experienced. There had been apprehension and tension prior to this pivotal river, but although the guides directed the experience and the participants played their roles, the river did not provide the challenge or potential danger anticipated. Shane sought to highlight the positive and novel aspects of this disappointing experience: 'I mean "Helicopter Kayaking", I've never had a helicopter pick me up and drop me off on a creek run before'.

The second heli-kayaking river experience quickly erased the disappointment from the first river. It fulfilled participants' expectation of prestigious kayaking with all the clients either getting wet in or walking around rapids in the first hour. There was obvious potential danger, as guides directed and matched the challenges to the participants' skill levels and had the whole group walk around one rapid. The day was full of tension and nerves, with the less confident participants seeking reassurance that they had the skills to complete rapids and openly vocalising their apprehension; 'I don't like this, this is way too hairy.' The tension for the guides was in directing the over-confident participants, who over-evaluated their skills and under-evaluated the potential danger. By the end of the day, these participants had had minor 'epics', parting company with their kayaks, but through skilful guiding in places they were all quickly rescued. The more competent participants were also given additional options to test their skills, and in these cases the skills test was not in completing a rapid but in judging whether to take or decline the option or choosing how the rapid was kayaked.

By the end of the day the participants were ecstatic with the experience, including those who had had 'minor epics'. They had taken the challenge of the prestigious West Coast heli-kayaking trip and had been successful. The pivotal experience of the tour was over; the hardest 'work' had been done. There were more rivers to be kayaked, still four days of the tour to go, but metaphorically the participants could see the end of the river. It was time to start telling the stories, stories of experiencing a prestigious destination that only the élite kayakers and a few of their peers had experienced. This latter tour period was not focused on the discipline of challenging practice, but on the carefully crafted constructing of their experience-based stories of this tour.

Creating Experience Stories

Kayakers like to sit around and talk about; where have you been? What rapids have you done? What near escape from the jaws of death have you encountered? It's part of the experience! People like to hear where you've been: 'Oh you went to the Futaluefu? [Famous river in Chile]' or 'you went to New Zealand?' or 'you went to Nepal?'. Everybody then starts to ask you what it was like, thus highlighting the importance of experience stories in the kayaking culture, and also the importance of symbolic capital stories of prestigious kayaking destinations.

On this trip, after the heli-kayaking experience on the West Coast, the participants' socialising developed a routine of scripting, telling and re-scripting their tour stories, stories that almost exclusively focused on heli-kayaking. Digital photos were reviewed and selected and arrangements were made for their exchange. Images taken from the helicopter or of participants arriving at the riverside by helicopter were particularly desired as this feature was unique and confirmed their participation in West Coast heli-kayaking. These images replicated those of the kayaking élite whose promotion of the West Coast had drawn the participants to this tour. What the participants did not have, however, were on-the-water action images that were identical or even similar to the kayaking élite. The participants were not skilled photographers. Also, they had completed some of the easier heli-kayaking rivers and even on these they had walked some of the rapids. For the participants to gain kayaking 'capital' from their stories they had to focus on the novelty of their helicopter experience complete with verifying images. Participants understood they had not experienced extreme, élite kayaking, yet this tour experience gave them the freedom to create experience stories that could, dependent on the audience, influence their capital in various fields.

The constraint on this freedom was that the stories had to relate to each specific audience and reflect their 'capital' in each audience's field. Each participant had a 'capital' position in the kayaking field and their kayaking 'habitus' or 'feel for the game' was critical to their stories' success. The stories had to demonstrate the valued qualities of their serious leisure, commitment, perseverance and gaining of skills, but they also needed to be believable in relation to their present 'capital'. As Eric remarked:

> This has been a very pleasant adventure but I wouldn't call myself an adventurer. I'd consider this more as a wonderfully packaged and relatively controlled environment. Um … again I would have been disappointed in this trip when I was twenty-two years old [approximate age of the majority of élite kayakers], but at forty-six, knowing I have different priorities and quite frankly a different skill level, it's actually a very enjoyable trip.

Eric's sentiment contrasts with Rachael's and David's who thought they 'were really adventurous' and used phrases such as 'extreme, hard-core and way out there' in describing the trip. For their kayaking peers with similar limited capital, as David described it, 'just being somewhere different and just the people that you are with creates the adventure'. David's and Rachael's non specific but adventurous descriptions of the kayaking would be accepted by their peers, while Eric's peers would require more specific information if he emphasised the challenge of the kayaking.

One feature that none of the participants emphasised was the part that the guides' direction had in the limiting of the negative potential outcomes and ensuring of success. The experience stories all had potential danger as a core, as this danger was what allowed participants to use their judgement and skill to be successful. To present an experience story in the kayaking social world where, as Bruce had complained, somebody tells you 'go right, go left' was not to present a story of adventure kayaking but of adventure tourism.

Adventure tourists, as David sought to describe, were 'dragged through like cattle', while kayakers had control of their experience and could measure its worth against the qualities valued as capital in the kayaking field. Adventure tourism stories emphasised heroics, action and thrills that did not relate to the participants' skills. As Robert expressed, 'People cannot grasp why I do what I do. You know they think I'm a complete nut, they think it's a very dangerous thing. I don't think so. I think it's relative, I don't jump into a rapid I don't think I can handle, I work my way up to it'.

The participants realised their non-kayaking audience would view their experience stories in terms of adventure tourism's thrills and heroics, and any storied description of skills or prestigious destination would not be comprehended. Rachael described adventure tourists as, 'a bunch of middle class, … middle aged people out somewhere they would not normally get to go'. More experienced participants, such as Eric and Bruce, were critical of the lack of self-control in adventure tourism activities such as bungee jumping or rafting. In Eric's view, adventure tourists were 'not involved in instantaneous and constant decision making about management of risk'. Yet these participants still sought the positive 'heroic and thrill seeker' response from the non-kayaker audience. As Phil pondered, 'I don't look at myself as an, ahh adventurer, but I know because of where I go and what I do, I would be looked upon in that way. I kinda like that'!

This paradox between distancing themselves from adventure tourists while also enjoying other tourists' viewing them as heroic was evident in the more vibrant interactions with non-kayakers in the last days of the tour. The stories for non-kayakers exaggerated the difficulty they had experienced, with comments such as 'it is as hard as it gets, … five meter drops', or 'very few people have done the section we did'. These more exaggerated stories relayed in interaction with non-kayakers were told during two nights spent after the heli-kayaking in Queenstown, the hyped up 'adventure capital' of New Zealand. Towards the end of the tour, there was a willingness to interact with non-kayakers, reduce kayaking time and relax into tourist activities such as purchasing souvenirs and gifts.

Intra-group conversations at this stage turned to future kayaking tours, anticipating and comparing this tour together with past tour experiences to the next potential tour. They discussed which kayaking destination was, as Rachael phrased it, next to be 'ticked off the life list'. This assessing and anticipating of future options was the last uniting bond as the tour concluded and participants were taken to the airport for their flights home. The reality of the tour became only a memory, an experience story to be played with, within the freedom and constraints of the 'way of thinking' of the participants and their audience.

Conclusion

The participants' anticipation, lived experience and narrated stories of this tour were focused on the activity of kayaking. Kayaking underpinned the participants' behaviours, their language, their intra-group social interactions and the external image they presented. For the duration of the tour they were not accountants, police chiefs, engineers or even tourists, they were adventure kayakers. Whilst being dominant, kayaking was not their only 'field', however, as being an adventure tourist, or indeed a package tourist, were two more of the ways participants could act out or understand their experience. They negotiated these competing 'fields' as well as the complexity of their desired identity, in order to construct their experiences.

Kayaking will be at the core of participants' stories of the tour, and it is through these stories that they will seek to gain, retain or advance their kayaking social world status. In terms of Bourdieu's ideas, they will advance their 'specific capital' in the kayaking 'field'. This social world is part of their serious leisure participation, with a social ethos that could be described as more constrained and disciplined than free. To gain the 'capital', participants' stories must emphasise valued kayaking qualities, such as learnt skills, perseverance and the successful testing of their skills. They must demonstrate their accomplishment within the prestigious West Coast kayaking destination, providing evidence of their successfully challenging the inherent potential danger of the kayaking activity. They must be stories focused on their adventure as kayakers, and not on being guided tourists participating in kayaking. The stories of the tour will discount the guided and tourist aspects, and focus instead on the kayaking 'habitus' and feel for the game of kayaking. Such a feel must show successful experience, a success that is reliant on safety. As Robert pondered towards the end of the tour, 'if someone was injured or had died, would I still look back at the overall trip as an adventure or a disaster?' This safety is implicitly guaranteed in the tourism 'field', and especially in the packaged, guided product.

The participants had more freedom in their tour stories told to non-kayaking peers. These were stories of adventure tourism where heroism and thrill comparison replaced tests of skills and perseverance. The product of this freedom was the inability for these stories to confirm more than the generic adventure tourist image of thrill seeking risk-taking. It was not the ideal image participants sought from this tour experience, but it was an image that did differentiate them within the tourism 'field' and it was the tourism 'field' that was more prominent in the latter stages of the tour. By that time, the challenge and discipline of successful kayaking had been achieved and the participants could now relax and enjoy the destination. Yet even in this less intensely kayaking-skills learning focused period of the tour, the distinguishing feature of kayaking had to be presented to differentiate their adventure, even if the qualities of the activity were not assessed.

The differentiation of adventure is a constant in participants' stories of this tour experience. Images of kayaking adventure had brought them to New Zealand, but they endeavoured to limit the potential negative outcomes of this adventure experience through the structure of a guided tour. They also understood that owing to their kayaking they were seen as adventurous, as heroic risk-takers, although, as Eric expressed, 'danger actually we really try specifically to avoid'. The participants' stories presented holograms of adventure, reflections of the imagined reality of the kayaking élite. Their tour experiences were a negotiation where they played at the reality of adventure within the safety of the tour structure. As one participant said, 'Somehow it just seems safer to do adventure tourism than adventure'.

References

Bauman, Z. 1996. 'From Pilgrim to Tourist: Or a short History of Identity', in *Questions of Cultural Identity*, (ed.) S. Hall and P. du Gay, London: Sage Publications, pp. 18–36.

Bourdieu, P. 1977. *Outline of a Theory of Practice* (translated by R. Nice), Cambridge: Cambridge University Press.

Bourdieu, P. 1984. *Distinction: A Social Critique of the Judgement of Taste* (translated by R. Nice), London: Routledge and Kegan Paul.

———— 1990. *In Other Words: Essays towards a Reflexive Sociology*, (translated by M. Adamson), Stanford, California: Stanford University Press.

———— 1998. *Practical Reason*. Cambridge: Polity Press.

———— 2000. *Pascalian Meditations*, (translated by R. Nice), Stanford, California: Stanford University Press.

Canard, H. 2000. 'Tourism, Conservation and Recreation', in *Managing New Zealand's Wildlands*, ed K. Lloyd, Rotoiti, New Zealand: Federation of Mountain Clubs of New Zealand (Inc.), pp.15–21.

Celsi, R.L., L.R. Rose, and T.W. Leigh, 1993. 'An Exploration of High-Risk Leisure Consumption Through Skydiving', *Journal of Consumer Research* 20: 1–23.

Dann, G. 1996. *The Language of Tourism: A Socio-linguistic Perspective*. Wallingford: Cab International.

Donnelly, P. and K. Young 1988. 'The Construction and Confirmation of Identity in Sport Subcultures', *Sociology of Sport Journal* 5: 223–40.

Ewert, A.W. 1994. 'Playing the Edge: Motivation and Risk Taking in a High Altitude Wilderness like Environment', *Environment and Behaviour* 26: 3–24.

Foster, G.M. 1986. 'South Seas Cruise: A Case Study of a Short-lived Society', *Annals of Tourism Research* 13: 215–38.

Green, D.C. and L. Chalip 1988. 'Sport Tourism as the Celebration of Subculture', *Annals of Tourism Research* 25: 275–91.

Kay, J. and S. Laberge 2002a. 'The "New" Corporate Habitus in Adventure Racing', *International Review for the Sociology of Sport* 37: 17–36.

_____ 2002b. 'Mapping the Field of "AR": Adventure Racing and Bourdieu's Concept of Field', *Sociology of Sport Journal* 19: 25–46.

Pearce, P.L. 1991. 'Travel Diaries: an Analysis of Self-Disclosure in Terms of Story Structure, Valence and Audience Characteristics', *Australian Psychologist* 26: 172–75.

Ryan, C. 1995. 'Learning about Tourist From Conversations: the Over-55s in Majorca', *Tourism Management* 16: 207–15.

Schmidt, C.J. 1979. 'The Guided Tour: Insulated Adventure', *Urban Life* 7: 441–67.

Selwyn, T. 1996. *The Tourist Image: Myths and Myth Making in Tourism*. Chichester: Wiley.

Stebbins, R.A. 1982. 'Serious Leisure: A Conceptual Statement', *Pacific Sociological Review* 25: 251–72.

_____ 1992. *Amateurs, Professionals, and Serious Leisure*, Montreal: McGill Queen's University Press.

_____ 1996. 'Culture Tourism as Serious Leisure', *Annals of Tourism Research* 23: 948–50.

_____ 1999. 'Serious Leisure', in *Leisure Studies: Prospects for the Twenty-first Century*, (ed.), E.L. Jackson and T.L. Burton, College, PA: State Venture Publishing Inc., pp.69–79.

Wheaton, B. 2000. '"Just do it": Consumption, Commitment, and Identity in the Windsurfing Subculture", *Sociology of Sport Journal* 17: 254–74.

5

REFRAMING PLACE, TIME AND EXPERIENCE: LEISURE AND ILLUSION IN MALLORCA

Jacqueline Waldren

'Reike, massage, water therapy, yoga and relaxation techniques – see Maire and Heikle'. This is the sign on the side of a car parked along the dirt road to Cala Deia, Mallorca described as one of the most beautiful coves in the Mediterranean. Deia, a village on the northwest coast of Mallorca, has attracted exotic visitors since the last century (see Rusinol 1929). On arrival, it is not long before most visitors become aware of the fifteen hundred foot mountains that form the valley of Deia. Walking down to the cove through the valley is often described by new and repeat visitors as one of the great experiences of their holidays. The leisure, peace and quiet the area affords allows these visitors to discover sensations often lost in the stress and strain of city living. As they are confronted on their way to the cove with this invitation to partake in practices based on notions of self-discipline, dedication and self-improvement, a new dimension is added to their experiences. Although Turner suggested the apparently optative character of leisure is not incongruous with these practices (1969), I have found the mere suggestion of such formalised techniques quite 'out of place' in this landscape I have enjoyed over the past forty years. However, such an ethnocentric response needs unpicking and so in this chapter I try to understand the background that has led to the production and consumption of contemporary leisure in this idyllic village of Deia, Mallorca, and the impact the disciplining of leisure has had on locals, foreigners and seasonal visitors over the past decades. Leisure there, I believe, is experienced quite differently by locals, expatriate residents (including artists, writers, business people, actors, alternative therapists) and tourists,[1] and all seem to be competing to make their practices, visions and ideologies effectively transform one another.

Illusions of Space, Time and Place

Although since the last century travellers had often visited Mallorca and found
their way to Deia, 'it was a declining village, merely a name of a place where
resources were declining and little opportunity existed for its young people'
(Sabater 1990: 3). It was the 1960s before the development of extensive tourist
infrastructures including transport and accommodations services were expanded
on the coastal regions of the island and before tourism became more important
to the Balearic economy. Young members of the peasant population saw new
opportunities in the increasing tourism industry and many from Deia found jobs
in the various services required for tourism, thus moving to other areas of the
island to free themselves from the agricultural toils of their parents. Their vacated
houses were rented to foreign artists and writers who found the unspoiled beauty
and tranquility they were seeking in this rural setting. Those who stayed in the
village soon began to realise that the pastoral existence they so wanted to leave –
the terraced landscape, the climate, sun and sea and the quaint stone houses –
were what attracted visitors to their village. As more foreign artists and writers
settled in Deia, their perceptions and experiences of identifying with and
appreciating the village's ethos of 'peasant' life, 'natural' beauty 'exotic' residents
and 'perfect' climate became the basis of stories that turned into 'local myths'.

Forty years after, it is clear that the environment has become not only the
location of production but also the object of consumption, offering a spatial
narrative complete with legitimising myths of famous residents and local conflicts
(Hewison 1987). The mystic quality of the setting and the effect of the phases of
the moon on all forms of life were popularised by long-term resident Robert
Graves in his book *The White Goddess*, and his poetry and prose have become part
of 'the myth of Deia' told and retold by expat resident and locals to new and eager
listeners. Secret knowledge, whether about mythological goddesses, 'real'
characters who had been part of Deia's past, or gossip about last night's conquests
give foreigners a sense of identity with others with whom they share these secrets
and intimacies. Tales of witches, Diana cults, and energy forces coming from the
mountains abound among the members of the foreign colony and promote and
validate long-term residents' positions as culture brokers to new arrivals.

Robert Graves' home is in the process of being made into a museum, which
will feature his working space, original manuscripts and the assorted artefacts that
commemorate his wide-reaching literary and social activities. Visitors will be able
to enter his studio, see the quill pen he wrote his poems with and observe the
wall-to-wall shelves of ancient books, among which are the Greek and Hebrew
texts he interpreted. Many locals have never entered the Graves' house and the
interpretation of his life, his identity and his history in their village may arouse
some interesting responses. Like Graves, many expatriates in Deia established life
styles that transcended locality and temporality with transnational identities and
cultural diversities.

Self-Revelation and Social Identity

The search for self-revelation, knowledge and independence has brought more and more people to Deia over the past century. The sensual experiences of walking along the shore, feeling the wind in your hair, tasting the salt on your lips, making love under the stars with the sound of waves breaking against the sand, climbing cliffs or standing on a rock facing out to sea are classically associated with islands (see Löfgren 1999). Artists in Deia not only painted or described these illusionary images, they re-figured and re-negotiated landscapes and seascapes, and they began to inhabit them as well. The special light, the play of the sun, moon, water, and mist on the landscape, the cheap cost of food, wine and accommodation and the quaintness of the local folk attracted them and kept them captivated. One American artist who lived in Deia for fifty years said:

> The very complexity yet simplicity of the landscape made room for finding yourself, entering a trance-like or meditative state of mind ... the perfection of the olive trees disturbed me ... there were no two alike. The earth and its surfaces where things happen and are going to happen give new life to things, your own message or essence can be revealed.

He found that 'painting what you saw had limitations' and he described his artistic transitions as 'creating surfaces that suggested things and allowed for accidents'. He sought 'to reveal what was under the surface through a combination of intellectual approaches and childlike imagination.' He hoped to 'reduce things to simplicity' while looking for deeper meanings, not those just acceptable or pleasing.

> With other artists in residence, we formed a group of people, alienated from our own cultures, of diverse beliefs and backgrounds, we wondered if through our work we might find a commonality beyond our differences. We created disturbance, distorted perspective, broke-up panoramas, a return to innocence, away from the horrors and terrors of World War II and reflecting our uninhibited, free, imaginative sense of reality.' (W. Waldren unpublished autobiography)

Residents' quests for artistic liberation were mirrored in their new lifestyles. The expatriate concept of an 'authentic' existence in Deia has continued to evolve from the rather élitist 'ideal community of unfettered, economically independent, creative, intelligent, artistic persons' envisaged by Laura Riding and Robert Graves in 1929[2] to an eclectic gathering of locals, artists, writers, musicians, alternative therapists, retirees, remittance men and women, business people, tourists and seasonal visitors. Social groupings are ever-changing and stories about the exploits of expats in Deia over the years are told and retold in the cafés by locals as well as foreigners perpetuating the myth of Deia as a unique experience, a place created in the minds of its inhabitants and authenticated for those past and those still to come.

From the late 1960s, outside the mainstream or accepted norms of their own cultural backgrounds as well as the local culture of Deia, these resident expatriates were able to pursue the formation of identities based on creativity, self-knowledge, and freedom of choice in all things. Some were World War II veterans who, against varied political, social and economic currents, were out of sync with their home societies, and their bohemian, eccentric, expatriate lifestyles were shared with other individuals who reinforced their values and idiosyncracies and helped to make these characteristics expressions of their independence. New 'free identities' were possible and their life-choices were legitimated by the presence of others who shared their goals. The foreign men in Deia adored women, fell passionately in love, and were deeply saddened when their 'loves' had to leave the village (their holidays over). Men proclaimed the virtues of womanhood, idealising women. For example, Brad Rising, describing the 1960s in Deia in an undated letter to the author's husband, wrote: 'I lived in places all around the world but never did I see such beautiful and interesting women as there were in Deia … It was a place for love and we were true hedonists playing it up in one of the most beautiful scenes in the world.' Such foreign men shared the belief that Western society had lost ideas of intrinsic importance and that perhaps the myth, magic, and dreams of other people and places held some of the answers they were seeking.

The local ties to the soil and agricultural work, as well as the repression of sexuality in the 50s and 60s and religious and political control of individual freedoms, were in absolute contrast to the 'landscape' and license experienced by foreigners. As long as foreigners kept to their own activities, the locals were largely indifferent to their eccentricities. Their actions and behaviours were too far removed from anything Deia people valued. One man said, 'This is the only place where people like us can breathe. You can wear one red espadrille and one blue one here and the locals don't care; they're tolerant of strangers.'

Throughout the 1960s, time and space had different meanings for local Deia people and foreigners. Locals appreciated and resented their environment. The harshness of the landscape left little leisure time for mere admiration for those who must wrest their livings from the land. They appreciated its beauty and climate, its textures, the contrasts of stone and earth, mountains and sea. Despite its harshness, the landscape is conducive to producing ample crops, especially olives. But it requires many months of arduous labour and more months of waiting to collect and process the products. Citrus fruits grow in such quantities that they often go unpicked as labour sources decline.

For foreigners, the experience of picking their own oranges for juicing or collecting olives for processing allowed them to feel connected to nature. However, these were selected pastimes, not obligatory responsibilities. While some spent most of the day in the cafés or on the beach, others, like Robert Graves, maintained a ritual existence in their paradise. Rising at dawn, Graves, for example, would write until eleven, breakfast on olive oil, tomato (*p'amb oli*) and local bread or home made marmalade made from his home grown oranges. He would walk to the cove at the same hour each day where he would climb up to a preferred spot and dive off, swim about, climb back up the hill, work some more until lunch, and take a nap until his regular post collection at four pm.

Physical fitness was maintained by the foreigners and locals as the landscape gave no reprieves. Everything was reached by rugged, stony paths and hills. One woman said, 'I know we live in paradise but I still have to climb up seventy-four steps each time I return to my house.' Mind, body and spirit were forcefully united. Bodies moved through the landscapes carried in the mind, and incorporated visual pleasures derived from a multitude of stimuli. Sun and poetry offered a soulful retreat. Books on philosophy, art, poetry, astrology or science circulated among the expatriates. They sought liberation through knowledge and practice. The free and leisured life chosen by the expats in Deia was a form of discipline which provided structure and meaning to their lives and allowed them to experience their ideal existences in their chosen place.

Mixed and Competing Visions

By the mid-1970s, increased numbers of foreign residents, television, a more active café scene, and weekend music provided by Mallorquin and foreign musicians, began to invade the spaces and sounds of local life. Mallorquin personal identity, once based on family, land ownership or pride in one's work, had to be redefined to accommodate the new forms of income and lifestyle brought in by expat residents and tourism. It was clear that the qualities of sun and moon, mountains and sea were perceived differently by locals and visitors,[3] but these qualities were, nevertheless, the elements that brought (and continue to bring) locals, expats and visitors together in Deia.

Drawing on the claim of Tomas, Sheppard and Walter that 'landscape is never value-free, and can function as a force in the formation of ideology' (2001: 542) we see the expatriates' creation of Deia as a mythical locality, an embodied experience of the world in which there is ideally no Cartesian split between the mind and body, culture and nature.[4] The 'non-conventional' becomes 'conventional' for some of the people. 'The socializing role of bodily experience forms an ideology made material through landscape and may serve to naturalize in such a manner that it may be impossible to imagine a world that is different. Movement, memory and daily routine within a landscape may work to create particular senses of personhood as well as ideas about appropriate action in different contexts' (ibid.: 547).

Daily routine becomes an essential part of expatriate living. Whether one goes to the café first thing in the morning for half an hour to read the paper and have a café con leche, or spends hours in deep (or casual) conversation with fellow residents or newly arrived visitors, or rises at four am to write or paint before the sun comes up, each orders time and space to accommodate a self-realisation and personal accomplishment. One endeavours to be 'spontaneous' but finds that time is socially constructed and can go out of control if one is not self-disciplined. The locality of Deia is contained and made one's expressive domain through self-discipline. Self-discipline is needed to pursue creative activities. No clock-in or boss to set patterns and pressures but an inner drive to practice one's art, fulfil one's dreams, hopes, ambitions.

By the 1980s, the visitors to Deia were no longer primarily eccentric nor artistic[5] but rather people from different social and economic backgrounds seeking the beauty and tranquility of Deia as well as the opportunity to observe the artist's colony for which it was becoming known. Foreign residents included Australian, British and American artists, British, Austrian and American writers, German designers, photographers and architects. The 'locals' set about redesigning landscapes, traditions and heritage in the hope of attracting the leisured to experience the location and objectification of the body in an idyllic setting. The places and spaces become transformed, as do the people experiencing them. Leisure is sought after, and, like location, is carried in the mind, imagined and mediated in experience. Today, the cultural production of tourism in this Mallorcan village finds its inspiration in the particularities of local architecture and human environment relationships, with locals, expatriate residents and tourists conspiring together, often unwittingly, in pursuit of an authenticating experience where what is authenticated is one's self through the mental and physical experience of time, space and place. 'Authenticity in this sense, becomes a commodity in its own right, and the possibility of attaining it is projected onto objects or places bringing a whole world of myth and expectations with it' (Fees 1996: 121). However, what are ultimately being consumed are not objects or places but each person's sensations or illusions of them.

Some ask if ordinary [*sic*] tourists appreciate the magic, experience 'authenticity' or merely glide through these destinations. Perhaps no one is 'ordinary' after a visit to Deia. The return of many people year after year suggests an attachment explained by each individual, from his or her own perspective. Descriptions of Deia and one's experiences in the village differ according to age, nationality, gender, season of visit, area where one resides and time spent there. As more foreigners settle for shorter or longer periods in the village, leisure production and consumption opportunities increase. Consumption of property, art, food or fashion, costs money and establishes newcomers' identities. A lack of money (once an unimportant commodity among the early expats) keeps one on the margins of social life. Materialism once associated with the Western values many left behind has begun to creep into Deia life and the 'idyllic peasant' is a figure of the past. The outside world of modernity, travel, consumption and varied forms of leisure, pleasures and goods is now accessible, attractive and desirous to locals and to the children of foreigners raised in the village. Miller et al. note: 'The presumed certainties of cultural identity, firmly located in particular places where one found stable communities of shared values and traditions have been shown to be illusions. New theories of space and place need to reflect the multicultural (and transnational) influences that have impacted on these places' (1998: 19).

This transcendence of locality by expatriates who have created new lives in Mallorca has produced new forms of multicultural tradition that now includes gallery openings for painting exhibitions, classical and pop music concerts, poetry readings, as well as the marketing of mind and body transformations to the varied visitors who come seeking escape from urban life. Soft flowing garments, casual or eccentric attire replace tight or restraining clothing; minimalist or ethnic and colourful decors combine with rustic white walls and wooden beams within houses. Children and grown-ups share spaces no longer seen as public or private.

New Forms of Leisure in Paradise

The City Hall has built a cultural centre for exhibitions, conferences, lectures, music recitals, etc. with a gymnasium available below for aerobics, weight training, pilates and a music practice room for all residents. Visiting practitioners of alternative therapies post announcements on the City Hall bulletin board. Some are printed in English and others in Spanish, German and English. One poster offered 'a residential seminar on Psy-Energetic Integral massage (The Belnet method), a subtle mixture of California Gestalt, Massage, Cranio-Sacral Therapy and Energetic body balancing.' Today locals and foreigners partake of self-improvement activities and sports. The City Hall sponsors Tai Chi and folkdance classes for the over 55s and *petanca* (*boules*) for all ages with tournaments and performances presented at the annual village fiestas.

A Scottish fellow and his Chinese partner laid out oriental carpets, a massage table and a reflexology[6] bench on the beachfront for two months in the summers of 2003 and 2004. Their 'open-plan living room' on the beach attracted people to enter, book treatments between swims and 'experience feelings you didn't know you had, pain, pleasure, self-knowledge, release … '. The reflexology clients faced the sea while sitting on a bench placed on a carpet and were greeted by people who passed by, who openly showed a general interest in what the client was experiencing. However, the person having a massage was consciously ignored by passers-by, obviously embarrassed or reticent to show interest in what seems a private experience between masseuse and client despite being in the same public setting. These different reactions highlight the variations encountered in the observation of physical contacts in public places. This is similar to the reticence residents have in asking one another about the 'work' they do at home or studio before joining others in the cafés, on the beach or in the shops. One acknowledges an artist's work in annual exhibitions; a writer's books can be found in the local bookstore soon after publication. However, many never exhibit or publish, but continue to live the ethos of creative pursuits, adding to the myth of Deia as an artist's colony.

These examples suggest that this village is the site of the production and consumption of leisure both by residents and visitors. However, the products provided today are more a part of a global urban environment than of 'the natural wonders' extolled by artists and writers, and the consuming public reflect mixed and competing visions. Mallorcan, Catalan and Spanish residents of all ages, long-term residents and seasonal visitors, may walk in the same territory but often move in very different mindscapes (mental landscapes). The 'nature' each describes is imbued with cultural meanings. Gaspar Sabater, born in Deia, describes himself as a 'local emigrant' explaining that he belonged to a generation that were 'pulled out' of their villages where they were born and raised and forced to emigrate to towns for studies or to find work. 'I am an immigrant although I have never gone for good ... [nor have I] ... returned for good. I seem to be in the middle of a road between Deia and Palma. However, when I need to find myself, I walk down to the cove and pass hours contemplating the sea. There are few who have such luck' (1990: 4).

The experience of being in Deia is quite different for each individual in the twenty-first century. Time, once seemingly unlimited, is now seen to be fleeting (many of the early residents are in their eighties; five of their generation died in the last year). The routines some continue give priority to creative work and this older generation of foreign residents put greater value on their privacy. Some continue to frequent the cafés, attend gallery openings or other social events, concerts, and cocktail parties. It is at such gatherings that long-term residents rekindle the spirit of their early days in Deia, reminisce about the past and marvel at the experiences they shared.

Deia, for most who were not born or brought up there, exists only as they perceive it, a paradise for rest and relaxation or an exotic landscape designed to test their creative abilities, to discover or soothe their soul. 'The myth of paradise remains an important factor in marketing of destinations' (Selwyn 1994: 29), and this image has been eulogised as part of Deia's attraction since the last century.[7] 'Constructing paradise is just one part of a range of pressures on culture from tourism' (ibid.: 32). Places are embued with magical or mythical qualities by those who observe them more than by those who inhabit them. Shangrila is a mythical utopia created by Westerners. Once viewed, the struggle to get there is left behind and nature's landscapes begin to overwhelm one, accept one or drive one away. This myth or image of a perfect place, where one's spirit or inner being (the 'real you' rather than the construction of family or society) could flourish, has led many people to search for 'mythical' places.

For many I have spoken to, recalling exciting moments and beautiful memories experienced in Deia formed the basis of the mythological past and present that made Deia their idea of paradise. Paradise meant different things to each person but common themes seemed to include a place that combined nature's bounty, earthly pleasure, social harmony, free will and expression apart from the routinised life of the technological and scientifically explained world. In Deia, the paths and woods along winding streams seemed like the Garden of

Eden. In Deia, a long-time resident said 'the outside world became more and more distant as the inside became larger and more complete. Paradise and reality flowed into one another and the ills of the outside world were temporarily closed out' (Waldren 1996: 200-201). In his essay 'Liminality and Communitas', Turner suggests: 'Prophets and artists tend to be liminal and marginal people, "edgemen," who strive with a passionate sincerity to rid themselves of the clichés associated with status incumbency and role-playing and to enter into vital relations with other men in fact or imagination' (1995 [1969]: 128). Expatriate identity has become located in this experience of 'communitas' with others (wherever they are located in the world) who have shared experiences in Deia. Places are extended beyond borders and time and formed by these global to local social relations based on nostalgia and memories as well as future returns (see Appadurai 2000).

While becoming part of a 'global world', the various groups in Deia have tried to maintain an image of a traditional village, where families carry on communal activities within the ancient walls. The struggle for coherence in a changing world involves reflection, and re-evaluation of personal and social identity. Everyday life, local rituals and events, which are often private, become cultural performances. A tourist observing the landscape, a 'local peasant' at work, a potter in her studio, a wedding in process, feels 'gifted' in sharing in 'local life'.

However, although the landscape observed is evidence of a long tradition of terracing and planting, of cutting back and pruning, few visitors recognise that generations of locals have produced this 'virgin' landscape that so enthrals them. The 'peasant' observed, the potter and the couple getting married may well be foreigners who reside in the village or have hired the church for this ceremony only to return to their homes on other parts of the island or in other countries. This illusion of participating in other cultures is a common feature of tourism and often requires local collusion in creating the illusions. Cultural events are staged for tourist and local consumption. Local women artisans produce goods for sale as well as for their own use. Weddings, once confined to people resident in the village, are now organised for anyone who can pay the fees set by the city hall, church or hotel.

Today, the residents of Deia, and the visitors to the village both mutually support local businesses and engage in similar recreational activities. The primary differentiation between the leisure activities of local residents and seasonal visitors is the duration and scope of these activities. Thus, a potential for synergetic interaction between residents and visitors is recognised. Friday and Saturday nights find the cafés offering 'live music' and standing-room only as locals and foreigners crowd together to share the sounds of modern, pop, reggae, folk or flamenco music. Village fiestas attract locals, residents and tourists to street dances and comedy acts. There are more tourists at the cove these days than residents or regular visitors, although local women continue to meet on Sunday mornings to swim before lunch while residents swim early in the morning or around sun-set. Artists and writers might well wander down to the cove restaurant for lunch, have a quick dip and return to their home to work, nap or relax, but seldom spend time on the beach as once they did.

Government studies and tourist literature suggests that tourism has offered solutions to some economic crises but created other social problems in its wake; excessive pressure on beaches, services, water, electricity and land, as well as problems associated with urbanisation, escalating property prices, increased immigration, diminished church attendance, etc. Forests are being cleared, streams covered over with asphalt to provide controlled parking areas and 'natural landscapes' are being framed as reserves to attract visitors. All over Mallorca, highways are cutting into protected landscapes as traffic demands increase. With this emphasis on control and urban thinking, people who are trying to return to a state of nature (uncontrolled, wild) may seek other places.

Mallorcans and foreign residents are beginning to ask questions concerning the power relationships that affect how resources, including environmental resources, are identified and developed by individuals and groups, and by local, regional and national governments. As awareness of 'the environment' (as a resource to be protected) has been awakened, the interests of various groups of people have become evident. A Green Party has formed, and environmentalists are actively protesting against rubbish disposal techniques while encouraging the general public to be conscious of conservation and recycling necessities.

Paradise Lost?

Many of the artists and writers who moved to Deia during the past fifty years were trying to maintain some semblance of a 'simpler life' in contrast to the complex life in the cities from which they came. However, the 'modernity' and 'materialism' they were escaping have been brought in by local and foreign developers to meet the demands of an increasing number of foreign buyers, locals and tourists. Boutiques featuring ethnic clothes (from Ecuador, Mexico, Indonesia and China) and shops selling woven carpets from Mexico, books mostly in English, Spanish, German and a few in Catalan as well as newspapers from England, Germany, Paris and Spain vie for clientele among locals and tourists. A health food store features vitamins, herbal remedies, and natural fibre clothing alongside organically grown local vegetables and stoneground bread, and it advertises all the possible health treatments and classes offered by people around the island.

The elegant hotel La Residencia offers its guests guided tours of the village, tai chi on the lawn, water aerobics, massage, and mud rubs. The 'local bakery' features German-style multigrain bread, croissants and quiche as well as peasant bread, olives and sundry fruit and vegetables from Chile, South Africa, the Canary Islands and the Balearics. In the effort to contain the influx of cars and visitors the city council has imposed regulations appropriate to urban environments, and parking spaces and meters have been installed near the beach and along the highway that runs through the town. All these international goods add colour to the 'natural landscape' and pastoral image of Deia and define the public, including the local population, as cosmopolitan providers and consumers participating in the experience of Deia.

During the spring and summer season from April through October, the demand for houses and hotel accommodation far outnumbers the available places; however, the variety of requests clearly reflects the myriad ways leisure can be consumed. Some visitors want 'simple' peasant houses built of stone, quaint furnishings and few modern conveniences, while others seek remodelled or modern renditions of 'traditional' houses with modern appliances, swimming pools, motor boats and servants. In the village there are three five star hotels and two simple pensions (with shared wc/showers), and rooms in private homes. One of the five star hotels features two suites with private pools. Resident artists let their houses for a month in the summer and live off the income the rest of the year.

The visitor is guided through nature along newly stoned dirt paths quaintly marked by handmade painted wooden signs that indicate the distance and time the walk will take to the cove, or farther on into the mountains or to other villages. One can drive to the cove down a paved road which ends abruptly and becomes a dirt path that leads to swimming, boating, basking in the sun, and eating fresh fish by the shore. Wine flows cheaply and sangria is often requested. Back in the village, food choices range from paella, to refined 'local' nouvelle cuisine, tapas (a melange of country specialties in small portions), pizza or pasta. 'Culture' is available in large or small doses: classical concerts in the church or at nearby ancient estates, an archaeological museum, a church museum, art exhibitions, and live music in the café on weekends provided by 'local' (Mallorquin and resident British) bands. Many enjoy celebrity-spotting for those well-known people who have bought homes or are regular visitors to Deia: The Eurythmics, Michael Douglas, Catherine Zeta-Jones, The Corrs, Andrew-Lloyd Webber, Richard Branson, and even the King and Queen, Prince, his wife, and the Infantas of Spain can be seen in Deia's now famous restaurants.

The local press capitalises on Deia's 'exotic' qualities as well as the visitors pursuing the famous in order to show the rest of the island and the world at large just how wonderful Mallorca (and especially Deia) must be if all these exciting celebrities (who could really go anywhere they liked) have chosen Deia over and over again. The Hotel La Residencia's recent publicity brochure tells the visitor:

> As you approach La Residencia, poised high upon the hilltop, yet nestled gently between the sea and a rugged backdrop of silent cathedral like mountains, your first impression is one of being cocooned from the rest of the world. Swept away to another space, another time. Scarcely a whisper from the village below with its cafés and restaurants, galleries and boutiques. Echoes of the past and Deia's rich textured history resonate off the weathered stone, the Spanish tile, the wooden shutters, the handwrought ironwork; while a gentle blend of subdued colours and flowing fabrics,

period furnishings and objet d'art wake up and party to an eclectic mix of contemporary art splashed boldly on whitewashed walls.

The places and spaces have become transformed, as have the people who experience them. Leisure, it is hoped, will be sought after and like location be carried in the mind, imagined and mediated in experience. Expatriate life is much more difficult today for the artists and writers who came seeking a new existence. In their youth, these men and women may have sought self-knowledge through frequent and exciting sexual liaisons; they were encouraged to see themselves in terms of their sexuality,[8] which was interpreted as the core of the self (Caplan 1987). With added years and less stamina, most have sought additional understandings of selfhood. Women are seen to have a key role to play in the transformation of self and society and those who have 'born and nurtured' and survived the changes still provide the inspiration and support system that allows them or their men to pursue art, poetry or research. Few struggling artists can afford to live in Deia today. Land and house prices have risen beyond their means. Thus the actions of ageing artists and writers become the myths of the present and the 'colourful characters of the past' give the village its ethos. Turner's description of how liminal beings appear to be 'reduced or ground down to a uniform condition to be fashioned anew and endowed with additional powers to enable them to cope with their new station in life' (1982: 45) fits quite accurately with the glorified role of resident artists and writers in Deia's village lore.

We have seen how nature, time and space are socially constructed by those who live, work and play in Deia. The Deianencs once dominated by the demands of the agricultural cycle and the crops associated with the changing seasons are now, like the resident artists and writers, more attuned to the climatic seasons that draw increased numbers of visitors to their village. As days get longer, warmer and residents and visitors return, working hours increase to provide the services required by the visitors, shops and cafés and restaurants remain open longer hours catering to the varied tastes and preferences of the visitors. Expats may spend more or less time in the cafés or at the cove, and dine at home with old friends in the evening. It is sometimes difficult to maintain daily routines with so many distractions but those who want to write and paint draw on their self-discipline and inform friends not to visit during work time.

All of these presentations use Deia as a living background to their activities. This picturesque village in the mountains of Mallorca, which has been depicted by artists and writers and was home to an agricultural populace now oriented to the service industry, seems to be inhabited today by groups of people with quite different conceptions of the place they live. Land ownership has become a commodity sold to the highest bidder, and Mallorquins are trying to find ways to combine modernisation with traditional styles to allow them to market their heritage and gain from the profit it now offers.

Politically active locals condone these activities and myth-making as it gives them the reason, space, time and income to redesign landscapes, tradition and heritage in the knowledge that they will continue to attract the leisured to experience the location and objectification of the body in this idyllic place. They too are taking advantage of free time and increased incomes to partake of leisure activities. Fitness classes and walking as a form of holistic healing (as prescribed by the local doctor) are practised by retired locals and foreigners alike, while gymnastics and African dance are preferred by younger women. Newlyweds honeymoon in the Seychelle islands, the Caribbean, and further afield while others employed in hotels and bars travel to India, Bali and Goa during their vacations. Tourism is both catered for and partaken of by many locals of all ages.

Conclusions or New Beginnings?

All of the above have combined to form the lifestyles and oral history associated with Deia. A sense of a gathering of locals and foreigners over time is kept alive by the seasonal visits of new people to whom the stories can be told and who can add to the myth of the creative past of Deia by recounting these tales over and over again. The past is portrayed in many forms which add new dimensions to the present. During the summer of 2005, two films made in the sixties have been shown in Sa Fonda, a café that was one of the early inns offering rooms in the village. One film made in 1960 by Mati Klarwein, an Israeli artist, depicts a fictional group of artists' lives and 'exotica' (wild parties celebrating the full moon, guitar music and creative dancers). All of the actors are the early foreign residents of Deia. The second film is the highly acclaimed 'Aguirre' directed by Herzog. It portrays the conquest of Peru where the part of the priest is played by Del Negro, an American actor, painter, photographer who has returned to Deia yearly since 1965. The first film has become a local 'cult film', a culturally significant, highly stylized set of events where all the players are familiar foreign artists, musicians and writers from Deia's past. The second records an historical, culturally significant set of global events produced as a professional high budget Hollywood film where one of the stars is a familiar foreign resident. Yet, together they reflect the intertwined and varied lives of the people and times in and beyond Deia forty some years ago. The reality of dispersed groups, tensions, and conflicts is balanced by this on-going story of characters in this artist's colony whose dreams, magic and realities have been lived or lost over time. The heterogeneity of the process of 'communitas' is highlighted as people from all levels of society and from all walks of life form strong bonds, free of the structures that normally separate them. Deia is seen as a space capable of accommodating diverse meanings and practices (cf. Coleman 2001: 23).

Many Mallorquins have sought out the aid of herbalists, astrologers, and tarot card readers over past centuries but the arrival of foreign practitioners has added new dimensions to these practices. The recent addition of alternative therapy practices made available in the village by foreign visiting and resident practitioners is beginning to offer ways to encompass the realities of progress with the ideals of paradise. Most of these therapies legitimate their messages with historical and geographic examples of what human beliefs ought to be, Chinese, Celtic, Japanese, and so on. These perspectives are often mixed and clearly contrasted to (so-called) Western values and practice. The most successful are those that can be integrated into Western materialism and consumerism within a traditional set of values: transcendental meditation, yoga, reike, reflexology. A Beijing-trained reflexologist and masseuse explained that: 'The Chinese medical system embraces a philosophy very different from that of the West. This philosophy is based on an awareness of the laws of nature and more particularly on the order of the universe.' Another important tenet of traditional Chinese medicine is that 'it regards man [*sic*] as a 'whole being', as an indivisible combination of mind/body/ spirit, where it is impossible to treat one aspect without affecting the others. The patient is also seen as an inextricable part of the environment' (Fulder 1997: 126).

Not all therapies are so clearly expressed: A large-framed young woman replete with multiple piercings of the ears, nose, eyebrow, tongue, and breast, as well as sporting tattoos on forearm and lower back, complained (in a social situation) to a woman practitioner of aromatherapy, massage, reike, healing and various other alternative treatments of recurring stomach pains. She explained that having practised a cleansing diet of raw fruits and vegetables, rice, soy milk and tofu she was still experiencing discomfort. The 'teacher' suggested she needed to release her 'yang' qualities (associated with femininity in this instance) which were submerged by the excessive amount of hard metal objects with which she was pierced. 'The material was unyielding, breaking any free flow of her energy despite efforts to adapt her diet,' said the teacher. Articulated in this manner the young woman had no hesitation (after years of aggressive defence of her free choice in body decoration) in removing her 'jewellery' the next day. By the time she had arranged a formal office visit with the practitioner (a week later), her stomach was feeling better and she was ready to tackle the myriad of other issues that were upsetting her life. The search for her 'yang' qualities remained a driving force throughout her 'therapy' during the next few months and included the purchase and wearing of softer clothes, the growing of her hair, and enhancement of other 'feminine' attributes.

The practitioner questioned the dispersed ideals and subjectivity assumed in the 'individualist stance' of her patient, and suggested a more holistic search for balance within and without. She used dress, aromatic oils, and decoration to transform her and create positive images by drawing on a number of different tools: Chinese philosophy, holistic medicine, contemporary fashion, youth culture, aromatherapy, and so on. It is entirely consonant with these views that emotional problems can be traced to physical origin and physical symptoms explained as emotionally induced. This varied approach encouraged the patient to alter her external identity, revealing and improving her new self-image and experience as well as her internal well-being.

What do these new therapies have to do with the lifestyles created by expats and locals over this century? Are they as incongruous as my opening description suggested? After reviewing the ethnography it seems they may have more in common than recognised at first glance. Primarily, everyone concerned in the production and consumption of leisure in Deia is highly reflexive. Both in the past and the present they have been searching for values they found missing in their home settings. Drawing on nature, imagined environments and others' cultural traditions, ancient and modern, all are using various forms of language, art, ritual, bodily involvement and philosophic templates to aid in self-discovery. They are one and together performing lifestyles that they themselves have designed in an imaginary landscape of their own. The expatriate residents of Deia came seeking the combination of mind, body and spirit and through their tenacity, disciplining of leisure, and self-made existences they not only fulfilled their dreams they also paved the way for future generations who seem to be once again seeking different experiences and knowledge about themselves and their place in the wider scheme of life.

Notes

1. The terms 'local' and 'resident' have many meanings and I have dedicated an entire book, *Insiders and Outsiders* (1996), to the discussion of these categories. 'Tourists' too is a broad category discussed in the volume *Tourists and Tourism* which I co-edited with Abram and MacLeod (1997). Following also Fulder's definition: 'Alternative or complementary are used to mean the aggregate of non-conventional healing systems and methods and therapy is used for one of them'(1997).

2. See Waldren 1996: 158.

3. This set of shared values in what appears to be unstructured lives can be associated with Turner's 'communitas' (1969). In the following passage Turner clarifies the ideas of liminal, communitas and anti-structure: 'I have used the term "anti-structure," … to describe both liminality and what I have called "communitas". I meant by it not a structural reversal … but the liberation of human capacities of cognition, affect, volition, creativity, etc., from the normative constraints incumbent upon occupying a sequence of social statuses … Anti structure expresses the idea that for people to relate to one another, there must be acknowledgement at some deeper level, of their common humanity' (Prince and Riches 2000: 36).

4. See Bourdieu's 'habitus' 1977, Heidegger's 'dwelling' 1972.

5. Rusinol mentions the nonchalance of the locals at the eccentric character of visitors to Deia early in the 20th century, noting that: 'Times have changed very much since the days when the sight of a man oddly dressed or behaving queerly would cause a commotion amongst the villagers … Savants, archaeologists, artists (above all, artists), herbalists and meteorologists, there is no manifestation or human knowledge that has not passed through Deya' (1958 [1905]). Deya is the Castillian spelling used until 1975 when Catalan (Mallorqui is a dialectal variant) once again became the written and spoken language of the island.

6. Reflexology is a form of ancient Chinese medicine involving treatment by massage or pressure points in the feet. It is proposed that there are reflexes in the feet for all parts of the body and these are arranged in such a way as to form a map of the body in the feet.

7. Arthur Rhodes, an English artist resident in Deia, had an exhibition he called Paradise Revisited in August 2005. His paintings depicted various renditions of 'The Garden of Eden' filled with the landscape, terraces and olive trees of Deia and nubile females seducing a helpless Adam. His paintings clearly admired and made fun of the many references to Deia as paradise.
8. This was 'sexuality' as defined by Turner: a polymorphic instrument of immediate communitas rather than as the basis for an enduring, structured social tie (1990: 153).

References

Alexander, J.C. and S. Seidman eds. 1990. *Culture and Society: Contemporary Debates*. Cambridge: CUP.
Appadurai, A. 2000. 'Grassroots Globalization and the research imagination.' *Public Culture* 12, no.1 (Winter).
Bourdieu, P. 1977. *Outline of a Theory of Practice*. Cambridge: CUP.
Caplan, P. 1987. *The Social Construction of Sexuality*. London: Routledge.
Coleman, S. 2001. 'Pilgrimage: Bringing 'Structure' Back In', *Anthropology Today* 17, no. 4 (August): 23.
Fees, C. 1996. 'Tourism and the Politics of Authenticity in a North Cotswold Town' in Selwyn, T. (ed.) *The Tourist Image: Myth and Myth Making in Tourism*. Chichester: Wiley.
Fulder, S. 1997. *The Handbook of Alternative and Complementary Medicine*. London: Vermilion.
Hewison, D. 1987. *The Heritage Industry: Britain in a Climate of Decline*. London: Methuen.
Lock, M. 1993. 'Cultivating the Body: Anthropology and Epistemologies of Bodily Practice and Knowledge', *Annual Review of Anthropology* 22: 133–200.
Massey, D. 1994. *Space, Place and Gender*. Cambridge: Polity.
Miller, D., P. Jackson, N. Thrift, B. Holbrook and M. Rowlands. 1998. *Shopping, Place and Identity*. London: Routledge.
Prince, R. and D. Riches (eds) 2000. *The New Age in Glastonbury: The Construction of Religious Movements*. Oxford: Berghahn Books.
Rusinol, S. 1958 (1905). *The Island of Calm*. Palma, Mallorca.
Sabater, G. 1990. *Prego 2000*. Mallorca.
Selwyn, T. 1996. *The Tourist Image: Myth and Myth Making in Tourism*. Chichester: Wiley.
Tomas, T., P. Sheppard and R. Walter. 2001. 'Landscape, Violence and Social Bodies: Ritualized Architecture in a Solomon Islands Society', *Journal of the Royal Anthropological Institute* 7, no 3 (September): 545–72.
Turner, V. 1995 (1969). *The Ritual Process*. Hawthorne, NY: Walter de Gruyter, Inc.
———— 1990. 'Liminality and Community' in J. Alexander and S. Seidman, (eds) *Culture and Society: Contemporary Debates*. Cambridge: Cambridge University Press.
Waldren, J. 1996. *Insiders and Outsiders: Paradise and Reality in Mallorca*. Oxford: Berghahn Books.
———— 1997. 'We are Not Tourists, We Live Here' in S. Abram, J. Waldren and D. MacLeod (eds) *Tourists and Tourism: Identifying with people and places*. Oxford: Berg.

PART III

ENACTING NATIONALITY

6

ANIMAL AND HUMAN BODIES IN THE LANDSCAPES OF ENGLISH FOXHUNTING

Garry Marvin

A rich anthropological literature examines the processes and associated practices of hunting animals for food but little attention has been paid to the hunting of wild animals in the modern world, when the activity moves from being part of a subsistence strategy to becoming a sporting practice.[1] In this movement hunting becomes set apart from utilitarian concerns and enters that space and time occupied by play, games, sports and other leisure activities. It becomes subject to rules and regulations that mark it as a non-necessary and essentially non-productive activity,[2] engaged in primarily for the inherent pleasures of the event itself.

Although all human hunting practices involve a contest between the hunter and the hunted, in sports hunting the contest is elaborated as the central feature of the event. Someone hunting a wild animal for food has to compete against that animal's natural abilities to remain undetected or to flee before she/he can kill it. However, in this situation the hunter does not seek out that competition as an end in itself – the meat hunter seeks to minimise the contest. The sport hunter, although wishing to kill, engages with the hunted animal in a very different way. Here the contest and competition are deliberately sought out and elaborated. Rules, regulations and restrictions are imposed to create the sporting challenge that is fundamental for hunting to be a leisure activity. The primary interest of the sport hunter is not that of obtaining meat, nor even that of killing an animal as a trophy (although that is important in many forms of hunting) but rather an immersion into the very difficulty of the encounter and the pleasure and satisfaction that come with overcoming these self-imposed difficulties. There is certainly the intention to kill an animal but how that animal is found and killed is far more important than the mere fact that it is killed. Hunting as a sport has competition (differently created and differently configured in different forms of hunting) as a crucial element in its construction and as such it can be analysed and interpreted in terms of those games which Roger Caillois, in his classic study *Man, Play and Games* (2001), classes as *agôn*, games which are:

> competitive, that is to say, like a combat in which equalities of chances is artificially created, in order that the adversaries should confront one another under ideal conditions, susceptible of giving precise and incontestable value to the winner's triumph (ibid.: 14).

English foxhunting has a unique cultural shape as a sporting event and this chapter explores some of the configurations and reconfigurations of human and animal bodies, identities and relationships in English rural spaces out of which it is constructed.[3] In terms of Caillois's definition, chances of equality are created through allowing the fox the possibility of evading the attention of the hounds or of out-manoeuvring them when it is pursued. Although not quite so easy to define as it is in human versus human sporting contests there is the notion of a 'winner' in the sense that either the hounds find and kill a fox and thus 'win' or that a fox, once it becomes the object of a hunt, may escape alive and thus 'win'.[4]

Foxes are routinely killed as part of working practices – those of pest control – in the English countryside. The intention is to kill foxes effectively but this is not hunting. Foxes are also regularly hunted by packs of hounds according to the rules of foxhunting – but, I would argue, the killing of foxes is not the central concern of this event. Both sets of practices involve killing foxes in the countryside but both are very different events. What I will examine here is how the engagements between humans and foxes within foxhunting are shaped into a complex performance. I will consider what has to be done to raise the killing of foxes to a leisure pursuit rather than it remaining a practice related to work in the countryside. Part of the answer has to do with animal bodies – how they are conceived, imagined, created, responded to and allowed to interact in the spaces of the English countryside.

Foxkilling – Foxhunting

Consider the case of a farmer who decides that foxes are a pest on his or her land – maybe they have been killing too many lambs, poultry or game birds. S/he may go out with a gun, perhaps accompanied by a dog, and walk quietly and unobtrusively through parts of the countryside known to be frequented by foxes at particular times of day. If a fox is seen within the range of the gun the farmer will simply shoot it.[5] There is no attempt to engage with the animal other than making sure it does not escape to a safe distance. The aim is to be effective and efficient – the relationship between human and fox is kept to a minimum. This is, of course, a cultural practice but it is not highly marked and not much elaborated. It is an everyday, working activity, an operation of pest control.

Consider the foxhunt. Scores of costumed riders meet in front of a farmhouse, country house or perhaps a pub. The most striking feature of the gathering is the pack of several dozen hounds gathered around the horse of the Huntsman.[6] The Huntsman is attired in formal riding clothes and is noticeable in his vivid red jacket.[7] The other riders, mounted on their horses, greet one another, take the drinks and snacks offered to them by those who host the Meet. Those who plan to follow the hunt on foot will similarly be offered refreshments and will join in the socialising. It is a convivial and highly public gathering. After perhaps half an hour the Huntsman blows his horn, calls his hounds to him and leads them into the countryside. The riders follow at a distance behind him. The Huntsman arrives at a small wood and, through his voice and horn, encourages his hounds to seek out the scent of a fox. If some of them catch a scent they will begin to whimper excitedly, other hounds are drawn to them, they all begin to follow the scent and the whimper becomes a more convincing baying. They begin to increase the pace and the Huntsman gallops after them. Once the Huntsman and hounds have been given enough distance, so that they can work without interference, the other mounted riders will be allowed to follow. The countryside suddenly resonates with the baying of the hounds, the excited horn calls, and the sounds of horses galloping, crashing through undergrowth, or jumping streams, hedges, fences and walls. The Hunt is in full cry.[8] The hunted fox may be at a considerable distance from this activity but if the hounds are able to hold onto the scent they will begin to gain ground. The fox may become evasive, change the direction of its flight, cross and re-cross its path, run across ground that disguises its scent or seek the safety of terrain where it is difficult for hounds to follow. If they are still able to hold the scent then there will come a moment when they can see their prey and will surge forward, increasing their speed to catch and kill the fox on the move. The Huntsman and those riders who have survived the challenges and obstacles presented to their horses will arrive to see the hounds tearing at a dead fox.[9]

Here, the relationship between human and fox is highly complex and highly ritualised. It is mediated through other animals – horses and hounds – there are formal rules governing the encounter, and rules of etiquette covering everything from proper clothing and forms of address between people to acceptable and unacceptable forms of behaviour.[10] In foxhunting, humans do not engage with foxes quietly, efficiently and unobtrusively. They announce their presence in the countryside, they expect (and require) the fox to flee, to be difficult to find and to capture. They willingly obey rules that limit the possibilities of hounds easily killing the animal. They seek the challenges and difficulties of getting across the countryside at speed on a horse – through these challenges and difficulties comes the possibility of excitement. Finally, they expect that foxes will often escape. Foxhunting is structured in terms of a contest between humans and foxes that is not allowed to develop in everyday life, and in the contest is the sport.

Configuring the Animals – Undisciplined, Disciplined and Ill-disciplined Bodies

Before moving on to a fuller exploration of the sporting quality of foxhunting it is necessary to attend to the animals – the foxes, hounds and horses that willingly or unwillingly participate in it – and how they relate to the human participants in the context of the event that these humans have constructed for their enjoyment. An important aspect of the cultural sense of foxhunting is expressed through animal bodies and through the interrelationships between these bodies. In this section of the chapter the concern will be to consider how humans create the disciplined *bodies* of the hound and the horse and how they attempt to maintain a disciplined *relationship* with them in order to engage with, and finally control, the undisciplined fox. Domestication involves the creation of docile, manageable, animal bodies that do not normally challenge the domination of their human masters. It will be argued here that although both hounds and horses may be classified as domesticated animals, in both their creation and their dependence on humans they are expected to offer a challenge, in terms of control and domination, to humans during foxhunting. The fox is a wild animal – its body is created through natural processes and maintained through its own volition and it lives its life independently (in the main) from humans. As the fox occupies the central place in the configuration of animals in this event I will begin with it.

The Fox

For many in the English countryside (especially those whose livelihoods depend on raising animals of various kinds) the fox is regarded as a pest that needs to be controlled. Wild animals ought to remain distant from humans but the 'problem' with the fox is that it does not keep its distance – it is an intruder into the affairs of humans – and there is a long history of country people complaining about the fox.[11] The complaints revolve around the fact that foxes often kill animals that belong to humans. For centuries they have been hunted down (although not necessarily hunted in any formal sense) and killed as a nuisance, a pest.[12] In this sense the wild animal, an undisciplined creature (not subject to human control) is an illdisciplined creature – it engages in an illicit, inappropriate and unacceptable practice by preying on domesticated animals, which is construed as theft, and by intruding into spaces it should not. This unacceptable predation brings it to the attention of certain people who seek to control it.

I have suggested that one form of this control is to kill the fox as efficiently as possible. As with other forms of pest control, there is no notion here of allowing the animal a possibility for escape. The only challenge is to reduce the animal's chance of escaping the death that the human wishes to inflict on it. In hunting, however, the relationship with the fox is expressed in a very different manner – the everyday concern about how to control foxes must be set aside in order for there to be a sporting event. The fox *must* be allowed to present a challenge to humans. It must be allowed to fully express its wild animal nature – it must be difficult to find, pursue and catch. As with all sporting events there must be a tension between intention and the attempt at its resolution – there must be difficulties, problems, doubts, successes, failures – since without such a tension there is no excitement and no interest. It is essential in foxhunting that the fox be allowed the possibility of escape and it should be hunted as a free, unrestricted, wild animal following its natural instincts – this time as prey rather than predator. It must be possible for the fox to hide from the attentions of its pursuers and, if this is not possible, to evade, outwit, or out pace them. The fox must be in control of its own body while humans attempt, through the hounds, to wrest that control from it. I will return to this process later when I further consider the sporting nature of hunting in the context of its arena of performance.

Hounds

The fox is one key centre of attention in this event but the nature of the attention that humans pay to it is directed through another set of animals – hounds. Unlike the person attempting to kill foxes as part of a pest control operation the relationship between humans and foxes in foxhunting is not a direct one. Here, humans do not directly seek out foxes, attempt to pursue them or kill them – this is the role of the hounds. It is through the complexity of the relationships that develop between hounds and foxes that part of the sporting nature of the event develops. Hounds are created, literally embodied, for their performance in this event and, I would argue, this is a *performance* rather than a simple working task. Hounds should not merely hunt in an effective manner; they are also judged, by all the participants in conversations during a hunt and in conversations after the event, as to whether they do this in an aesthetically pleasing and interesting manner.

Notions of bodies and discipline intersect in various ways with regard to the foxhound. At the first level they are pedigree animals created, as a result of human imagination, desire, will and skill, out of a canine form. Present-day foxhounds are the result of generations of human decisions about how such an animal should/will look and how such an animal might be produced by selective breeding.[13] Each of those responsible for this breeding[14] have clear ideas about the physical configuration of a foxhound (its 'conformation') but this is not equivalent to the sorts of agreements that obtain in the case of breed 'standards' set, for example, by Kennel Clubs. The views of each foxhound breeder will differ slightly in terms of 'conformation'. There will be differences of opinion about height, weight, length of leg, shape of face, type of coat etc. and the breeders in each Hunt will attempt to breed to and for their own ideal.

All of them though, at this basic level, will speak of trying to breed a robust and athletic animal that is appropriate for hunting foxes in a particular terrain. Most Hunts will hunt on two days a week, some as many as four, and each hound may have to run thirty, forty or even fifty miles on each day. Such activity demands an athletic animal body. At the level of the animal body the breeders will also operate in terms of an aesthetic concern with the colour of the animal's coat. Some will favour particular colour combinations, for example, black and tan; some will seek to produce hounds of one colour, for example, all-white hounds. Such a concern does not effect the way that hounds hunt but it does contribute to the overall look of the pack and breeders will refer to the ideals of a 'level pack' – a quality that combines the similarity of 'conformation' with that of the similarity of 'look' and one that contributes to the creation of a particular pack identity.

This creation of the physical foxhound is only the first stage of human concern. Beyond the body of the hound, breeders are also seeking other qualities in their animals. Of primary concern here is what is referred to as 'nose'. Foxhounds search for their prey not by sight but by scent, and good scenting hounds – those with good 'nose', are highly prized. Although it is less exact than creating the body of the hound, breeders do seek to breed for this quality of nose. An even less tangible quality desired in hounds is that of 'fox sense'. Although hounds should, ideally, simply follow the scent left by a fox, this line of scent can become confused or lost. This eventuality might be because of rapidly changing climatic conditions – sun might cause the scent to evaporate or rain may cause it to dissipate – or the fox, when it realises that it is the subject of the attention of hounds may, while fleeing, run through an area (for example where there are other animals) that disguises its scent. If hounds do lose the scent then it is expected that they will try to resolve the problem. At the point where they lose the scent they should set off in a direction they think the fox might have gone in order to recover the line of scent. This is referred to as 'fox sense'.

A final quality needs to be mentioned here – that of 'voice'. When hounds find the scent of a fox they should communicate this to others of the pack by the sounds they emit. The imagery is complex and cannot be explored here but this is referred to as 'speaking' and is interpreted as a sign of the developing relationship between hounds and fox.[15] But these sets of canine sounds are also referred to as 'the music of hounds' and as such are part of the total aesthetic of hunting. Breeders speak of how different hounds have soprano, tenor and bass voices and how they, the breeders, seek a melodious chorus and a melodious pack. This is part of the performative aspect of foxhunting and many of those who participate in foxhunting comment on the thrill and pleasure of hearing this 'music of hounds.'

The preceding section has dealt with some of the aspects of the embodied hound but the notions of bodies and discipline also need to be explored in the context of the relationships between the human and the hound. It is essential, in order to hunt correctly and successfully, for the Huntsman (the person responsible for the care of the hounds and for the practice of hunting) to produce and maintain a disciplined *pack* of hounds. The numbers of hounds kept by each Hunt will depend on how many days a week are actually spent hunting, but each will keep several dozen animals and many will have scores. All hounds are kept collectively in purpose-built kennels – dogs are kept together in one section and bitches in another. The kennel is, in Foucauldian terms, a site, an institution of surveillance and discipline. The Huntsman must develop two, related, sets of discipline with regard to the hounds in his charge – discipline within the kennel and discipline outside the kennel. The potential for disorder among such large numbers of hounds kept together is enormous. He and his staff must make sure that no hierarchies develop, that no fighting occurs, that the animals live together amicably and harmoniously. The pack, at rest in the kennels, must be maintained as a docile group of animals. Here, it is reasonably easy for the Huntsman to impose his will and maintain discipline over them because the animals are contained. However, the maintenance of discipline becomes more problematic when the hounds are taken out to hunt.

The processes of training, or as the fox hunt world prefers to call it, 'educating', hounds to hunt foxes is not a particularly elaborate one – fundamentally they learn what is expected of them from following older, experienced, hounds. When young hounds first join the pack they learn pack discipline from the periods of exercise. Each day hounds, as a group, are taken from the kennels by the Huntsman and an assistant (sometimes on bicycles, sometimes on horseback) for exercise through country lanes and fields. At this time young hounds might be 'coupled' with older hounds (a 'couple' consists of two collars connected by a leather thong or a chain) so that they do not wander off from the pack or stop to investigate anything that attracts their attention. By the time these hounds are ready to start hunting they will be used to keeping together with the pack and they quickly learn to follow more experienced hounds when they find the scent of a fox. They should also learn to respond immediately to the commands, given by voice or horn, of the Huntsman.

Concern about the maintenance of the discipline within hunting is revealed in one particular 'wrong turn' that can occur. If hounds are suddenly attracted to an animal such as a rabbit, hare or deer and begin to start chasing it this is referred to as 'rioting' – a situation of disorder and ill-discipline. The Huntsman is expected to intervene immediately to stop this improper hunting. Hounds should have their hunting instincts disciplined such that they only follow the quarry that is of human concern and not one that is of their concern. Hounds should not hunt to follow their own purposes, they should be acting as agents of their human masters. If such control does break down then it should be restored as quickly as possible.

Hounds are bred to hunt foxes but they should hunt them in a particular manner. Here discipline must be related to the performative nature of the event. The relationship between the Huntsman and his hounds is much admired and much discussed by those who go hunting. Indeed for many it is an appreciation of this relationship and how it is expressed on the hunting field that is central to their enjoyment of hunting. Foxhunting *aficionados* speak of 'the invisible thread' that connects the Huntsman with his hounds. There is no physical link between the two: collars and leashes – the accoutrements of control that are essential in most human/domestic dog relationships – play no part in this relationship. The Huntsman controls the hounds through his personality, skill and the previous relationships he has developed with them. But taking them out to hunt constitutes a challenge to this control and discipline. The hounds must be free to find the scent of the fox wherever it might be and they must be able to follow it wherever it might lead, and yet the Huntsman must attempt to maintain contact with them – they must not be totally hunting on their own even though they might be at some distance from him.

The Huntsman must maintain a delicate balance between freedom and control. For example, he may direct his hounds into a small wood and he will follow them. They will begin to search around for the possible scent of a fox. He must have a deep understanding of the local terrain and environmental conditions, as well as of the behaviour of his hounds. They may wander around in a lackadaisical manner. Is this because they are being lazy and unfocused? Do they need encouragement from his voice or horn? Should they be left alone for a while to work things out for themselves? Is it that there really is no scent there and should they be called back and moved along to another site? If a particular hound begins a hesitant whimper, perhaps indicating that it is beginning to find a scent, should the Huntsman encourage the rest of the pack to join this individual? All of these procedures will be judged, by those who have come hunting, as part of his performance. There will be discussions about whether the Huntsman understands his hounds, whether he is over-patient with them and keeping them in one place when it is obvious to everyone else that there is no scent to be found. On the other hand, he might be judged as being impatient with them and too quick to move on when they have had no chance to really work through an area that still has potential, with a faint scent still lurking there. He will also be judged on whether he maintains contact with them or not when they really get into the stride of hunting. Sometimes hounds will follow a strong scent and then suddenly lose it. At this point they might appear to be confused, they may mill about purposelessly, and look back to the Huntsman for guidance. Some Huntsmen will immediately try to help them by taking them in a particular direction; others will encourage the hounds to solve the problem for themselves. All of this will be commented on.

This complex set of relationships between Huntsman and hounds is at the centre of the event – it is this that constitutes the event in which others can participate. As was touched on before, it is not the basic fact that foxes are killed by hounds that is the central concern of the event. What is important is the development of the relationship between the fox and the hounds. This depends, in large part, on the quality of the disciplined pack of hounds previously created by the Huntsman and how this quality is expressed in each individual hunt. The whole style of the Huntsman and the style of his hounds when hunting is the subject of intense interest, scrutiny, judgement and evaluation by those engaged in hunting.

The Horse

Although many people participate in this event by following the action on foot, the fullest participation occurs on horseback. I suggest that the place of the horse in modern English life is enormously complex. For example, there are definitional problems about whether the horse still has a place as a working animal in England or whether it has moved more centrally into a world of leisure. Certainly horses are little used as creatures for the essential transportation of humans, as beasts of burden or for drawing carriages of various sorts. Police horses might be regarded as pertaining to the world of work, but should military horses, only used for ceremonial purposes, be seen as working animals? Race horses and competitive show jumping horses participate in sporting events, but is the nature of their participation actually one of work, with their 'job' that of being a race horse or a show jumper just as jockeys and professional human show jumpers work in these events? Hundreds of horses are kept in riding schools to service the leisure interests of people but such animals are also working animals.

My concern here will be to consider the relationships between humans and horses within foxhunting and to focus on the issues of discipline and control. As with all equestrian events it is essential that humans create a docile, disciplined, horse body. The processes involved in the full domestication of the horse are more complex than those necessary for the domestication of livestock such as cattle, pigs and sheep because of the nature of the relationship that the human desires with the animal. All domestication involves the use of selective breeding to produce the required animal body and such animals should also be domesticated in the sense of having tractable bodies so that humans can work closely with them. The horse is certainly a domesticated animal in this sense but humans must work further with the body and with the character of each horse in order to be able to ride it. It must be tamed and trained in order to accept the accoutrements of the processes of discipline – bits, bridles, saddles and reins that the rider uses to control the horse. At the centre of the human/horse relationship is the meeting of two wills and two bodies. It is an intensely close, individual, and embodied relationship.

Most people involved in a leisure relationship with a horse do not seek for this relationship to be a particularly difficult one and they are rarely able to ride their horse in a challenging environment. Most merely walk or canter through the restricted spaces of the English countryside with the occasional exciting gallop across land that is open to them. In foxhunting, however, the mounted participants seek out the challenge of riding in a more complex, difficult and potentially dangerous landscape. It is important to point out here, something that will be developed below, that foxhunting opens areas of the countryside to members of the Hunt that are normally closed. Most horse riders have a restricted access to the countryside. They only have access to country lanes, tracks, bridleways or publicly owned rural spaces such as national parks and woods. On a hunting day, landowners (by prior arrangements with the Hunt) allow riders onto their land – but there are limitations.

Nowadays, hunting riders may not simply gallop, 'rough-shod', across the countryside wherever and however they choose. They are very much the temporary guests of the landowner rather than people who, because of their social status and economic power, can demand and command access to the countryside. There is a new discipline in hunting and the authorities of each Hunt must make sure that their members ride in a considerate manner across the land of the farmers and other landowners who have allowed them to be there. Riders will be guided across the countryside by a nominated official from the Hunt. The riders must maintain a distance at all times between the Huntsman and his hounds. Hounds will run wherever they choose in order to follow the scent and the Huntsman will try to keep close to them. It is worth pointing out that only the fox may run exactly where it chooses. It has the total 'right of way' across the countryside because this is its home, its natural place of being, and it becomes the animal that leads or guides the event. Interestingly the fox is often referred to as the 'pilot', in the sense of one who guides or leads others through unknown or difficult terrain. Hounds will choose their own route but they should, ideally, only be going where the fox has been before. The riders will follow but they will not be allowed to pursue a direct route if this would lead them across fields with crops or fields with livestock which might take fright. But, given these provisos, the riders will attempt to keep up with the hounds and do so in as direct and fast a manner as possible. The fox, hounds and Huntsman create conditions to which the riders attempt to respond. This creates challenge and the excitement.

In attempting to keep close to the central action the riders and their horses must contend with the challenges posed by the landscape. There will be open expanses for galloping, obstacles such as ditches, streams, hedges, walls and fences that need to be jumped, there will be slopes and turns that need to be negotiated at speed, and places where horses can easily lose their footing. The excitement centres on the rider attempting to remain seated and in contact with his or her horse and the challenge revolves around the will, nerve and ability of both horse and rider. The rider relies on a skilful and disciplined relationship with the horse in order to rise to the challenge but he/she must also allow for the possibility of control collapsing if there is to be any excitement at all. Merely walking or trotting across unchallenging countryside would be considered dull by most riders. During the event headstrong horses may take off at the gallop and not respond to commands of the rider, they may refuse to jump an obstacle or swerve at the last moment, they may jump the obstacle in an ill-judged manner and throw their riders. Skilful and daring riders are admired but descriptions of who was thrown off at a particularly imposing hedge or who couldn't get their horse to jump anything also form part of the narrative of a day's hunting. Those participating in this equestrian side of hunting do not expect to see their fellow riders jumping fences in the aesthetic manner that they would expect of a show jumper – simply getting over and continuing is often enough. This is not an equestrian *spectacle* or an exhibition of equestrian skills: there is no distanced viewing of the event.[16]

Landscapes of Performance and Sport

I now begin to explore the relationships between these disciplined, undisciplined and illdisciplined bodies – both human and animal – within the landscapes that constitute the performative, sporting, arena of the event. Unlike bullfighting, cockfighting or other animal baiting, or animal racing in which the animal contestants are removed from their 'natural' environments and placed in specially constructed arenas, contests between humans and animals that are framed as 'hunting' take place in the lived space of the animals concerned. It is significant that foxhunting as a sport takes place in the same rural spaces as the fox-killing as pest control, but these spaces are reconfigured in terms of how the humans and animals may engage with them.

Although there is clear evidence of foxhunting in England prior to the eighteenth century, it was in that century that the event really developed as a popular country pursuit. By the mid-nineteenth century it had become so popular that several major landowners and owners of packs of hounds felt the need to codify and to regulate foxhunting. One of the things they did was to divide the countryside into 'Hunt countries', carefully mapped and named territories within which only one registered Hunt had the right to hunt. England is still mapped and divided into Hunt countries and these constitute an important landscape of hunting, and through that a landscape of identification.[17] Interestingly these Hunt Countries do not relate to county boundaries, although they might have county names within their names – East Cornwall or Cambridgeshire with Enfield Chace – they are different forms of mapping. Many, for example, do not have county names at all and will use other identifications – the Blackmore and Sparkford Vale, the Fitzwilliam, the Cottesmore. Not only are these important hunting spaces and administrative territories but they are also significant territories of identification and belonging. For example Hunt people at events outside of their 'country' will often use their Hunt country as a primary identifier: 'We are from the Blackmore Vale country' rather than 'We are from Dorset' or 'We are from the Fernie country' rather than 'We are from Leicestershire'. They use this form of identification with a particular, meaningful, space of countryside to identify themselves to certain strangers but the identification with a particular 'country' is also felt as an intense connectedness with particular landscapes and the lives within them. The meaningfulness is particularly important in the construction of a sense of belonging to, and of being of, somewhere.

In the main, foxhunting is enacted across the worked, agricultural, spaces of the countryside. Although some Hunts (depending on where in England they are located) will enter 'wild' countryside – for example moors and forests – most foxhunting takes place across fields, along hedgerows and through woods. Such landscapes form part of the everyday landscapes of most of those who participate in foxhunting. For many, they will be the landscapes with which they are directly involved in terms of work, as farmers and others connected with the agricultural world. For others they will be landscapes through which they travel in their daily life, landscapes which, on certain days, become reconfigured for the performance of the Hunt. Most people who participate in hunting do not travel around the country hunting in different places. The majority belong to the Hunt in the area in which they live and have their social life (much of it connected to events organised by the Hunt or informally with other members of the Hunt). Many of them belong to families who have lived in an area for generations and have hunted across the same countryside for generations. It is a countryside with which they are very familiar and with which they are intensely connected. To belong to a Hunt is a more complex belonging than that involved in most sporting clubs; it is to belong to a locality and its physical, social and cultural landscapes.

The majority of those who hunt do not leave the spaces of their everyday world on a hunting day to go elsewhere but rather they are drawn into the spaces and places of these everyday worlds to engage with them in differently configured, more active and more intense ways. They pay attention to the countryside in a more concentrated way and sense it differently as it becomes an arena for the performance of foxhunting. Everything about the countryside takes on a new significance when hunting begins. All the participants pay close attention to, respond to and comment on sounds, smells and sights, the changing weather conditions and the textures of the land over which they are riding or walking. On a hunting day the whole landscape becomes a challenge in a way that it is not on a daily basis. A central concern will be with where foxes might be found. Where have they been found before? Where might they be found today in this particular weather? The challenge is to find them. Having found a fox, the test for the riders is how to follow it. They do not necessarily follow the roads, pathways and tracks that connect places in everyday life, that allow people to get from one place to another. When hunting they are not making a journey to somewhere but rather they are attempting to follow, in the most direct way possible, where the fox leads them. Fences and hedges which are there to divide, contain and restrict movement across the worked landscape of the countryside become a challenge to the flow of the hunt. Their everyday purposes are subverted and they become obstacles to be jumped. Some fields can be galloped across, some must be skirted around. Streams that would normally not be crossed must be jumped or waded across. Woodland with dense undergrowth must be pushed through, often at speed. All of these challenges are experienced as individual tests. Will, for example, a rider have the nerve to jump a high hedge at the gallop or be willing to encourage his or her horse down a steep embankment? To do so might risk a fall and injury; not to do so might risk losing contact with the hunt. Much of the pleasure and excitement of hunting is in this direct bodily engagement with the landscapes of the countryside.

The conditions for this engagement are created by how foxhunting has been constructed as a sport rather than as a mundane activity. The most important aspects of this construction are in the nature of the indirect encounter between humans and the fox in which the fox must be unrestrained and allowed the freedom of escape across the countryside. As was mentioned in terms of the everyday working practice of fox-killing, the aim is to allow little chance of the fox escaping. The fox, as a free wild animal, attempts to hide from potential enemies or, if it does become visible, to flee from them, and it thus constitutes a challenge to the humans who attempt to find it. However, that notion of challenge is not further elaborated in pest control operations. If a fox runs across a field in front of a farmer armed with a gun, he or she will simply shoot it. There is no notion of giving the animal a 'sporting chance' to get away. The person with the gun may or may not have the necessary skills to kill it, or the conditions might not be right for a successful kill, but the encounter is not seen as a test of that person's ability. The potential fox killer wants to be successful on every occasion and to be so with the minimum of effort and difficulty. Skill, chance and luck of course play their part but this is work, not play and it is solitary, not social.

In order for fox killing to become the sport of foxhunting the challenge that the fox presents has been culturally elaborated as a set of rules and guiding etiquette about 'fair play' and acceptable practice.[18] Underlying these rules are a set of ideas concerned with what constitutes a 'proper' engagement with the fox. The most important aspect of this is that, according to the rules of hunting laid down by the governing body of the sport in England: 'Foxhunting as a sport is the hunting of the fox in its wild and natural state with a pack of hounds. Nothing must be done which in anyway compromises this rule' (Masters of Foxhounds Association Rule Book).

This rule means that foxhunting requires an extensive area in which to operate. It is an event that must range as freely as possible across the countryside. Its arena is fluid rather than fixed and encompasses wherever the fox chooses to go. This dimension is fundamental to the event and marks it as very different from any other form of fox killing. The relationship with the fox should take place across time and across space. If hounds, on entering a wood, suddenly discover and kill a fox this is not regarded as 'proper' hunting. Ideally the foxhunt should proceed from hounds finding the scent, through the following of the scent across the country, perhaps the loss and the refinding of the scent; it should build up a momentum and gain in pace as the hounds close in on their prey and end with the hounds, finally having seen the fox, surging forward to kill it on the run. A *developing* relationship between hounds and fox, closely followed by the other participants, is essential if the event is to create the excitement that makes it a sporting contest.

This form of hunting is highly intrusive in the countryside. Most other forms of hunting involve disguise, camouflage, silence, a blending into the landscape – an attempt to be a non-presence. Not so with foxhunting. The costumed riders are highly visible, the hounds are not silent (indeed they are encouraged to be vocal), the Huntsman can be heard cheering on his hounds and encouraging them with his horn. All of the activity of foxhunting *announces* the presence of the Hunt in the landscape. This might be interpreted as the Hunt announcing its presence to the fox. The fox must be encouraged out from invisibility to visibility; it must become an active participant of the event and be allowed to show its skills and qualities when the subject of attention. It must enter the competitive configuration of humans, horses and hounds.

In terms of foxhunting as a formal and highly disciplined event it is important to emphasise that here the participants do not have a direct, or an individual, relationship with the fox – their relationship with it should be through the hounds. For most people this consists of attempting to follow the hounds which are themselves attempting to follow the fox. Nothing should interfere with this relationship. There is a proper order to things and anyone attempting to insert themselves between the fox and the hounds (or between the Huntsman and the hounds) would be swiftly reprimanded. Humans on the hunting field are expected to be disciplined and to exercise self-control. For example, during a day's hunting, individuals, either on foot or mounted, may well encounter a fox. If they are mounted they are certainly not permitted to chase after the fox – that is the work of hounds. The first reaction on encountering a fox is to remain still and silent. The person should understand that hounds might well be following the scent of that particular fox. To move about or to shout excitedly that they have seen it might cause the fox to deviate from its path or interfere with or confuse the hounds. It may well be that hounds are hunting a different fox and to draw attention to the one they have seen might cause the hounds, if they are nearby, to leave the developing relationship with the hunted fox to begin again with a fresh one. There are appropriate ways for an individual to call the attention of the Huntsman to the fact that a fox has been sighted but that person has to have a good understanding of what is going on around him/her before doing so.

In this arena of hunting only the fox may do as it chooses and it is only brought under control at the moment of its capture. All other bodies are either subject to the discipline of others or to self-discipline. But these notions of discipline are ideal ones. Maybe the hounds will lose the Huntsman or not hunt as they should, while a horse may decide to bolt and the rider may be thrown. The event is predicated on discipline of various kinds but these disciplined relationships are put to the test during the hunt and much of the interest and excitement revolves around whether the participants can create, maintain, hold onto, an initial discipline and control in this volatile situation. The volatile situation is not a natural one, it is one of their own creation, one created in order to test themselves and the animals with which they seek to interact.

Conclusion

My concern in this chapter has been particularly with the non-human animal body. Such a focus seems to be fundamental for understanding the structures and processes of foxhunting, how it is configured as a sport and how it is engaged with and responded to by human participants. In terms of participation in this form of hunting, I think there are two interconnected strands. Some people are primarily interested in the dramatic processes of hunting itself. They are interested in watching the ebbs and flow, the engagements and disengagements between hounds and foxes – the hound-craft and the fox-craft of the event. People enjoy watching the uncertainties and difficulties as hounds attempt to find a scent, keep it and pursue their fox. But this, the dramatic centre of the event, creates another set of possibilities, the challenges of following the action of hunting from horseback, that form the equestrian event that others attend to participate in.

Animal identities – fox, hound and horse – are created *for* this event and *as a result of* this event. But such identities cannot be divorced from their human creators. Embodied foxes are not physically created by humans but they are imaginatively created. Their identity reflects human imaginings and concerns. Hounds and horses are created in more complex ways. They do not exist as 'natural' animals: they are intensely cultural creations. Their very existence and the form this existence takes is a result of human desire, imagination and will. They too have their identities shaped in terms of human concerns. The animal body is thus a site of human identity(ies) as much as it is a site of animal identity(ies). Human identity(ies) is/are then further expressed through the relationships developed with these creatures. At least part of what is going on in hunting is a celebration of the animal body – a human creation – and a celebration of particular animal/human relationships. This is not a distanced or intellectual celebration but one expressed through a close (often directly embodied) engagement with these animals and experienced through all the senses. Hunting is a sensual and emotionally charged practice for both the human and the animal participants that is enacted, expressed and experienced across the landscapes of the countryside, and it is the place of its enactment that gives rise to the other celebratory quality of the event. Foxhunting derives its cultural sense from concerns of the countryside with which it connects and interconnects. For those who participate in foxhunting this is not simply an event set, as a spectacle, in the countryside. Rather it is profoundly *of* the countryside, a celebration of a lived and enduring engagement with it.

Notes

1. Important exceptions are Matt Cartmill (1993) and, more recently, the ethnographic work of John Knight (2003 and 2004).
2. This is not to deny that many animals are eaten by those who hunt them but such hunters are not *primarily* in search of food.
3. The ethnographic data presented in this chapter are drawn from material gathered over several years of participant observation research with three Hunts in England and from interviews with the participants and officials of many others.
4. In foxhunting the notion of success implied in the term 'winning' is more usually spoken about using an opposite term, 'defeated'. The hounds defeat the fox or are defeated by it.
5. This particular scenario is used for the sake of illustration. Farmers and other landowners will kill foxes in this manner but they might also, in some controlled cases, use snares and often they will ask others with specialist skills to shoot foxes at night. This practice involves finding a fox, pinning it in a beam of light from a powerful lamp and shooting it. Other practices of fox control involve putting terriers into 'fox earths (the tunnelled-out spaces in which foxes shelter) in order to drive the fox into nets from where they can be shot, or using dogs such as lurchers to flush out foxes so that they can be shot.
6. The term 'Huntsman' is used to refer to the person who is responsible for working with the hounds and guiding them to hunt foxes on a hunting day. This is referred to as 'hunting the hounds'. At present all Huntsmen in the country are men and I have found only rare occasions when women have performed this role. In most Hunts there is only one Huntsman (who can be an amateur or a professional) although it is possible that in a Hunt with several Masters of Foxhounds (the titular heads of the Hunt), who are also Huntsmen, they might share the actual hunting of the hounds. It is impossible to develop the point here but it is interesting to note that although there are no female Huntsmen there are many female Masters of Foxhounds.
7. There is no space here to elaborate on the complexity of dress codes. There are other people, Masters of Foxhounds, Hunt Servants and subscribers to the Hunt who have been invited to do so by the Master who are significantly marked out by red coats. Although most Hunts mark out such people with a red coat, a few Hunts mark them out with coats of other colours. The significant point is that they *are* marked out from other riders.
8. Hunt with a capital 'H' refers to the fox hunt as a social entity rather than to the practice of hunting itself.
9. Although a common term for this is 'eating', the fox the hounds do not actually consume the flesh of the fox although they might tear parts of its flesh, or parts of its body, from it. It is not a food source for them.
10. The over elaboration of means compared with ends, the rule-governed and formal nature of the event, the use of special dress, special forms of address between people, a specialist lexicon, use of music and other elements are the 'alerting qualities' that suggest one is in the presence of a ritual event (see Gilbert Lewis 1980).
11. See for example Chaucer Nun's Priest's Tale, Cummins (1988); Fissell (1999); Hufford (1987); Terry (1992).
12. It is not possible, within the limits of this chapter, to consider the arguments made by those who participate in foxhunting regarding the event as effective pest control but see Marvin (2000) for an elaboration of ideas of the fox as a problem in the countryside.
13. For a classic account of issues concerned with the breeding of foxhounds see Duke of Beaufort (1980).

14. The foxhounds used for hunting are not bred by breeders independent of Hunts. Each Hunt breeds its own hounds (although male and female hounds may be loaned to other Hunts for cross-breeding) and the decisions about what sorts of animals to produce will usually be made by the Master(s), the Huntsman, or a combination of the two. Most people who are members of Hunts or who participate in hunting will have views about the qualities of the hounds being bred and they will discuss these with fellow hound *aficionados*, but they have no say in the breeding policy.

15. There is no complex anthropomorphising of these animal vocalisations. They are simply interpreted in terms of how the hounds are reacting to and responding to the scent or the sight of the fox.

16. See Marvin (2003) for a fuller discussion of issues relating to the participation and performance of both riders and foot followers.

17. Although these 'countries' constitute demarcated territories, it does not mean that the Hunts associated with them may hunt wherever they please within them. For example there may be landowners who disapprove of hunting and forbid the activity on their land. Actual access to specific areas must be negotiated between the authorities of the Hunt and local landowners.

18. See Cartmill (1993: 29–31) for an exposition on some of the fundamental principles of hunting as sport.

References

Duke of Beaufort 1980. *Foxhunting*, Newton Abbot/London: David and Charles.

Caillois, R. 2001. *Man, Play and Games*, Urbana and Chicago: University of Illinois Press.

Cartmill, M. 1993. *A View to a Death in the Morning: Hunting and Nature through History*, Cambridge, Massachusetts: Harvard University Press.

Chaucer, G. 1960. 'The Nun's Priest's Tale' in *The Canterbury Tales*, Harmondsworth: pp. 232–49.

Cummins, J. 1988. *The Hound and the Hawk: The Art of Medieval Hunting*, London: Weidenfeld and Nicolson.

Fissell, M. 1999. 'Imagining Vermin in Early Modern England.' *History Workshop Journal* 47: 1–29.

Hufford, M. 1987. 'The Fox' in A.K. Gillespie and J. Mechling (eds) *American Wildlife in Symbols and Story*. Knoxville: University of Tennessee Press.

Knight, J. 2003. *Waiting for Wolves in Japan: An Anthropological Study of People-Wildlife Relations*. Oxford: Oxford University Press.

_____ 2004. 'Representations of Hunting in Japan' in J. Knight (ed.) *Wildlife in Asia: Cultural Perspectives*. London: Routledge/Curzon.

Lewis, G. 1980. *Day of Shining Red: An Essay on Understanding Ritual*, Cambridge: Cambridge University Press.

Marvin, G. 2000. 'The Problem of Foxes: Legitimate and Illegitimate Killing in the English Countryside' in J. Knight (ed.) *Natural Enemies: People-Wildlife Conflicts in Anthropological Perspective*. London: Routledge.

_____ 2003. 'A Passionate Pursuit: Foxhunting as Performance' in B. Szersznski, W. Heim and C. Waterton (eds) *Nature Performed: Environment, Culture and Performance*. Oxford: Blackwell, pp. 46–60.

Terry, P. 1992. *Reynard the Fox*, Berkeley: University of California Press.

7

PLAYING LIKE CANADIANS: IMPROVISING NATION AND IDENTITY THROUGH SPORT

Noel Dyck

Introduction

Whether actively pursued or incidentally encountered, engagement with sport constitutes a salient feature of everyday life for a sizable proportion of children, youth and adults in cities and communities across Canada. This chapter examines how varying forms of involvement with sport may be marshalled to shape domestic representations of Canada as a nation as well as to mediate the paired and often problematic identities of 'Canadians' and 'immigrants'. Although Western social science has traditionally relegated sport to a supposedly frivolous category of mere 'fun and games', such a perspective is badly dated and conceptually callow. Within Canada, as in many other nations, participation in and contemplation of sporting activity has become a powerful vehicle for defining and celebrating nationhood. What is more, sport provides complex organisational and expressive capacities for enunciating and embodying opposing ideological propositions about appropriate relationships between Canadians 'old' and 'new', propositions articulated in terms of acceptance or avoidance of the disciplined practices that comprise sport.

On the one hand rests a decidedly positive and hopeful depiction of sport that envisions it as an accessible and effective vehicle for fostering the social and cultural integration of immigrants and their children into athletic and recreational sport activities valued by many Canadians (Minister's Task Force on Federal Sport Policy, 1992). According to this scenario, the team relationships, camaraderie and shared values forged by athletes on the field of play may also be shared by parents on the sidelines, be they native-born or immigrants. Moreover, it is believed by aficionados of sport that competing in the same games under the same rules will give rise to forms of cultural intimacy capable of furnishing shared experiences, understandings, idioms and identities. These, it is surmised, can be transported away from the gymnasia, pools and rinks of athletic competition and applied beneficially in other realms of everyday life. From this perspective, sport participation is defined as a voluntary and highly enjoyable field of endeavour that, if made equally available to all residents of Canada, would help to bring 'us' together in smaller and larger ways. Herein lies the cherished prospect of building a civically integrated society by harnessing the recreational pleasures and associative powers ascribed to sport.

There is, however, 'another hand' upon which perches a less idyllic rendering of the nexus between immigration, nationality and sport in Canada. The implicit expectation that immigrants can and should join in the sporting activities preferred by other Canadians may be held with an intensity that acts to blur the line between hospitality and expectations of assimilation. An instance of this was evoked by a story appearing in the sports section of the Vancouver *Sun* newspaper on 7 November 2000. In a weekly column on local high school sports, it was reported that:

> Richmond High's once-proud and successful senior boys' football program appears to have been thrown for a devastating loss. How devastating? The Colts may have played their last game ever last Friday in Victoria against the Mount Douglas Rams ...
>
> The problem, according to [the] head coach ... is a steady decline in the number of student athletes who have turned out for football at the school in recent years.

The head coach attributed this regrettable development to several factors, one of the more significant of which was the growing population of Asian immigrants in the area: 'We have an exploding Asian population and those kids' interests are in other sports.'

Evidently, a sense of regret and cultural distance may emerge not only when the belief that immigrant children would benefit by taking part in Canadian sports is disappointed but even more so when such an outcome is interpreted as jeopardising a community's ability to maintain traditionally popular sport programs. Accordingly, sport activities may cease to be simply optional and sociable leisure activities and become instead emotionally and symbolically charged markers of ethnic difference, opposition and intolerance.

To delineate the articulation and interpenetration of sport, nation, immigration and identity in Canada we must delve into sundry aspects of what may be entailed in 'playing like Canadians' both on and beyond the venues of athletic travail. Precisely because sport is constituted by embodiment and self-discipline, play and pleasure, it remains a subtle medium for proposing and improvising identities and arrangements that may suit groups and individuals better than those put forward by state and sport officials. This raises questions about not only the capacity of sport to serve as a site for the production of identities but also of where instrumentality in sport ends and improvisation begins.

How We Play the Game

The prescriptive potential of sport is vividly captured in a celebrated work of Canadian literature, Roch Carrier's *The Hockey Sweater* (1979). Set in a rural Quebec village in the 1940s, the tale humorously recounts the dilemma of a dedicated young fan of the Montréal Canadiens who outgrows his hockey sweater. When his mother orders a replacement from a mail-order company, what arrives is not the coveted '*bleu, blanc, rouge*' of *Les Canadiens* but rather the hated colours of the arch-rival Toronto Maple Leafs. Unable to prevail against his mother's stand that one hockey sweater is as good as any other, the young player is fated to suffer ignominiously at the hands of fellow devotees of *Les Glorieux* at the neighbourhood ice rink.

As well as presenting a warm and empathetic account readily grasped by anyone who has revered a particular team or sports hero, *The Hockey Sweater* serves as an allegorical marker of traditional cultural and linguistic tensions between French and English Canadians. Originally published in a book of short stories, it was subsequently turned into a popular animated film by the National Film Board of Canada (*The Sweater*, 1980) and published as an illustrated book for children (Carrier 1984). Most recently, an excerpt from the story has been enshrined on the reverse side of the Canadian five dollar bill along with images of children and adults skating and playing hockey: 'The winters of my childhood were long, long seasons. We lived in three places – the school, the church and the skating rink – but our real life was on the skating rink.'

The notion that the 'real life' of Canadians remains inextricably linked to ice hockey continues unabated. The Canada-Soviet Union hockey challenge tournament of 1972 produced not only some memorable games but also a viscerally inscribed sense of pride mixed with more than a little relief when the Canadian team managed to record a narrow but dramatic series victory in what was seen as the summit of success in 'our game'. Nevertheless, Canadian fans' abiding hope that their team might continue to triumph at international levels of hockey competition remained vulnerable even after 1998 when professional players were finally permitted to take part in Olympic hockey tournaments. This fragility became especially evident during the hockey matches at the Salt Lake City Olympics of 2002. The failure of the Canadian men's hockey team to win an Olympic medal of any kind four years earlier at Nagano prompted a certain degree of apprehension on the part of all but the most optimistic of Canadian fans.

It was in this context that the matter of hockey sweaters once again took the fore. A newly created national all-sport radio broadcast network opted to focus upon Team Canada's participation in the Olympic tournament and had obtained radio broadcast rights to Canada's games in the preliminary round. As a promotion the radio network sponsored a listeners' contest that offered as prizes one Team Canada hockey sweater signed by a player from the men's team and another signed by the captain of Canada's women's team. The contest invited listeners to send in email messages indicating why they wanted to win one of the signed jerseys and to indicate what they would do with it if they won the prize. On the morning following the Canadian women's team's gold medal victory and just before the men's semi-final match, the two winning entries were read out during a radio broadcast. Indeed, a number of other entries had been shared with the audience during the previous week, including several of a humorous vein.

But the two winning entries were serious in tone. The first, from a girls' hockey club in rural Manitoba, noted just how much the Canadian women's team's determination to show that girls can play hockey at the highest level had meant to their players. The entry traced the gradual growth of their club and promised that, if won, the jersey signed by the women's captain would be prominently displayed in their local hockey arena to inspire generations of girl hockey players to come. The radio announcers readily endorsed the sentiments expressed in this submission.

The other winning entry came from a listener with a South Asian surname who identified himself as having immigrated to Canada with his family at age four. He noted just how much he had wanted to overcome the differences that separated him from other children in the east Ottawa community where he had grown up. And it was, he said, hockey that allowed him to do this: from the street hockey games that he played, to the hockey cards that he collected; from the devotion he shared with his friends for the *Montréal Canadiens* of the late 1970s and to a particular player from that team in that era; from the 'house' or recreational hockey league within which he participated. All of these, his entry stated, enabled him to be like other Canadian kids. He recalled how during the late spring as *Les Canadiens* played for yet another Stanley Cup Championship, he and his friends would play hockey on the street while a car radio playing at top volume in a neighbour's parked vehicle would allow them to keep up with the exploits of their heroes on the ice. Moreover, since his father worked Saturday nights he was allowed to stay up late to watch the weekly televised 'Hockey Night in Canada' match with his mother, all the while sorting through his hockey cards.

As an adult, he had become an officer with the Canadian Department of Foreign Affairs and on many occasions had managed to move past the stiffness that sometimes accompanied diplomatic functions by talking hockey with his non-Canadian guests or hosts. An otherwise severe looking Finnish diplomat whom he had encountered had warmed instantly to a discussion about the relative merits of Finnish players playing in the National Hockey League. As for what he would do with the jersey were he to win it, the contestant noted that since he was about to be transferred to the Canadian embassy in Washington, he would undertake to wear his Team Canada jersey proudly throughout his first day on the job no matter how Team Canada fared in the Olympic tournament. After presenting this winning letter in its entirety, the radio hosts warmly applauded its inspiring message, noting that in their opinion this entry better than any other revealed the special powers of hockey in Canada.

This entry evoked the positive and hopeful view of sport that portrays it as being invaluable for promoting social and cultural integration and, thereby, national unity. In fashioning a finely-nuanced vernacular account of continuing personal engagement with Canada's sport, the contestant exhibited a deep understanding of how Canadians who care passionately about hockey tend to talk about it and of how an appreciation of this and other sports might afford an immigrant with the social and symbolic means to assert a Canadian identity in a manner that went beyond being merely convincing to become emblematic. Touching upon elements that encase the supposed centrality of hockey in Canadian life – family, community, informally played 'road' or 'pond' hockey, and pride in representing Canada to the world – the entry managed to articulate the complex emotions of a highly charged week of Olympic competition in a way that expanded the boundaries of the category of 'Canadian' in the very process of differentiating it from other national identities.

From this perspective sport is likened to a mode of socialisation that by acquainting immigrants with the cultural values and social preferences of the host society offers them an informal but potent means for attaining social mobility through cultural assimilation. Conversely, immigrants' failure to engage with or participate in the games and sports of the host country, whether by choice or by exclusion, may be interpreted as effectively maintaining their cultural distinctiveness and separation within the new society. Indeed, for immigrants and their children to play games and sports brought with them from their native lands rather than those generally favoured in their new country may be construed as an act of deliberate boundary marking that signals serious limitations in the extent to which they will seek incorporation into the new setting.

These ostensibly dichotomised models of immigrant participation or non-participation in sport and of the use of sport either to promote or to forestall immigrant integration into host societies can be illustrated by use of accounts provided by sport historians (e.g. Eisen and Wiggins 1994; Adair 1998). The field of immigration and sport can also be informed by conceptually adjacent anthropological and social science literatures on sport and ethnicity (e.g. Fleming 1995; Werbner 1996; Andrews et al. 1997; Anderson 2003), sport and nationalism (MacClancy 1996; Bairner 1996), and sport and colonialism (Mangan, 1986, 1992). Indeed, work conducted in all of these fields serves to establish the differing ways in which sport involvement or non-involvement can be utilised to shape individual, group and even national identities. Clearly, the literature indicates that sport has been wielded in different places and times to promote recognition of similarity and/or difference, to foster unity or to spark conflict.

The prospect of mobilising sport as a means for fostering the integration of immigrants into Canadian society rests upon one of its less celebrated features.

The embodied pleasures and entertainments that engagement with sport affords athletes and spectators are, of course, manifest. But this demonstrated wherewithal to generate sought-after experiences serves not only to sustain recruitment of willing players and fans but also to capture the interest of those intrigued by the disciplinary potentials infused within sport. At the heart of athletic performance rests the attempt to exercise control over stylised uses of the body so as to accomplish desired movements, practices and outcomes. Whether the training of sporting bodies ensues primarily from self-direction, from externally controlled regimes of coaching, or from a combination of the two, nonetheless, the shaping and management of the athletic body presumes some inclination towards compliance and thereby projects an idiom of biddability. The transformative logic that proposes the sculpting of malleable bodies may accordingly be extended to guide the disciplining of other aspects of sport participants' deportment and behaviour both on and off fields of play. Thus, sport can be seen to furnish an attractive and pliable medium for mounting projects of social and political engineering under the rubric of play.

In Canada sport is enlisted in support of a range of social ventures promoted variously by families, community groups and state agencies. In urban and suburban neighbourhoods, organised community sports for children and youths have been pitched to mothers and fathers as wholesome and beneficial activities with which to augment the conscientious performance of parental child-rearing responsibilities. Rhetorically garbed as reliable provisioners of 'fun' and 'healthy' physical exercise for young athletes, these characteristically adult-organised sport associations also undertake to nourish the 'self-esteem' of girls and boys (Dyck 2000) and to otherwise prepare children to meet the competitive challenges said to await them in the world of adulthood (Dyck 2003). By routinely requiring substantial levels of parental support, both in terms of time and money, community sport activities constitute social settings within which mothers and fathers can also publicly demonstrate to their contemporaries and themselves the extent of their devotion to and sacrifices for the social and athletic development of sons and daughters. Just as couples are seen to be transformed into families by the arrival of children (James 1998), so too do observably 'supportive' mothers and fathers of young football players, swimmers and martial artists substantiate not only their assiduousness as parents but also perhaps a status as procreators of talented young athletes.

Participation as a coach, manager or official within a community or provincial sport organisation is a credential proudly listed by candidates for political office in the Lower Mainland of British Columbia. Although municipal governments devote significant resources to building and maintaining hockey rinks, soccer fields, baseball diamonds, gymnasia and swimming pools for community use, there is often public pressure for even more to be provided. Local governments wish to be deemed as 'responsive' in providing sport facilities and services that suitably manage the whereabouts and safely harness the energies of child and youth populations, for these are generally rated as services that reassure tax-paying parents. Municipalities that serve as informally selected immigration-reception areas also expect sport, recreational and educational facilities to play a part in fostering integration and acceptance of immigrants into local communities.

A more extravagant declaration of the role that sport might play within and on behalf of Canadian society is enunciated in a federally commissioned study of amateur sport. Noting the pervasiveness of sport within Canadian society, the report identifies competitive sport as 'an expression of our nature, our search for fun and fair play and of our national character' (Minister's Task Force on Federal Sport Policy 1992: 9–22). In addition to offering Canadians the opportunity to test and develop themselves 'physically and personally', the Task Force labels sport as 'a basis for social interaction, community building, developing intercultural relationships and local pride'. As well as developing feelings of national unity and pride, sport is showcased as helping Canadians 'face the reality of globalization by developing competitive skills and behaviours that are rapidly becoming essential to our economic survival'. Turning to children's sports, the Task Force concludes that modern social conditions have combined 'to erode the moral development of Canadian youth'. The Task Force calls upon sport to redress this societal gap 'by accepting a leadership role in instilling values and ethics in Canadian youth'. Clearly, sport participation is here envisioned as much or more as an all-purpose, virtually 'magical' solution to all manner of individual concerns and national problems than as a source of leisure and fun. Although ostensibly acting as forms of recreation and enjoyment, children's sports are in effect conscripted for decidedly disciplined purposes of reshaping not only youthful bodies but also prospects for national unity and economic development.

The proclivity to employ sport as a device to facilitate the integration of immigrants into Canadian society materialises out of a set of cultural understandings about the nature and virtues of sport as not only a form of pleasure but also a beneficent mode of civic engagement. Nonetheless, a basic question arises here concerning the assumed efficacy with which sport is to be mustered for social purposes. In short, what seems to be relatively unproblematic in published accounts about the ways in which sport can be employed to observe, create and/or cross social and cultural boundaries becomes decidedly complicated and equivocal when encountered directly during ethnographic fieldwork.

Instrumentality and Sport

These concerns with the conjectured responsiveness of sport to intentional orchestration can be illuminated by reference to several ethnographic encounters gleaned from field research in the metropolitan Lower Mainland area of British Columbia. The first occurred during a surprise birthday party organised for an Indo-Canadian friend by his wife. The guests included a number of fellow immigrants from India and their families along with a few non-immigrant friends and colleagues from work. A huge and delicious buffet meal was served from the kitchen, but the party's activities were centred in the living room. The evening featured a range of Indian cultural performances, including Hindi songs presented variously with or without accompaniment by Indian musical instruments, an exhibition of traditional dancing to recorded music, and a number of lengthy and rhetorically stylish testimonials to the birthday celebrant.

Yet, in the kitchen a television set remained tuned to a professional ice hockey match that featured the local team, the Vancouver Canucks. At different points during the evening I returned to the kitchen for food and drink and each time obtained a detailed update of the state of the game from several pre-teenaged Indo-Canadian boys. They described the winning 'wrap-around' goal scored in overtime by the Canucks in technically perfect terms that would have done any local sports broadcaster proud. It was not the case that all of the children or youth, or even all of the boys, attending the party remained in the kitchen in front of the television set. Several of the younger boys and all of the girls watched the events in the living room with varying degrees of interest. But the young hockey fans left their seats in the kitchen only occasionally and briefly to retrieve cookies and sweets that had been removed to the front room. For them, the extended presentation of Indian culture unfolding in the living room was decidedly less compelling than the Canucks' game with the Oilers.

The second encounter took place during a weekend afternoon sports tournament staged at a Sikh temple located in one of Vancouver's suburbs. I was attending the tournament to witness for my first time the traditional Indian game of *kabaddi* (see Alter 2000). Entering the temple grounds with my brother, it appeared that, except for a couple of uniformed police officers, we were among the few non-Sikh spectators in a crowd of some two thousand people. Nor were there any women in the audience, although boys of all ages and some young, pre-adolescent girls were in attendance with fathers, uncles, grandfathers and older brothers. Seated on a small hill near the encircled playing area, I had an opportunity to appreciate the subtlety and skill that characterise this quickly shifting and feinting game of touch tag.

I also overheard a number of discussions between children and fathers who were loosely and sporadically monitoring their children's whereabouts as the matches proceeded. A number of young children who tired of watching the game on the field began to perform unsupervised gymnastics on an elevated metal hand-rail near the back of the ground, a development that in due course elicited tumbles and tears from several youngsters and irritated intervention by their fathers. One of the men seated near to me who had previously responded enthusiastically and at some length to several of my questions about the rules and tactics of *kabaddi* and where the different teams attending the tournament came from, told me that this had been a particularly long and trying day for him. Early that morning he had taken his ten year-old son to the tryouts for the local youth ice hockey league. Not only is ice hockey a rather expensive sport, he informed me, but it also requires that parents of child and youth players provide transportation to and from games scheduled as early as 6.00 a.m. throughout the long winter season. *Kabaddi*, he noted, required in contrast no expensive equipment and could be enjoyed on warm afternoons. Our conversation and his afternoon at the tournament eventually terminated when this father determined that his tired and increasingly fractious younger son and daughter could no longer be placated simply with promises of a trip to the local swimming pool if they just played quietly and let him watch the *kabaddi*.

The third encounter took place on a flight departing Vancouver for England. During the ten-hour trip I conversed for a time with the passenger seated next to me, a man who had immigrated to Canada from Asia with his family when he was a child. Hearing about my employment as a social anthropologist and my interest in the social construction of children's sport, he noted that his parents had been so determined that he should succeed in academic pursuits that they had not allowed him to play any sports outside of school physical education classes. On graduating from high school, he proceeded to university where he completed a bachelor's degree in business studies before qualifying as an accountant.

It was only after he had taken a well-paid position in municipal government that he concluded that his work relations and career prospects would be enhanced if he was able to engage in the informal discussions of sport that cropped up recurrently during his work day. And so he had set out to systematically acquaint himself with some of the sports – including ice hockey, basketball and Canadian football – that are prominent features of the professional sports scene in British Columbia. With persistent application he had learned not only something about the general form and rules of these sports but also the names of particularly popular local athletes and appropriate clichés to choose when discussing their exploits. Ironically, the cultural separation insisted upon by his parents during his childhood was deftly repaired by this man in adulthood through careful application of the habits of study acquired during his sequestered youth.

Before turning to consider the broader implications of these ethnographic encounters it is necessary to note two pertinent aspects of contemporary sport in Canada. The first is that there is a tremendously broad and mixed range of sporting activities available to participants and spectators, particularly in larger urban centres. Although ice hockey may have notional predominance within the media-stoked public consciousness during the winter months, in fact, native-born and new Canadians alike collectively take part in so many different formally and informally organised games and sports that a personal declaration that one is active in or has an interest in sport cannot be readily deciphered without further interrogation. Is one a participant in or an enthusiast of figure skating, skiing, orienteering, volleyball, triathlons or a particular discipline within the martial arts, to name but a few of the available options? Does one have a relatively simple sport 'career' or one that combines a *mélange* of enthusiasms and experiences in different sports at different times? Thus, an involvement or interest in sport, which is generally deemed a positive trait in Canada, leaves one with considerable leeway with respect to how this might be socially constructed and culturally expressed.

The second point concerns the (by now) virtually required participation of parents and other adults in support of children's community sport activities (Dyck 2000, 2002, 2003). Mothers and fathers who may have successfully avoided all manner of entanglement with sport during their own childhood and early adulthood may, nonetheless, yet be conscripted into standing on the sidelines during endless soccer games involving their son's or daughter's team or in assisting with the staging of weekend-long meets for their teenager's swim club lest they be deemed to be uncaring and non-supportive parents. In practice, what this means is that possessing some larger or smaller experience of direct or indirect involvement in sport is by no means unusual in Canada.

But why do the ethnographic instances outlined in this chapter sit uneasily with the previously introduced dichotomised models of immigrant participation or non-participation in sport? The principal problem, I believe, revolves around taken-for-granted presumptions about the purposive use of sport that run through the literature on immigration and sport and, perhaps, other sectors of academic writing on sport. When one conducts retrospective investigations and analyses of immigration and sport, it becomes tempting and easy to impute a rationality and intentionality to given choices that can be argued to have had some particular outcomes. Thus, it is claimed that nineteenth-century Jewish immigrants to the United States discovered and took up baseball (Levine 1992) and, for a time, boxing as sporting activities that offered cultural insights and avenues of social mobility into American life.

Nevertheless, when one is working not retrospectively but in the present, the sheer complexity of social relationships and cultural meanings that constitute a field such as immigrants' involvement with sport serves to beggar an ethnographer's ability to contain and analytically manipulate these activities in simple or simply instrumental terms. Accordingly, an ethnographic account of a sports tournament in British Columbia that reports the playing of *kabaddi* before an audience of several thousand Sikhs, a game that the vast majority of Canadians have never heard of, let alone seen, provides tantalising corroboration of what might be labelled cultural resistance to the forces of assimilation if one applies existing theoretical models to this finding. But the problem with ethnography is that it almost invariably provides its practitioners with more types of information and contradictory insights than can be neatly stored within our existing conceptual vessels. Hence, a Sikh father arrives at a *kabaddi* tournament only after having met the financial and logistical requirements to enroll his son in the coming season of youth ice hockey, a definitively Canadian sport. Similarly, an Indo-Canadian cultural occasion co-exists, living room to kitchen, with a professional ice hockey broadcast. And an Asian-Canadian accountant adjusts for a lack of involvement in sport during his childhood by learning to 'talk' Canadian sport as an adult.

The myriad meanings and social relationships that embody the activities and discourses of games and sport, like other forms of human endeavour, are complex, diverse and widespread. Undeniably, sport is and long has been associated with ethnic, nation-building and colonial projects. Yet, on the basis of my field research, I suspect that efforts to apply sport calculatedly in these and other contexts has begotten as much in the way of ironic, incidental and contradictory outcomes as it has produced in the way of intended results. Anthropologists and other students of sport may, therefore, be well advised to take a somewhat less sanguine approach to the anticipated design with which sport can be used for different purposes. Particular games and sports can be entered into or avoided for any number of reasons, but the consequences of doing so are neither transparent nor readily manageable.

The emotional pull and valence offered by sport, similar to nationalism, can be attractive as a vehicle for forwarding particular social and political agendas. But just as nationalism can jump up to bite the hands of those who would have it do their bidding (Cohen 1996), so too can sport both attract and invert efforts to direct it towards overriding purposes. The emotional range and depth invoked by sports readily lends itself to the expression of primordialist sentiments and declamations of belonging. Ethnicity and nationalism are frequently interwoven into sporting events and contexts. But it would certainly be a mistake to reduce sport merely to a readily programmable expression of ethnicity or nationalism.

The Vagaries of Sport

From the perspective of participants, what occurs within and is valued about sport is linked firmly, albeit in highly individual and sometimes idiosyncratic ways, to particular locales and life circumstances. The mere fact of a person joining in or remaining outside of a selected game or sport does not, in itself, tell us much about the personal implications and consequences of such a choice. For instance, a young Indo-Canadian male, identified here by the pseudonym of 'Muntaj', grew up in a small town in northern British Columbia where his immigrant father and other family members worked in the forestry industry. As a teenager in a town where South Asians were in a distinct minority, Muntaj's love for and proficiency in sport led him to win a position on the local high school basketball team. Basketball is arguably the most popular and prestigious of sports played in British Columbia high schools, and Muntaj's inclusion on the team took him to league games and tournaments around the province. Travelling many weekends during the season, he formed close relationships with his teammates that in some respects distanced him from his parents:

> You know, when you're at school, you're always constantly hanging out or when school's over, you're playing more basketball. As far as my own family is concerned, I'm not quite sure of the relationship … I was constantly gone so it was kind of difficult for my parents … I guess it's an interesting relationship with my father … since I was working at the mill at that time too, [and] he would have preferred that I work more instead of playing basketball. And focus more on my studies …

But Muntaj was determined to play because he loved the sport:

> The coach had asked me in my Grade Ten year … whether I was going to play, and that summer I had come down [to the Lower Mainland] and visited my cousin who was getting married. And I was talking to him about it, how I was considering playing basketball in my senior [school] years. And he told me, 'Just do it. You'll enjoy the experience. You'll always reflect back on it when you're older and think about what a positive experience you had and the great fun you had. Whether you win or lose, it's the whole experience that you will remember.' And that's been the case. Even now I kind of reflect on the days where you would be on the bus travelling throughout British Columbia, going to these different tournaments and remembering all the fun I had. So I'm glad I was given that advice because I definitely enjoyed it and look back on it as a positive experience.

Asked what impact playing basketball had had upon his life, Muntaj identified what he had learned from the game: 'There's quite a diversity of players from different backgrounds. I think you get a tolerance for other people, not simply people from other nationalities but I mean like different personalities. You realise a [given] kid is kind of different and you've got to give a little and take a little to make things work.'

Yet, just as he had sought advice from a family member about how to navigate differences between him and his father on the relative merits of playing basketball rather than focusing solely on part-time employment and school work, so too did Muntaj discover a way to reconcile family and sport within his own experience:

> I learned that you need to work hard at everything in order to accomplish anything. But I kind of learned that from my dad too, coming here from India, coming to a new country is a big move. You realise how hard it is to work and establish yourself. I think basketball taught me a lot too because our coach always emphasised that if we always work hard and constantly practice, it only makes you better over time.

Following high school Muntaj managed to combine work with university studies, without having to give up either his love of basketball or the wearing of his turban.

While soccer or association football may be known as the 'world game' and although it has been played in Canada since the nineteenth century, this sport tends to occupy a tertiary status at best in the pantheon of sports preferred in Canada. Much as in Australia, where soccer is identified as an 'immigrant' game (Moore 2000), and the United States, where soccer is widely played by suburban boys and girls but struggles as a professional spectator sport (Andrews et al. 1997), soccer in Canada tends to attract television audiences during World Cup and European Championship tournaments. When these finish, however, popular attention turns once again to hockey, football, baseball and basketball.

Immigrants who arrive in Canada equipped with prowess in and love for soccer are likely enough to discover opportunities to 'find a game' and play the sport at either youth or adult levels. Nonetheless, the context and salience of soccer in Canada may differ fundamentally from what was taken for granted in their home countries. 'Reza', who fled his homeland during the Iranian revolution, notes that Canadian and American players tend to emphasise strength and stamina rather than technical skills on the soccer field. His fond memories of playing soccer as a child on the streets of Tehran parallel in several respects nostalgic renderings of 'pond' hockey. Yet, as an adult soccer player in Canada he has had to choose between playing on 'Iranian' teams or concealing his identity and playing for a 'non-ethnic' or 'Canadian' team in local men's leagues. The attraction of playing for a 'non-ethnic' team has been that it made Reza 'feel good about living in Canada because there was an environment in which I could have social relations which went beyond my own close circle of friends who are mostly Iranians'. In contrast, his experience of playing for an explicitly 'Iranian' team in British Columbia had featured less sociability and greater emphasis upon attaining winning results so as to ensure the promotion of the team to a higher division of play. Reza has, accordingly, opted and gradually learned how to play 'non-ethnically':

> I have mostly played for non-Iranian teams since I left Iran. [But] it's always [said by teammates that] 'you're an Iranian'. So when I played for an over-thirty [years of age] team, I made sure that if they liked Reza, they would like Reza. They didn't know where I am from until the third or fourth game. So on this team, they never turned around to say to me 'You goddamned Iranian', even as a joke. Whereas on another team it was, 'Oh, you Iranians are all the same.'

For Reza sport has provided an important way for dealing with the dilemmas entailed in immigrating to Canada.

Conversely, for 'Vern', a committed amateur curler, immigrants represent a promising resource for resolving logistical problems confronting his favourite sport. A long-time member of a suburban curling club, Vern serves as a volunteer official and is especially interested in ensuring the organisation's viability. In recent decades large numbers of Chinese immigrants have settled in this particular suburb, and Vern's club decided to try to attract some of these newcomers by holding open houses at the rink to showcase the sport of curling. The open houses were only partially successful:

> Well it was effective to show it off. Gosh, we had big crowds of people come in here and we had people here to tell them about it [in both Mandarin and Cantonese]. But they came down, had a look, and wandered away. Our biggest mistake was that we didn't give them an experience of the actual sport itself. We brought them down here, they looked at the big circles on the ice, and things like that. 'Oh, isn't that nice. Very nice. Very nice. Where's the coffee and donuts? Goodbye.' Yeah. And nothing happened.

Determined to overcome this setback, Vern next fielded a request from Taiwan – a country that had inexplicably formed a national curling federation, even though it lacked either a curling rink or any curlers – to assist in creating a Taiwanese curling team. Searching throughout the Vancouver area, Vern was unable to locate any Taiwanese curling enthusiasts. Yet as a certified curling instructor, he remained confident that he could create such a team if only he was able to locate five willing Taiwanese trainees. And his wish was answered when he discovered Taiwanese engineering students enrolled at a local university:

> They volunteered. Young guys. Easy to teach. We were doing okay, so that worked out well. And that kind of spawned the second run at trying to introduce the Chinese to curling here because I had these young fellows going. Why not expand it to a whole bunch of other people? So once again, we decided to have open houses.
> … So anyway, what happened was that we ran three open houses in a row, and this time we ran the open houses along with an on-ice trial. So they came here, got shown around the club, got taken out on the ice, got to throw a couple of rocks. It's slippery out there. You've got to be really careful.

With the assistance of the young members of the Taiwanese curling team – who had by now experienced international competition – Vern managed to recruit new members to the club: 'As a matter of fact, when I come down here to do this on Sunday afternoons, I'm the only Caucasian in the house. Oh, myself and the icemaker, the fellow that cleans the ice out there. He's the only other one.' Although immigrant Chinese participants still represent only a small proportion of the membership of the club, Vern is pleased with the progress made to date and optimistic about future prospects:

> It's been effective. And it will be more effective next year, next fall. Because I've already got a program put together for next fall. And we'll do the same thing again. We'll hold two or three open houses, the people that are curling with us right now, they'll be asked to bring their friends and neighbours and all this sort of thing.

What, among other things, the experiences of Muntaj, Reza and Vern serve to elucidate is the banality of generalised rhetorical discourses concerning the nature and implications of immigrants' choices with respect to taking part in sport in Canada. The syncretic and improvisational possibilities afforded by sport reach far beyond simplistic and sterile models of sports as pliable mechanisms for either promoting or resisting integration.

Conclusions

In Canada the tendency is to leave it to immigrants and their children to fit themselves into the existing structure of sporting opportunities and practices. While some do so, others decline this ostensibly open offer. In situations where the number of non-participating 'new' Canadians becomes striking or, as in the case mentioned at the beginning of this chapter, when traditionally popular 'Canadian' sporting pastimes may be impacted upon supposedly owing to a lack of interest in these activities on the part of 'new' Canadians, then a more worrying line of questioning may commence. 'Why don't they take part?', 'What is the matter with them?', 'Why aren't they like us?' The lines thus drawn between 'us' and 'them' serve to erode the possibilities for the more playful qualities of sport to generate pleasurable experiences, sporting relationships and shared informal identities between individual Canadians, whether 'old' or 'new'.

Many factors could, of course, be suggested to explain why participation in any given community sport activity may be neither logistically feasible nor culturally attractive to all 'new' Canadians. Indeed, some of the same factors may also serve to account for why not all 'old' Canadians and their children choose to take part in particular sporting activities or in any form of sport at all. For instance, the financial and temporal costs associated with sport serve as an implacable barrier to participation for many Canadians. But be that as it may, the sporting scene in Canada has also become far more complex and varied than static expectations and assertions constructed in terms of 'us' and 'our games' can ever acknowledge. For example, few 'old' Canadians, be they sport bureaucrats or ordinary citizens, even know the name *kabaddi*, the sport played enthusiastically before crowds of Indo-Canadians in the Lower Mainland of British Columbia. Nor did the sport reporters who so proudly hailed the gold medal victory in wrestling of a Nigerian-born Canadian competitor at the Sydney Olympics in 2000 seem to know that as a refugee immigrant to Canada, Daniel Igali had also become a highly proficient player of *kabaddi*. Similarly, substantial numbers of elderly Chinese-Canadians appear early in the morning at certain parks in Vancouver to practice *tai chi* without any apparent need of having this activity organised through community recreation centres. The point is that the looming collapse of a football program at a high school in Richmond does not, as the head coach's statement recognised, mean that immigrants and their children have no interest or involvement in sport. It does, however, suggest that we may need to scrutinise some familiar notions of what does and doesn't constitute sport and its appropriate place in Canadian society.

Sport participation in Canada, or anywhere, is hardly a culturally neutral matter or simply a set of physically playful activities. Sports are frequently burdened with explicit and implicit meanings and ideological values, both in terms of preferred and prohibited practices and practitioners. Sports tend to be enthusiastically partaken of and loyally supported. But they are often not much reflected upon. What is more, the recent escalation in the attribution of 'magical' properties to sport in Canada makes it difficult but, nevertheless, essential to distinguish between the rhetoric and the often surprising and unpredictable realities of sporting activities at the community level.

We need to take account of the insights provided by Bourdieu and Passeron (1990), Willis (1977) and other critical analysts of educational systems, a parallel social sphere that has also been burdened with the expectation that schools could provide all manner of solutions for all manner of problems. What they have discovered is that, contrary to the best of intentions, educational systems charged with immodest extra-pedagogical responsibilities of social engineering tend to reproduce rather than to resolve inequalities and social differences. The lesson here is that we need to move beyond the profuse but obscuring rhetoric of sport and instead view these activities as comprising complex and diverse social and cultural undertakings in their own right that are, nonetheless, inextricably implicated in much broader social, economic and political contexts.

Sport is unlikely in itself to be able to resolve the broader social inequalities and tensions that its activities so vividly mirror. But studying sport can furnish us with important insights into the dynamics of a wide range of fundamental social processes, including, for example, the dilemmas of contemporary parenting; child and youth peer relations; ethnic, gender, racial, class and regional differences as well as commonalities; the impact of political policy from various levels of government; the nature of community organisation; the creation of transnational networks; and much, much more. Given the vitality of sport and its capacity to highlight the impact of these various processes, dynamics and relationships within its activities, what is astounding is that scholars and policy makers have for so long been willing to consign this fascinating and instructive sector to the margins, where it is abandoned to superficial platitudes. Nor should the improvisational capacities of sport to propose and to invent and embody all manner of preferences, postures and relationships be overlooked. The time for sustained and careful study of sport is surely long overdue.

Acknowledgements

Research for this chapter was funded by a grant from the Vancouver Metropolis Project. I wish to express my appreciation to Les Podlog, who served as a research assistant, and to Vered Amit for her comments on earlier drafts of this essay.

References

Adair, D. 1998. 'Conformity, Diversity and Difference in Antipodean Physical Culture: The Indelible Influence of Immigration, Ethnicity and Race During the Formative Years of Organized Sport in Australia', *Immigrants and Minorities* 17, no. 1: 14–48.

Alter, J.F. 2000. 'Kabbadi, A National Sport of India: The Internationalism of Nationalism and the Foreignness of Indianness', in *Games, Sports and Cultures*, (ed.) N. Dyck, Oxford; New York: Berg, pp. 137–61.

Anderson, S. 2003. 'Bodying Forth a Room for Everyone: Inclusive Recreational Badminton in Copenhagen', in *Sport, Dance and Embodied Identities*, (eds) N. Dyck and E.P. Archetti, Oxford; New York: Berg, pp. 23–53.

Andrews, D.L., R. Pitter, D. Zwick and D. Ambrose. 1997. 'Soccer's Racial Frontier: Sport and the Suburbanization of Contemporary America', in *Entering the Field: New Perspectives on World Sport*, (eds) G. Armstrong and R. Giulianotti, Oxford; New York: Berg, pp. 261–81.

Bairner, A. 1996. 'Sportive Nationalism and Nationalist Politics: A Comparative Analysis of Scotland, the Republic of Ireland and Sweden', *Journal of Sport and Social Issues* 20, no. 3: 314–34.

Bourdieu, P. and J. Passeron. 1990. *Reproduction in Education, Society and Culture*, London; Newbury Park, CA: Sage.

Carrier, R. 1979. *The Hockey Sweater and Other Stories*, Toronto: House of Anasi Press.

———— 1984. Illustrated by S. Cohen, *The Hockey Sweater,* Montreal: Tundra Books.

Cohen, A.P. 1996. 'Owing the Nation, and the Personal Nature of Nationalism: Locality and the Rhetoric of Nationhood in Scotland', in *Re-situating Identities: The Politics of Race, Ethnicity and Culture*, (eds) V. Amit-Talai and C. Knowles, Peterborough, Ontario: Broadview Press, pp. 267–82.

Dyck, N. 2000. 'Parents, Kids and Coaches: Constructing Sport and Childhood in Canada', in *Games, Sports and Cultures*, (ed.) N. Dyck, Oxford; New York: Berg, pp. 81–115.

———— 2002. 'Have you been to Hayward Field?: Children's Sport and the Construction of Community in Suburban Canada', in *Realizing Community: Concepts, Social Relationships and Sentiments*, (ed.) V. Amit, London; New York: Routledge, pp. 105–23.

———— 2003. 'Embodying Success: Identity and Performance in Children's Sport', in *Sport, Dance and Embodied Identities*, (eds) N. Dyck and E.P. Archetti, Oxford; New York: Berg, pp. 55–73.

Eisen, G. and D. K. Wiggins, (eds) 1994. *Ethnicity and Sport in North American History and Culture*, Westport, Connecticut: Greenwood Press.

Fleming, S. 1995. *"'Home and Away': Sport and South Asian Male Youth".* Aldershot: Avebury.

James, A. 1998. "Imagining Children 'At Home', 'In the Family' and 'At School': Movement Between the Spatial and Temporal Markers of Childhood Identity in Britain", in *Migrants of Identity* (eds) N. Rapport and A. Dawson, Oxford; New York: Berg, pp. 139–60.

Levine, P. 1992. *Ellis Island to Ebbets Field: Sport and the American Jewish Experience*, New York, Oxford: Oxford University Press.

MacClancy, J. 1996. *Sport, Identity and Ethnicity.* Oxford; New York: Berg.

Mangan, J.A. 1986. *The Games Ethic and Imperialism*, Middlesex: Viking.

———— 1992. *The Cultural Bond: Sport, Empire and Society*, London: Cass.

Minister's Task Force on Federal Sport Policy, 1992. *Sport: The Way Ahead. An Overview of the Task Force Report,* Ottawa: Minister of State Fitness and Amateur Sport and Minister of Supply and Services Canada.

Moore, P. 2000. 'Soccer and the Politics of Culture in Western Australia' in *Games, Sports and Cultures*, (ed.) N. Dyck, Oxford; New York: Berg, pp.117–34.

Werbner, P. 1996. "'Our Blood is Green': Cricket, Identity and Social Empowerment Among British Pakistanis", in *Sport, Identity and Ethnicity*, (ed.) J. MacClancy, Oxford; New York: Berg, pp.87–111.

Willis, P.E. 1977. *Learning to Labour: How Working Class Kids Get Working Class Jobs*, Aldershot: Gower.

8

A Relaxed State of Affairs?: On Leisure, Tourism, and Cuban Identity

Thomas F. Carter

The crowd exploded in a thunderous cry of anger and disbelief. Another close call had gone against the home team. One man leapt onto the backstop separating the field from the seats behind home plate. Stadium officials plucked at the back of his shirt in an attempt to pull him down as he vainly tried to jam his hand through the gaps in the wire mesh to get his hand closer to the umpire. Several irate fans clambered onto the roof of the dugout sheltering the home team's players. Conga drums continued beating out a rumba-like rhythm and a couple of shrill whistles punctuated the roar of voices. Some wiseacre was wildly generating a high pitched scream from a hand cranked air-raid siren. Several thousand voices spontaneously organised a chant, directing their spleen at the umpires who were, in the minds of the fans, once again jobbing their team. '*Asesino! Asesino!* (Assassin!) reverberated throughout the night air, drowning out the public address announcer attempting to calm the crowd. Four middle-aged American tourists spun in their front-row seats to face the emotional tidal wave washing over them on its way onto the diamond. Leaning across the short gap between my seat and hers, one woman shouted into my ear to be heard over the crowd's thunder. Eyes glowing, Diane asked in a slightly reverential yet conspiratorial voice, 'Is it always like this?'

On the surface, the gist of her inquiry was about the raw emotional spectacle of thousands of fans screaming, playing music, and dancing in response to and in attempts to evoke specific events on the baseball diamond. The eroticism of sweaty bodies glistening in the stadium's lights, moving to powerful rhythms, was undeniably palpable yet also completely unintentional on the part of the thousands of men involved in this sporting spectacle. Indeed, any suggestion of such eroticism would have horrified them, for it would entail a reversal of the sexual gaze prevalent in Cuban society where men look and comment upon female bodies.

Beneath the surface, dynamic social forces informed Diane's simple question. The very presence of two middle-class American couples at a baseball game in late 1990s Havana calls upon historical relationships between Cuba and the U.S., current political relations between the two countries, and various understandings of being Cuban. Using their presence at the stadium, I explore the contradictory 'game' played throughout Havana between the 'home team', *habaneros* (residents of Havana), and the visiting team, foreign tourists. In particular, I contrast baseball fans' own senses of being Cuban with the powerful tourist imaginings of Cubanness. At stake in this 'game' is how Cubans will be defined and understood, which ultimately reflects the relationship between Cubans and the rest of the world. At the core of this 'game' are questions regarding the implementation of power within leisure, tourism, and identity. I use American tourists' presence at a site not normally associated with emergent Cuban tourism, the baseball stadium, to draw attention to the specifically contradictory disciplinary forces within leisure in Cuba. The events at the stadium illustrate the unique circumstances in which capitalist and socialist conceptions of leisure shape understandings of Cubanness.

The spectators in the stadium are not the only players in this 'game', however. The Cuban state plays a significant role shaping leisure and has a significant stake in the outcome of how it is practiced. Like many American tourists, Brenda, Richard, Diane, and Carl, came to Cuba to experience 'socialism before it disappears' without realising the social reality they encounter radically differs from everyday Cuban life. Tourists do not suffer the indignities of food shortages, rationed soap, frequent blackouts, or other difficulties that life in 1990s Havana forced many to endure. Most Cubans remain somewhat distanced from foreign tourists – a social distance reinforced through physical and moralistic means. The explicit presence of Cuban police constrains more intimate interactions with foreign tourists on the part of many Cubans while state-run tourist companies dominate the kinds of interactions individuals have with foreigners. In addition to these institutional controls, socialist moralistic codes of expected and acceptable behaviour also play a significant role in Cubans interactions. Whether by individual choice or institutional force, such enforced distancing turns Cubans' everyday interactions into a living history performance in much the same manner as the various late nineteenth- and early twentieth-century fairs and expos transformed non-European peoples into exotic displays for North Atlantic consumption. In a sense, the socialist state is engaged in creating a 'society of the spectacle' (Debord 1983) for foreign consumption. Any movement into and through various sorts of public space where tourists appear – such as beaches, shops, restaurants, hotels, museums, plazas, parks, and stadiums – turns Cubans into caricatures of their 'true' selves. Simultaneously gazing at and gazed upon by others, Cubans are transformed into representatives of an idealised 'culture' assumed to be dying if not already extinct.

Tourists do not to experience everyday life in socialist Cuba but travel through a hyper-real (Eco 1986) version of Havana. While hyper-real experiences can be construed to form a core element of all tourism (Urry 1990), tourist experiences of Cuba remain specific to spatial, historical, and cultural circumstances. American tourists' hyper-real imagined Cuba differs from other foreign tourists' imaginings of Cuba because of the historical relationship between Cuba and the U.S. Cuban authorities promote tourism primarily as an 'unspoilt' Caribbean site of sun and sand. Attached to this hedonistic beach leisure is an undertone of illicit sex that has resulted in Cuba returning to its pre-Revolutionary international reputation as a site for sex tourism. In contrast, American tourists' desire to 'see Havana as it really was before it all changes' is a distinct form of Cold War nostalgia tied to a romanticism rooted in the centuries-long relationship between the U.S. and Cuba. This contemporary nostalgia is embedded in Cold War ideology; nonetheless it is inextricably linked to earlier colonial discourses on race, empire, and eroticism (cf. Kuppinger, this volume).

The Cuban government supposedly erased such discourses in the creation of the socialist 'New Man', a social being motivated by moral principles rather than material desires (Guevara 1992). Revolutionary ideology has consistently emphasised that its citizens need to make sacrifices for the good of the Revolution. Tourism, however, is predicated upon instant gratification and the government's promotion of foreign tourism contradicts its legitimating discourse. The government, it would appear, expects its citizens to maintain a moral distance and not succumb to the instant gratification of capitalist consumption thereby creating a situation on the ground rife with contradictions between socialist expectations and the burgeoning illicit service industry, known popularly as *jineterismo,* oriented towards meeting foreigners' 'needs'. In exploring the contradictions between the disciplining frameworks of socialist conceptions of leisure and Cuba's increasing presence in the international tourism industry, I draw on Katherine Verdery's analyses on the transformation of Eastern European socialist states and their subsequent postsocialist realities (1996, 1999) and Chris Rojek's work on the concept of leisure (1995, 2000).

While extremely useful as comparative material, the experience of Eastern European socialism cannot be extrapolated to Cuba despite the Cold War rhetorical ideology that explicitly linked Cuban socialism with the Soviet bloc. The various trajectories of various former socialist states in Eastern Europe make it all too clear that generalisations relating to that region are inadequate and suspect. Similarly, our understandings of leisure are commonly predicated upon such activity occurring within a capitalist worldview, which does not accurately reflect the lived reality on the ground in Havana. Leisure as it is understood in Cuba is informed by socialist ideology. The government's cultivation of tourism, however, leads to distinct contradictions between the ideology of socialist leisure and the consumption of Cubans commodified by foreign tourists. Cubans are acutely aware of these contradictions: they appear to be vast and irresolvable and are experienced everyday. The requisite transformation of Cubans into objects of foreign gaze for profit within a socialist state lies at the heart of this untenable contradiction between the government's ideals of social persons and the interactions resulting from locals' pursuit of foreign goods through tourism. Ultimately, the moral legitimacy of the state could become unsupportable in its open commodification of its citizens.

A New Kind of Leisure for the Socialist (Modern) 'New Man'?

Human history is not so much about scarcity, poverty, and inequality as it is about abundance, conspicuous consumption, and transgression (Rojek 2000). There has always been a surplus of energy and unused resources. Leisure provides an answer to how one might usefully organise this excess. Furthermore, this 'answer' is historically specific to time and place; it is only within modernist ideology that work and leisure are binary opposites. Work, defined by effort, discipline, seriousness, and duty, is a matter of social and/or contractual obligation. Via work, individuals assume formal social roles and contribute to the maintenance of society through labour. In contrast, personal pleasure and free choice tend to define leisure. Individuals are not obligated to engage in specific activities and have no need to meet either the control or demands of socially dictated rules, routines or responsibilities. In leisure, people explore, experiment, create, and play within individually chosen practices. Thus, work and leisure are thought to be mutually exclusive, separate realms dominated by a different ethos and motivations. Leisure and work are temporally and spatially separate practices.

The ideological articulation of a clear-cut theoretical cleavage between work and leisure in industrial capitalist societies created new social spaces for alternative forms of social organisation (Thompson 1966; Clarke and Critcher 1985). Beginning with the advent of the industrial revolution, the modern era resulted in productive processes becoming increasingly alienating while family life diminished through the processes of urbanisation, wage-labour, and the bureaucratisation of social control and education. Possibilities multiplied for the formation of social groups based on leisure practices as a result of these changes. These common interest groups (sport clubs, religious and political associations, musical ensembles, and others) all competed for individuals' attention. The leisure smorgasbord obscures the simple reality that, caught up in the modern world as these groups are, the time and space devoted to leisure remains bound by instrumental rationality even as it is ideologically separated from activities undertaken for pecuniary gain.

The difficulty with this dichotomy is that, in practice, leisure does not differ from work in terms of how its organising ethos informs it. A basic framework to any modernist leisure-based activity remains the achievement of specific goals. Within capitalist ethos, a primary purpose of rest and relaxation is to renew individuals' energy levels in order to replenish their capacity for increased productivity. Thus, an individual lying on the beach 'doing nothing' is in actuality 'recharging his or her batteries'. From this orientation then, there simply is no such thing as 'free time' because non-work time requires an individual to honour the work ethic by 'doing something', even if its appearance suggests the individual is not actually doing anything productive at all. Any given leisure practice, then, is not an autonomous activity displaying the availability of time a la Veblen (1899), but an ideologically disciplined activity performed to bestow status upon the practitioner (Bourdieu 1984).

Although leisure may not be free and self-determining as is often assumed, its social constraints are more relaxed than other spheres of social life, such as work, family, or politics. This relaxed space of social activity, however, remains a tightly circumscribed framework that operates not only in terms of words and signs but involve material social processes. States more or less forcibly 'encourage' certain leisure activities whilst suppressing, marginalising, and undermining others. These constraints have enormous, cumulative cultural consequences for how people identify themselves and their 'place' in the world (Corrigan and Sayer 1985: 3–4).

Socialist Leisure – Reordering Production, Consumption and Time

Socialist leisure, then, is a set of regulated practices that comprise much more than mere economic relations. The aspects of leisure discussed above remain the same whether we are discussing such activity in the context of capitalist- or socialist-organised economies because both are predicated upon modernist discourses. However, because socialist societies organise their economies with different emphases, how leisure is structured differs from leisure within capitalist societies. As an explicit critique of industrial capitalism, Marxist-Leninist socialism shifted how many of these concepts were to be organised and understood. This difference, in turn, has enormous impact on Cuban identity in light of the government's increasing reliance on foreign tourism.

Socialist time attempted to reconfigure industrial capitalist time (Thompson 1967) in two ways: more modestly in how space and time are marked or punctuated, and more momentously by changing the very parameters of spatiality and temporality themselves (Verdery 1999: 39–40). The usual ways of altering the punctuation of time include the creation of wholly new calendars via establishing holidays that punctuate time differently, promoting activities that have new work rhythms or time disciplines, and giving new contours to the 'past' through rewriting history and revising nationalist genealogies. The extent to which socialism organised space and time differently from other kinds of society became readily apparent upon the demise of socialist regimes. The tearing down of socialist-era statues made it clear that Soviet statuary had particular qualities distinguishing it from other monuments. Their gigantism and the kind of time they froze made socialist space and time-ordering distinctive (Yamplosky 1995).

Cuban leaders attempted to accomplish all these things with varying degrees of success. In particular, they were successful in ordering socialist time by abolishing certain holidays and moving other festivals to different times of the year. Christmas was removed from the socialist Cuban calendar soon after Castro assumed power because of its associations with conspicuous consumption in capitalist societies, including pre-Revolutionary Cuba. It was reinstated as a holiday in 1998 as part of the political negotiations surrounding the upcoming visit by Pope John Paul II.

Carneval, that quintessential Caribbean festival normally celebrated as pre-Lenten spectacle of excess and licentiousness, was moved and made more specific to each municipality. Havana's *Carneval* was moved to the weekend closest to 26 July. The temporal shift of *Carneval* meets the state's political and economic agendas. It unites the celebratory exuberance of that festival with the anniversary of the formation of the *Movimiento de 26 de Julio* [July 26 Movement] – Castro's guerrilla movement that initiated and implemented the Cuban Revolution. It also moves the celebration into *tiempo muerte* [dead time], the fallow period within the sugar industry, thereby preventing the loss of labour due to celebrants missing work. The usual time of *Carneval* occurs right at the crucial moment of the cane harvest and therefore workers celebrating instead of labouring would jeopardise an entire year's sugar production.

Revolutions, whether heralding the ascension or declension of socialism, throw open the very notions of time that underlie history, potentially altering several different basic understandings. The imposition of new rules on the uses of space and the creation of arrhythmic and apocalyptic temporalities instead of cyclical and linear rhythms displace understandings of social processes that enable people to shape their histories in terms of which they act. The revolutionary state continues to attempt to provide ordered regimes to its citizenry's leisure activities, thereby reducing the risk of potential revolt against its legitimacy. At its core, the Cuban state's attempts to regulate leisure, particularly its control over sport-related activities including spectatorship, amount to an overt implementation of body politics. In this regard, it is no different than the U.S. (Sage 1990) or China (Brownell 1995).

Because socialist discourse remained a modernist ideology, the separation of work and leisure into two separate categorical activities remained a key feature of Revolutionary ideology. Cuban leaders' plan to transform Cuban society included an explicit discourse on how leisure should be ordered. Leisure was to be managed and used in a constructive, educational manner; in other words, leisure activities had to be 'productive' within a Cuban socialist context. In 1966, Cuban officials introduced new legislation redefining 'leisure time'[1] and instructed the populace on what was acceptable use of that time. 'Whatever a person does during his free time is closely related to his attitude towards work and society. Free time will be instrumental in forming the social outlook of the new man: a man capable of living in a communist society' (*Granma Weekly Review* 1966).[2] Based on Marx's definition of 'leisure time' as 'that which man has available for his education, his intellectual development, for the fulfillment [*sic*] of social functions, for social relations and for the free exercise of his physical and intellectual forces' (quoted in Bunck 1994: 200), Cuban leaders clearly advocated that leisure was to be put to efficient and valuable use. Towards that end, the state attempted to manage and monitor citizens' free time. Citizen seminars taught the value and 'proper' use of leisure time. Leisure was to be devoted to reading, family, sports, political activities (in support of the Revolution), or other 'intellectually valuable' choices, of which several hours of volunteer work should be included. An individual's activities away from work were held to be as vital to the formation of the Cuban 'New Man' as labouring at one's profession.

The Revolution's efforts at creating new persons required changing social attitudes towards leisure. The restructuring of leisure practices was inextricably tied to the reorganisation of Cuba's economy under socialist principles. Socialism's inner drive was not to accumulate profit, like capitalist ones, but distributable resources. Redistribution, as Eric Wolf reminded us, is less a type of society than a class of strategies implemented through a variety of means (1982: 96–98). The promise of redistribution was one reason that socialism worked differently to capitalism. The socialist social contract guaranteed people food and clothing but did not promise quality, ready availability, and choice. Thus, the system's *modus operandi* tends to sacrifice consumption, in favour of production and control over distribution.

In emphasising production and distribution, socialist regimes wanted not just eggs but also the goose that laid them. The main concern for socialist bureaucrats was not merely getting their hands on requisite resources, but on those resources that generated other resources. While capitalism's inner logic is to accumulate surplus value, socialism's inner logic centres on accumulating means of production. Consequently, 'efficiency' is defined in entirely different terms. Socialist efficiency means 'the full use of existing resources' or 'the maximisation of given capacities' rather than producing the most using the minimum amount of resources (Verdery 1996: 20–26). While one of the most important resources is labour, socialist managers hoard labour just like any other reproductive resource because they would never know exactly how many workers they will need, rather attempting to extract the maximum amount from the minimum number of labourers. Forty workers working in two eight-hour shifts, six days a week, might be sufficient to meet a factory's monthly production goals – if all the necessary raw materials were on hand. But this never happens. More often, many workers will be idle for part of the month, and then, in the last eight days, when the required materials are finally on site, the factory requires sixty-five workers working twelve-hour shifts to meet the monthly quota.

To combat such situations, the state continually cajoles and prods people into participating in Party-organised rituals confirming socialist fervour. Work-unit competitions and voluntary workdays designed to optimise 'leisure' are often met with disdain because they regulated individual leisure time and provided no apparent tangible reward for participation. Instead of securing consent, such intrusive practices of supposed commitment had the opposite effect; sharpening Cubans' consciousness and resistance to the 'official cult of work' (Burawoy and

Lukács 1992). In imitation of Party bosses, many developed a contrary attitude of non-work and tried to do as little as possible for their pay.

Consequently, socialist states have displayed an inherent tension between what is necessary to legitimate their rule – redistributing products to the populace – and what is necessary to bureaucrats' power – accumulating products at the centre. Particularly important has been preventing resources from falling out of central control in order to expand productive capabilities rather than consumption. As the earlier example regarding managerial 'efficiency' illustrates, it was more important to have an excess supply of labour to call upon *if* the need arose than to maximise the production process by producing more goods with less labour. This perspective became apparent when the state legalised and then attempted to restrict the emergence of independent contractors/businesses through bureaucratisation and heavy taxation (Peters and Scarpaci 1998, Jatar-Hausmann 1999: 76–80).

The problem with tourism, of course, is that it is an industry geared towards the consumption of resources without reproducing or increasing the productive capabilities of the institutions consuming such resources. The nascent Cuban tourism industry is in direct competition with other Caribbean tourist sites offering sun, fun, and sand. Internally, though, Cuban tourism is not really competitive despite the existence of three different tourism-based companies, each of which is run by a particular ministry of the Cuban government. Since the state sets prices and controls what packages, sites, and transport will be available, the tourist has no advantage in attempting to compare prices for a rental car, for example, because the prices for both the car and the availability of such a car are centrally controlled. Tourist complaints are often met with a simple retort that 'you should talk to the man with the beard'. The only domestic competition for the tourist industry is the informal sector or second economy.

As provider of many consumer needs, the second economy is parasitic and inseparable from the state-run economy. 'Needs', as we should know, are not given: they are created, developed, and expanded. In capitalist economies, this is what advertising accomplishes, convincing consumers of their need for goods that they did not know they needed. In practice, socialism may exacerbate consumer desire by frustrating it, thereby making consumption the focus of populace effort, frustration, and discontent. The second economy emerges precisely because socialist states tend to devalue consumption creating so-called 'pockets of capitalism' (Pérez-López 1994). Increasingly visible in Cuba, most of these nascent entrepreneurs, ironically, will not survive unless the socialist umbrella remains to serve as both a supplier of scarce goods and inadvertent protector from larger competitive agents. As Cubans became increasingly desperate during the economic crisis of the 1990s, many grew increasingly alienated from the state and critical of it, resulting in an increased politicisation of consumption, which also resulted in a challenge of official definitions of what 'needs' they had.

Thus, consuming goods confers an identity that sets individuals apart from the regime, enabling a person to differentiate the self as an individual in the face of relentless pressures to homogenise everyone's capacities and tastes. Acquiring objects has become a means to constitute an alternative Cuban self against socialist ideals. The appearance of *jineteras* (literally, 'those who ride', from the verb *jinetear* [to ride], originally used in context with horses) has been downplayed by the state as disgruntled youth who want luxury goods and not basic necessities. *Jineteras/jineteros* are not simply prostitutes of either gender but specific Cubans who provide services for visiting foreigners outside the state-supervised economy. These services can range from providing transportation to supplying goods (rum, cigars) or services, including sexual ones. The state's struggles to provide the populace's basic needs allow Cuban consumers to simultaneously find goods unavailable elsewhere and demonstrate contempt for the government. Although state discourse provides a moral condemnation of such behaviour, its promotion of tourism contradicts such moralistic positions. From the state's as well as individual Cuban's perspective, tourists are resources to be hoarded. Relations with foreigners (tourists and others) are cultivated precisely because they are a potentially renewable resource. Those individuals hustling outside the state-controlled tourist industry provide a more intimate relation and, consequently, may be more likely to transform tourists into renewable economic resources.

The tension within Cuban tourism is this inherent contradiction between socialist-informed production of tourist-related facilities and a capitalist notion of how goods are to be consumed. In socialism, the locus of competition centres on purchasers, and to outcompete others an individual needs to befriend suppliers. Thus, it is not the reservations clerk in a hotel who should be 'friendly' and ingratiate themselves to the clientele, but the hotel clientele who need to smile and ingratiate themselves to the desk clerk. The apparent 'indifference' is something of a shock to foreign tourists. 'They don't quite have the hang of good service yet,' was Diane's summation of their hotel experience. That hotel staff expected a tip *before* any services were to be provided was completely lost on her and her companions.

Consuming Cubans: Tourism in Cuba

Although the political economy of tourism remains a relatively understudied subject, contemporary leisure travel is clearly comparable in its significance to other flows of global capital, labour, coercion, information, knowledge, and value across social, cultural, linguistic, regional, and state boundaries. There are direct continuities between earlier forms of colonial domination and surplus extraction and the global inequalities produced and perpetuated by Caribbean-sited tourism-oriented development (Fanon 1968: 153–54). This 'hedonistic face of neocolonialism' is painfully ironic since one of 'the rationales for tourism development in the 1960s was export diversification away from reliance on primary products' (Crick 1989: 322, 319). The entrance of the Cuban state into the international tourism industry is simply the latest move of the 'repeating island' phenomenon of replicative economic exploitation that began with cane plantations and continues to this day (Benítez-Rojo 1996).Whether through official channels or as *jineteros*, Cubans involved in the tourist industry live less off the production of sugar that the government still exports than off the *caramelos* (literally, 'sweets' but more accurately translated in this context as 'favours') that many find themselves supplying, willingly or unwillingly, for powerful foreign demand. The transformation of tropical luxury goods into European social necessities was a decisive moment in the emergence of the capitalist world economy (Mintz 1985) and therefore a major factor in the development of Western ideologies of individual self-identity through nonessential consumption (Sahlins 1996).

Some aspects of these transformative processes within European and North American imaginations can appear relatively benign, such as the Cubans' appropriation of Ernest Hemingway's passion for the island as an attraction and iconic embodiment of foreign expectations and behavioural norms. Papa Hemingway's spirit of colonial domination and consumption of Cubanness is promoted by the state tourist agencies. Visitors can walk the grounds and peer in the windows of the author's house in San Francisco de Paula, and replicate the man's drinking exploits consuming *mojitos* and *daiquiris* in the *Bodeguita del Medio* and *Floridita*. Tourists can also hire fishing boats out of the Hemingway Marina, replicating the deep-sea fishing trips Hemingway engaged in and eulogised in *The Old Man and the Sea* (originally published in 1952). This form of nostalgia, however, is merely a more subtle thread of discourse that reproduces colonial power relations. Other aspects, however, are much more prominent and pervasive.

At the heart of the Cuban re-entry into the tourism industry lies a discourse of imperialist nostalgia, a nostalgic construct that denies humanity to Cubans much as colonial, race-based discourses once did. Imperialist nostalgia revolves around a distinct paradox: the individual mourns for what has been deliberately destroyed (Rosaldo 1989: 68–87). Most commonly associated with metropolitan individuals engaged in colonial domination, imperialist nostalgia is a peculiar manifestation of 'the white man's burden' in which 'modern' nations stand duty-bound to bring so-called traditional ones into the future. Such forms of longing appear hauntingly similar to modernist notions of 'progress'. In the ideologically constructed world of ongoing progressive change, putatively static societies, such as communist states, become reference points for defining contemporary modern identity. 'We' valorise innovation then yearn for more stable worlds, whether these exist in our own imagined past, in other cultures, or in a conflation of the two. When these so-called modernising processes destabilise societies, the agents of such change experience the transformations of other cultures as if they were personal losses. American tourists' interest in Cuba is predicated upon this particular form of nostalgia, recognising that Cuban society is rapidly changing. Normally a dimly remembered memory of days-gone-by when Cuba was a hedonistic playground for American tourists, such nostalgic discourse has become more explicit in the American perception of a post-socialist world (Prieto Gonzáles 2003).

In the American imagination, Cuba was the exotic, erotic, tropical Other in the decade leading up to the Cuban Revolution (Pérez 1999: 168–98, Schwartz 1997). It was a place of license and loose morality filled with night clubs, brothels, bars, and casinos. Within those places, tourists mingled with prostitutes, pimps, politicians, gangsters, racketeers, and policemen in a sinuous dance of corruption. The reputation of Havana as the 'red light of the Caribbean' and 'the brothel of the New World' offended many Cubans. The irony of the Cuban government's entrance into the international tourism industry is that, in some ways, the socialist state has reproduced this lurid reputation of pre-Revolutionary Cuba. After dedicating decades of ideological discourse towards the erasure of racial bigotry and ethnic stereotypes, the Cuban tourist industry now emphasises and capitalises on such stereotypes, especially Afro-Cuban performances that further emphasise the tropical eroticism and exoticism of Cuba. Resorts offer shadowy, mysterious religious rituals based on *santería* to amuse tourists with 'direct contact' with magic, spirits, and African ritual. Typical tourist itineraries include 'cultural performances' enacted by one of several national folkloric groups, rumba and other dance shows at the reborn *Tropicana* and *Sans Souci* cabarets, and visits to Guanabacoa, a Havana suburb, to see a folklore museum devoted to Afro-Cuban religion. Galleries and street artists pander to these tropical images by producing works of art for foreign consumption.

The Cuban government actually promotes such global perceptions through promotional campaigns emphasising the exotic beauty of Cuba and Cubans. In 1991 both *National Geographic* and *Playboy* magazines used pictorial 'essays' to document the islanders' natural charms. Below a photograph of a young woman dressed all in white, dancing with her hands flung high above her head, the caption in a *National Geographic* piece reads, 'Slow, fast, and then faster, sacred *bata* drum rhythms seize a dancer in Santiago de Cuba seeking communion with the Afro-Cuban divinity Babalú-Aye' (White 1991: 94–95). *Playboy's* pictorial of voluptuous semi-nude coloured women did nothing but reinforce foreign notions of exotic eroticism, particularly since the photo essay was done at the invitation of Cuban tourism officials (Prieto Gonzáles 2003: 24–26). *National Geographic* has returned to Cuba several times in the past decade further emphasising the island's exotic tropicality, most recently in a November 2003 issue (Winter 2003), while *Playboy* has not returned. Castro actually defended Cuba's new status in a bizarre twist of logic, stating that it [sex work] was unfortunate yet acceptable as long as it satisfied tourists. He asserted that *jineteras* could not be considered prostitutes because 'prostitution is not allowed in our country' (*Washington Post* 1992) and no one forces these women to sell themselves to their customers. 'Those who do so do it on their own, voluntarily, and without any need for it'

(*Washington Post* 1993). Nonetheless, they were 'highly educated hookers and quite healthy' because of their access to the state's health care system. Beyond sex work, the sensual exoticness of Afro-Cuban bodies remains a core aspect of Cubanness in the minds of foreign visitors. The sensuality and exoticness of Afro-Cuban bodies in particular is one emphasis of Cubanness more directly resultant from foreign imaginings than any constructed self-image.

The creation and maintenance of a Cuba as a tropical Other is a result of class and ethnic distinctions shaped by tourism patterns in Cuba and cannot be separated from interrelated gender and racial hierarchies that have direct historical antecedents in colonialism (Stoler 1995). These widespread historical colonial contexts of gender and ethnic subordination collude to help construct young Afro-Cubans as objects for historically dominant foreigners. In an insidious convergence of local and global conceptions, a complex heritage of Cuban perceptions of non-white sexuality and female dishonour – rooted, ultimately, in slavery (Martínez-Alier 1989) – renders female sexual agency a pervasively 'racialised practice' (Fernández 1999), particularly when visibly focused on and remunerated by foreign men. Owing to tourist demand, the commodification of Cubans proceeds along an axis defined by racial stereotypes and is consequently experienced by many *habaneros* themselves as linked to conceptions of blackness. This is a significant change from the classy *mulata*, whose body traditionally formed the screen for projections of male Cuban sexual fantasies (Kutzinski 1993) and the image of the Cuban nation (Villaverde 1977). In the popular Cuban imagination, the figure epitomising the emergent forms of dollar prostitution is some very dark-skinned girl from the countryside or solidly black barrio of Havana whose vulgarity and awkwardness immediately gives her away as black trash. A common stereotype is that such girls cannot even walk on high heels.

A consequence of the Cuban government's emphasis on tourism, then, is that the island itself has become a sort of nostalgic living history museum, resulting in the commodification of the Cuban populace as a whole. Cuba has become the new, 'hot' spot (in all its connotations) in sex tourism, challenging the South East Asian spots for European and North American male attention. For Cubans to now engage in sex work practically means to assume a non-white identity by association, and not just in the minds of foreigners enacting their own fantasies of erotic authenticity. A Cuban study (cited in Fernández 2001) found that Cubans' personal attitudes about race and attractiveness significantly affect the hiring process of state-run tourist enterprises, leaving darker skinned Cubans on the margins of this lucrative sector. Instances of discrimination were more prevalent in the emerging sectors of the economy, i.e. tourism and other dollar-related industries, than in socialist/peso workplaces. Such practices reinforce both the perception and the embodied reality of illicit *jineterismo* as being predominantly populated by darker skinned Cubans, and of lighter skinned Cubans more readily obtaining official tourism jobs.

As Cuba's economy rapidly shifts its emphasis from a traditional base of agricultural exports to tourism, Cuban bodies are increasingly coming to function as transfer points of value extracted in the form of competitively priced services realised in the cultivation of foreign (primarily but not exclusively) male selves. To what degree people will individually compromise themselves morally in order to access *el fula* (the U.S. dollar) is a question Cubans are having to continually ask themselves. The negotiation for services between Cuban provider and foreign consumer is the physical manifestation of a power struggle over the identity of groups whose imputed low standards of morality, lack of self-control, and lack of civic virtue predispose them to engage in economies of predation. The Cuban modernity that foreign tourists penetrate is not merely structured by fantasies about erotically primitive black bodies; on the contrary, it actively produces such bodies in collusion with the Cuban state.

Imperialist Nostalgia for Cuban Baseball?

Brenda, Richard, Diane and Carl, the four tourists at *Estadio Latinoamericano*, never expressed any interest in the burgeoning sex trade in Havana. In a sense, therefore, this group was unusual. Many other tourists I encountered explicitly demonstrated through words and actions that 'companionship' was a primary reason they came to Cuba. Nonetheless, the foursome clearly took advantage of *jineterismo*. The simple fact that I was seated next to them was a direct indication of their participation in it. At the start of the game, I was seated in a section with a group of fans with whom I normally associated. Yasser, a young black man who sometimes also participated in the conversations of that *peña* (group, club, or circle as in 'social circle' (Carter 2001)), had been hired by the four to guide them to the game and get them back to their hotel. Yasser spotted me in the stands and brought me down to the guarded section where the tourists sat so I could translate for him. The very position of their seats in the stadium, in a section directly behind home plate with a security guard at each entrance, indicated their participation in these processes. Those seats are reserved for administrators, visiting dignitaries, and those who can afford to pay in dollars rather than pesos. Yasser arranged their seats, purchasing their tickets for them, skimming a couple of dollars off the top for each ticket. The four were thrilled at how inexpensive it was to sit that close to the action on the field without realising how much of a premium they had paid. Keen to ensure that they knew he could continue in their hire or provide other services for them if desired, Yasser desperately 'encouraged' me to visit with them and interpret for him. Thus, by the time the crowd erupted, I had spent most of the game answering questions and interpreting for the group.

These four, like most of the tourists I encountered in Havana, expressed regret that life in Cuba was not remaining the same. They knew that the post Cold War world was rapidly intruding yet refrained from acknowledging that American policies played any role in pushing Cuba into its precarious situation. Explaining why they were in Havana, Carl opined, 'We came because it was a chance to see things how they were. It's all going to change.' Carl was talking simultaneously about Cuba in general and Cuban baseball specifically. Several prominent Cuban baseball players had recently defected from the country. Their departure resulted in a bidding frenzy by professional clubs in the U.S. for their services. 'Once Castro dies, all of this will be gone. The Big Leagues will come in and the best will be gone.' Richard elaborated, 'We figured this was a chance to see some place somewhat mythical before it disappeared into history. Once Castro goes, everything will change. This was a chance to experience a bit of history before it's relegated to the books.' What these tourists did not realise was the simple fact that the Cuba they imagined they were visiting was more a product of their own nostalgic imagination and a historical past that no longer existed, if it ever did at all, than a lived-in present. Although they recognised that Cuba was changing, their perspective framed the island as one that had not yet begun to change when it had already radically altered since the collapse of the European socialist states. Their blissful ignorance did not make their experiences any less 'real'; rather, it indicated the power that nostalgia has in shaping social realities.

Like many forms of leisure, sport provides an opportunity for people to invoke nostalgia and express emotions vicariously without making deeper commitments. Lefebvre argues that emotional commitment to certain leisure forms is likely to be ultimately unsatisfying because they are mediated by ideologies of marketing and commodification (1991).

Lefebvre's premise is based upon capitalist orientations towards leisure, yet baseball teams, as well as other sports teams, can and do become the emotional axis of individuals' lives. The appeal of Cuban baseball to American tourists is its 'unspoilt' nature, i.e. the lack of rampant commodification of professional athletes, the uncertainty of franchise survival, and the rupture of community. Cuban players supposedly are still sufficiently enamoured with the game to play it simply because they love it. Furthermore, the players are actually home-grown, not paid mercenaries that play for the highest bidder, which further reinforces the perceived innocence affiliated with Cuban baseball. Thus, Cuban baseball in the American imagination represents a time when innocence had yet to be lost in American discourse and baseball was the national pastime.[3] In short, Cuban baseball, in American tourists' imagination, is temporally placed in the 1950s, which is ironic since this 'innocence' only became possible because of the Revolution. Pre-Revolutionary baseball was a professionally organised affair with players from all over the Caribbean switching teams in pursuit of the highest salary. The nationalisation and reorganisation of the sport is what made such misapprehensions possible. Tourists' sentiments evoke images of more innocent times that have been lost in the U.S. and they are completely and utterly false in Cuba as well. For these four American fans, their emotional ties involve an implicit attempt to establish one's innocence while simultaneously discussing what one has helped to destroy. Emotions need not be destructive, however. They can also constitute an essential element in the production of identities, thereby making it an important, renewable resource.

Producing Selves: Cuban Fans

In the echoes of the devastatingly difficult question relating to compromised morals that Cubans are having to repeatedly ask themselves, I now return to the roaring crowd and conclude with an exploration of how local fans actively produce Cuban identities that counter the invasive forces metamorphosing senses of being Cuban. By attending games at the stadium, Cubans embody a different kind of Cubanness, one that establishes a rather different moral position than those who hustle foreigners. It is an auto-reproductive kind of Cubanness shaped by the edifice that holds them. The stadium is not a place where one goes to watch but a place one goes to observe in company of compatriots and to be observed to be in company. The company one keeps definitively provides an answer to that moral conundrum. While many barely eke out a living, by appearing at the stadium, an implicit moral declaration is made – their morals are not as compromised as other Cubans'. When Yasser rather sheepishly approached me to request my assistance with the American tourists and led me down to where he had sequestered the tourists, he did so under the gaze of his usual compatriots. Like tourists, Cuban fans can certainly be considered consumers. They consume the sport spectacle played out before them under the stadium lights. They differ from tourists, however, in that fans are an interactive part of the production of these spectacles as well. As fans, they actively reproduce and not merely consume the spectacle thereby creating more powerful, energised sentiments of Cubanness.

What is commonly described as a 'fan' is a contemporary articulation of a social relationship historically constituted within the popular, involving relationships to such diverse modalities as labour, religion, morality and politics. There is no absolute reason for locating fandom primarily in the realm of commercial popular culture although it is so for the vast majority of people in capitalist societies. Increasingly, however, this is the only space where the fan relationship can take place (Grossberg 1992: 63). Nonetheless, the very notion of a fan assumes a close relationship between identity and caring (ibid.: 1992: 60). The social relationships within fandom are predicated upon the evocation of emotion. All too often portrayed as irrational and, even, psychotic (Jenson 1992), fans use emotions to view and experience the ballpark as community (Trujillo and Krizek 1994). Through this emotional prism, the stadium becomes a self-contained environment that accommodates thousands of regular 'residents' and acts as a place where friends and families come together to work, play, and share in community celebrations. Most of those in attendance are from the surrounding neighbourhoods, which are primarily working class. Transportation problems preclude others from further away from attending. It is easier and safer to watch on television at home than attempting to negotiate the difficult, dark journey to and from Cerro and the more affluent areas of the city. These fans' emotional ties are vital to the construction of individual and group identities; fully indicating that such emotionality is anything but irrational.

Emotions form and formulate much of the embodied discourse that circulates within the spectacle of Cubanness. They provide a way of talking about the intensely meaningful as it is culturally defined, socially enacted and personally articulated. These meanings are mediated and structured by cultural systems and social and material environments. Emotions also serve as a discursive space, more open than others, that links the mental and the physical and the ideal and the actual world. They serve as a way of orienting people towards things that matter rather than things that simply make sense (Lutz 1988: 5).

As elements of localised ideological practice, fans' eruptions involve negotiation over the meaning of events and inadvertently, intentionally or not, over rights, morality and control of resources. Shouting at the top of their lungs, fans' vocalised passion produces a vigorously embodied Cubanness that challenges the foreign nostalgic version thrust upon them. Cognizant of foreign perceptions of Cubanness, these vociferous performances are for their own consumption, not foreign. Certain teams and individual athletes embody specific Cuban qualities in their performances on the diamond yet these are by no means clear-cut or unambiguous (Carter 2008, in press). Baseball as a sporting spectacle is historically based and tied to nationalist discourses. The formation of a socialist state transformed some of the nuances of these sporting connections of Cuban nationalism, but did not truncate those connections, unlike other aspects of Cuban society.

The spectacle that is Cuban baseball is constructed and performed by and for Cubans, one in which a diverse range of emotions can be felt while simultaneously uniting fans in shared experience. Attending baseball games remained viable and acceptable within the socialist ideological formation of leisured activity because of these historical nationalist discourses. To engage in baseball fandom remains acceptable because these invoked passions are, effectively, a reproductive emotional resource. Tourism, in contrast, is 'wasteful' because it does not reproduce any such sentiments. Such 'waste' originates in morally positioned judgements from which no Cuban can be morally pure when survival requires violating state-defined normative moral behaviour. Yasser's fellow fans later commented on his behaviour that 'he has to make choices. We all do. It comes down to basic questions like "Do you want soap?"'. Fans are not alone is having to make such decisions. They, like all Cubans, do have alternatives for demonstrating Cubanness in less morally compromised (less 'corrupt' as capitalist actions are categorised in socialist ideology) ways. In short, emotion involves struggles over the entire range of issues that concern the formation of human groups.

In contemplating how leisure is disciplined, it cannot be treated as an isolated phenomenon from other social spheres of activity, most especially work. Furthermore, just as tourist practises are situated socially in specific times and spaces, leisure itself is specifically ordered in local times and places. Baseball fans create an enclosed society of the spectacle, but this spectacle is inhabited by vibrant, passionately active, and implicitly, but not necessarily, socialist Cubans rather than the morally compromised Cubans produced and consumed within international tourism. The answer to Diane's question at the beginning of this article, one I did not tell her, is that it is not always 'like this' in the stadium. Indeed, only the presence of tourists, such as the American Diane, makes it so. Their perceptions of the raucous, emotionally vociferous crowd transform Cubans into eroticised, exoticised Others – informed by neocolonial economic and Cold War political relations – that also transforms Cubans into disposable, passive, non-renewable consumables. The socialist morals disciplining leisure in Cuba directly refute this commodification of the Cuban people all the while the state complicitly aids these capitalist processes transforming Cuban society. The spectators' vibrant embodiment of Cubanness in the stands clearly refutes all attempts to reduce them to caricatured commodities for foreign consumption. Their vibrant, active involvement in their own leisure informs Cubans' own renewable sense of self – a reproducible Cubanness invested with emotion – that ultimately denies Diane's consumable, non-renewable version of Cubans and, ultimately, Cuba.

Notes

1. Compare this construction of time and leisure with Waldren (this volume) and Kane and Tucker (this volume).
2. All translations are my own unless otherwise noted.
3. It is doubtful such an era ever existed. Rather, I am referring to the mythological discourse of American baseball.

References

Benítez-Rojo, A. 1996. *The Repeating Island: The Caribbean and the Postmodern Perspective,* 2nd edn, trans. James Maraniss, Durham: Duke University Press.

Borneman, J. 1990. *After the Wall.* New York: Basic Books.

Bourdieu, P. 1984. *Distinction: A Social Critique of the Judgement of Taste,* trans. Richard Nice (trans.). Cambridge: Harvard University Press.

Brownell, S. 1995. *Training the Body for China: Sports in the Moral Order of the People's Republic of China.* Chicago: University of Chicago Press.

Bunck, J.M. 1994. *Fidel Castro and the Quest for a Revolutionary Culture in Cuba.* University Park: The Pennsylvania State University Press.

Burawoy, M. and J. Lukács. 1992. *The Radiant Past: Ideology and Reality in Hungary's Road to Capitalism.* Chicago: University of Chicago Press.

Carter, T.F. 2001. 'Baseball Arguments: Aficionismo and Masculinity at the Core of Cubanidad', *International Journal of the History of Sport* 18, no. 3: 117–38.

———— 2008. *The Quality of Homeruns: Cuban Baseball, Identity, and the State.* Durham: Duke University Press, (in press).

Clarke, J. and C. Critcher. 1985. *The Devil Makes Work: Leisure in Capitalist Britain,* London: MacMillan.

Corrigan, P. and D. Sayer. 1985. *The Great Arch: English State Formation as Cultural Revolution,* Oxford: Blackwell.

Crick, M. 1989. 'Representations of International Tourism in the Social Sciences: Sun, Sex, Sights, Savings, and Servility', *Annual Review of Anthropology* 18: 307–44.

Debord, G. 1983. *Society of the Spectacle,* Detroit: Black and Red Press.

Eco, U. 1986. *Travels in Hyper-Reality,* London: Picador.

Fanon, F. 1968. *The Wretched of the Earth,* New York: Penguin.

Fernández, N. 1999. 'Back to the Future? Women, Race, and Tourism in Cuba', in *Sun, Sex, and Gold: Tourism and Sex Work in the Caribbean,* (ed.) K. Kempadoo, Lanham, Md: Rowman and Littlefield Publishers, pp.81–97.

_____ 2001. 'The Changing Discourse on Race in Contemporary Cuba', *Qualitative Studies in Education* 14, no. 2: 117–32.

Granma Weekly Review, 23 October 1966, p.2.

Grossberg, L. 1992. 'Is There a Fan in the House?: The Affective Sensibility of Fandom', in *The Adoring Audience: Fan Culture and Popular Media,* (ed.) L. Lewis, London: Routledge, pp. 50–65.

Guevara, E. 1992 [1965]. *Socialismo y el Hombre en Cuba,* Atlanta: Pathfinder Press.

Jatar-Hausmann, A.J. 1999. *The Cuban Way: Capitalism, Communism, and Confrontation,* West Hartford:.

Jenson, J. 1992. 'Fandom as Pathology: The Consequences of Characterization', in *The Adoring Audience: Fan Culture and Popular Media,* (ed.) L. Lewis, London: Routledge, pp.9–29.

Kutzinski, V. 1993. *Sugar's Secrets: Race and the Erotics of Cuban Nationalism,* Charlottesville: University of Virginia Press.

Lefebvre, H. 1991. *Critique of Everyday Life,* Oxford: Blackwell.

Lutz, C. 1988. *Unnatural Emotions: Everyday Sentiments on a Micronesian Atoll and Their Challenge to Western Theory,* Chicago: University of Chicago Press.

Martínez-Alier, V. 1989. *Marriage, Class, and Colour in Nineteenth Century Cuba: A Study of Racial Attitudes and Sexual Values in a Slave Society,* Ann Arbor: University of Michigan Press.

Mintz, S. 1985. *Sweetness and Power,* New York: Penguin Books.

Pérez, L. 1999. *On Becoming Cuban: Identity, Nationality, and Culture,* Chapel Hill: University of Carolina Press.

Pérez-López, J.F. 1994. 'Islands of Capitalism in an Ocean of Socialism', in *Cuba at a Crossroads,* (ed.) J.F. Pérez-López, Gainesville: University of Florida Press, pp. 190–219.

Peters, P. and J. Scarpaci. 1998. *Cuba's New Entrepreneurs: Five Years of Small-Scale Capitalism,* Arlington: Alexis de Tocqueville Institution.

Prieto Gonzáles, A. 2003. 'La isla prohibida. Miradas norteamericanas sobre Cuba', *Temas* no. 32: 19–31.

Rojek, C. 1995. *Decentring Leisure: Rethinking Leisure Theory.* London: Sage.

_____ 2000. *Leisure and Culture,* London: Palgrave.

Rosaldo, R. 1989. *Culture and Truth: The Remaking of Social Analysis,* Boston: Beacon Press.

Sage, G. 1990. *Power and Ideology in American Sport,* Champaign, Ill: Human Kinetics.

Sahlins, M. 1996. 'The Sadness of Sweetness: The Native Anthropology of Western Cosmology', *Current Anthropology* 37: 395–428.

Schwartz, R. 1997. *Pleasure Island: Tourism and Temptation in Cuba,* Lincoln: University of Nebraska Press.

Stoler, A.L. 1995. *Race and the Education of Desire: Foucault's History of Sexuality and the Colonial Order of Things,* Durham and London: Duke University Press.

Thompson, E.P. 1966. *The Making of the English Working Class,* New York: Vintage Press.

_____ 1967 'Time, Work-Discipline, and Industrial Capitalism' *Past and Present.* 38: 56–97.

Trujillo, N. and B. Krizek. 1994. 'Emotionality in the Stands and in the Field: Expressing Self through Baseball', *Journal of Sport and Social Issues* 18, no. 4: 303–25.

Urry, J. 1990. *The Tourist Gaze: Leisure and Travel in Contemporary Societies,* London: Sage.

Veblen, T. 1899. *The Theory of the Leisure Class,* London: Allen and Unwin.

Verdery, K. 1996. What *was Socialism and What Comes Next?* Princeton: Princeton University Press.

_____ 1999. *The Political Lives of Dead Bodies: Reburial and Postsocialist Change,* New York: Columbia University Press.

Villaverde, C. 1977. *Cecilia Valdés,* La Habana: Editorial Arte y Literatura.

Washington Post, 9 August 1992, p. A31.

_____ 2 January 1993, p.A20.

White, P. 1991. 'Cuba at a Crossroads', *National Geographic* 181, no. 2: 90–121.

Winter, S. 2003. 'Cuba Naturally', *National Geographic* 204, no. 5: 60–83.

Wolf, E. 1982. *Europe and the People without History.* Berkeley: University of California Press.

Yamplosky, M. 1995. 'In the Shadow of Monuments', in *Soviet Hieroglyphics,* (ed.) N. Condee, Bloomington: Indiana University Press, pp.93–112.

PART IV

TRANSCENDING THE NATION

9

STAGED DISCIPLINE AS LEISURE: NOTES ON COLONIAL SOCIABILITY IN CAIRO[1]

Petra Kuppinger

On 1 January 1900 the Consul General and Minister Plenipotentiary of Germany in Cairo, Herr von Muller, lavishly entertained thirty hand-picked members of the German community at a dinner party in Cairo's famous Shepheard's Hotel. Thirty covers were laid out on a table with 'exquisite taste' in a 'magnificent' hall that had recently been added to the hotel.[2] A menu of thirteen items had been arranged and printed copies (in German) were handed to the guests. After the party, the consensus among the guests was that 'the chef had even surpassed his previous worthy efforts on occasions of this nature and the dishes, which were more particularly of a German character, were triumphs of culinary skill' (ibid.). Items on the menu included illustrious foods such as: Princess Soup, Rhine-Salmon with Chambertin Sauce, Potato Croquettes, Ox-Filet a la Zurich, Sorbet with Marasquino, and truffled Pheasant.

Herr von Muller's extravagant dinner party to welcome the year 1900 was just one of many occasions where the colonial élite and, in this case nationals working under the protection of the British colonial government, entertained, celebrated, performed, engaged in sports, or simply relaxed in settings that exclusively catered to their needs and comforts. Hotels, clubs and private villas perfectly duplicated their European models and therefore left nothing to be desired as elegant stages for upscale social events. Food, entertainers and all sorts of gadgets were shipped in from Europe to allow for the greatest possible conveniences and to underline the sentiment of being not in Egypt, but back home in Europe.

Such neatly orchestrated exercises of European turn-of-the-century bourgeois sociability, when set in a colonial context, raise a series of issues. First, there is the obvious point that it was largely the colonised who worked hard to realise these bourgeois social fantasies. While the chef who did the Potato Croquettes was probably French, Italian or Swiss, the person who peeled the potatoes more likely than not was Egyptian, Nubian or Sudanese (see also Nelson 1960: 4). The same holds true for waiters, cleaners, guards and armies of other workers who made colonial entertainment possible and for the most part so successful. Equally obvious is the fact that the Egyptian contributions to the success of colonial extravaganzas were neither acknowledged, nor ever mentioned, in the lengthy discussions of such events. Less obvious, but very significant, is the direct or indirect use of the colonised at such occasions to demonstrate successful pacification of colonial subjects, and the management of potentially dangerous colonised bodies. While parties, like Herr von Muller's, were conspicuous or even conceited productions of colonial dominance and control, the conscious display of the subordinated colonised suggests cracks or ambiguities in the edifice of collective colonial confidence, and in individual colonisers' sense of security.

In this chapter I will examine the role of colonised workers, who were used in various ways as displays of colonial power in the everyday and small-scale context of élite colonial sociability. I argue that, in addition to doing the hard labour of preparing, accommodating and cleaning at social occasions, the colonised were occasionally employed at such events to demonstrate to both themselves and élite colonial spectators that they were not only docile workers but also docile colonial subjects, who had been neatly integrated into the powerful and smoothly functioning colonial political body. On such occasions, the colonised workers were to represent the colonial success story of not only making people work, but making them move or perform according to the colonisers' design. Such performances reassured spectators that the colonised were no longer dangerous, irrational, or worse, criminal beings, but instead had internalised a modern order. I argue that minutely orchestrated movements and performances of the colonised served a fundamentally important purpose. They illustrated colonial success as the colonised worked as told, wore uniforms that obliterated their bodies, cultural origins and contexts, and moved in clearly circumscribed formations.[3] Thus, the performing individual became an impersonation or manifestation of the superior ordering power of the colonisers. Such shows of designed or prescribed movement were not mere entertainment for colonial spectators. They underlined the subordinate status of the colonised for leisurely consumption and, very importantly, served the daily maintenance of the colonial élites' subjectivities and confidence. In this context the question arises as to why, in early twentieth-century Egypt, when British rule was relatively firmly established, and a nationalist or anti-colonial movement was only emerging, the colonisers needed such everyday reassurances that they had successfully pacified colonised bodies. This question needs to be discussed in the context of larger debates about the making and maintenance of colonial subjectivities with their specific mindsets, identities and confidences (or lack thereof) in a larger imperial context. These issues transcend Egyptian and English borders, and pose further questions about how colonial subjectivities were constructed, and, most importantly for the current context, how they were maintained in the context of mundane everyday life.

In the first part of this chapter I examine debates about colonial subjectivities, and combine those with discussions about colonial displays or exhibitions of humans, in order to situate the everyday small performances/displays of pacified bodies in a broader context. Second, for a better understanding of the daily maintenance of colonial subjectivities and confidence, and of colonisers' senses of mission and superiority, it will be necessary to briefly introduce élite colonial social life and entertainment in Cairo as the setting of these moments of maintenance of subjectivities. Finally I will examine a few instances of orchestrated colonised movements that served the clear purpose of maintaining colonial subjectivities and confidence, and assured the colonisers of their everyday safety in the colony.

Confidence and Fear: Constructing and Maintaining Colonial Subjectivities

The staging of lavish ceremonies and events, and the display and exhibitions of colonised individuals as manifestations of colonial power and success have frequently been discussed (e.g. Breckenridge 1989; Cohn 1983; Corbey 1993; Mathur 2001; Mitchell 1989; Mitra 1996; Ranger 1983; Trotter 1990). My interest here is in tracing links between large scale events, live exhibits of colonised individuals in Europe, and everyday staged performances of the colonised in the colonies.

Before reviewing colonial spectacles, a few preliminary remarks are necessary. When I argue below that colonial élites had to deal with anxieties and the occasional recognition of points of tension and ambiguities, I do so with the clear understanding that these are moments of insecurity, and not sentiments that dominated the colonisers' everyday lives. Certainty was indeed the dominant sentiment, or at least the 'claim to certainty' or the 'apparent certainty' of matters.[4] Yet the understanding of the incomplete and precarious nature of the colonial project was pressing enough to be addressed on numerous occasions. Whereas Timothy Mitchell talks about 'disciplined, staring Europeans' at nineteenth-century exhibitions (1989: 12), I suggest that these spectators were frequently individuals who still needed to be disciplined/remade into proper imperial subjectivities. Simultaneously, I am aware that larger events and spectacles served multiple, and at times even contradictory, purposes. Raymond Corbey writes about the 'narrative plots' of events and exhibitions which varied with regard to their relative position within 'civilizatory, imperialist, missionary, and scientific discourses' (1993: 359). As much as narrative plots shifted within this broader discursive context, they also served multiple purposes for the audience. While I argue that they served the purpose of demonstrating the successful disciplining and control of representatives of the colonised peoples, I am far from maintaining that this was their sole purpose. I am interested in selective 'practices of discipline and the concomitant idiom of wildness and taming that were present more implicitly in many exhibits involving people' (ibid.: 354). This was one narrative plot among many others such as education, entertainment and the fascination with the exotic Other.

Large-scale spectacles like the 'Imperial Assemblage' in the context of Queen Victoria's coronation as Empress of India were crude displays of power and control.[5] Organisers 'realised that the Assemblage must be designed to make an impact upon the British at home as well as upon Indians' (Cohn 1983: 185). Cohn points to the dual audience of any colonial spectacle: the colonisers (and their co-patriots back home) and the colonised. Impressing one's message simultaneously on these different audiences was a challenge. Proof had to be given to the British that they were victorious, superior and safe in their hold of the colony. The message to the colonised was more difficult in that it contained contradictory elements. On the one hand there was the representation of their lost power over their country and destiny. On the other hand there stood the assurance that they had gained the superior guidance of the British, and the privilege and safety of an orderly life in a colony. Also impressed onto the colonised was the message of how they as individuals could benefit from subordination to the colonial project. The Assemblage, an event that had minutely been planned for months, centred on the final and complete political and symbolic subordination of the Indian princes/kings. They needed to be reconstructed from being rulers in their own rights, to becoming loyal servants to the crown. Colonial success hinged on the pacification of these leaders. Cohn notes the following:

> The presence of these descendents of the former great ruling houses of India imparted some of the flavour of a Roman triumph to the assemblage. The British conception of Indian history thereby was realized as a kind of 'living museum', with the descendents of both the enemies and the allies of the English displaying the period of the conquest of India. The 'rulers' and the 'ex-rulers' were fossilized embodiments of a past which the British conquerors had created in the late eighteenth and early nineteenth centuries. All of this 'history' was brought together in Delhi, to announce, enhance and glorify British authority as represented by the person of their monarch (1983: 193).

Cohn employs the term 'living museum' to illustrate the fact that the princes were not participants but mere decorative elements, manifestations of British power, and witnesses to their own defeat. Little additional commentary is required for such a large scale play on the colonial stage.

Apart from ingeniously staged large spectacles, the question emerges of how colonial subjectivities were made and maintained in the everyday reality of empire, both at home and in the colony. How was colonial power reenacted and staged on smaller, more mundane, occasions? How were ambiguities or tensions in the colonial project, at least superficially, addressed in everyday life situations? One important issue in this context is the consistent fear of the uncontrollable or savage nature of the colonised.[6] How could the British at home, and even more so those who ventured to live in the colonies, be convinced that their lives and those of their loved ones would be safe when living among the colonised, if the latter were indeed as savage as frequently portrayed? One avenue to demonstrate the successful civilising efforts undertaken in the colonies were life displays of the colonised back home. I will turn to those next.

Saloni Mathur provides an excellent account on how superficially successful, but intensely flawed such exhibits were (2001).[7] Examining the case of the Colonial and Indian Exhibition in London in 1886, she notes that the exhibition of Indian artisans did indeed attract thousands of spectators who could partake in the docile bodies producing Indian crafts.[8] As Europeans were staring at these staged scenes of colonised productivity, a look behind the scene disclosed a very different reality.[9] The men on exhibit were not craftsmen who had willingly come to London to enlighten the British about their crafts. Instead they were inmates of the colonial prison in Agra who were forcefully recruited to participate in the exhibit.[10] In an ironic twist, they had not learned the crafts they were exhibiting in local workshops, but had been taught these skills in colonial prison. Such moments of ambiguity (or even failure) in this exhibition point to tensions and divisions in the imperial society. The imperial subjectivities of the masses, or at least the middle classes, who observed the Indian craftsmen and internalised the statement about the coloniseds' productive and peaceful subordination, were not questioned; on the contrary, they were most likely strengthened. As such, the exhibit was a success.[11] Yet, there were also those who saw the disasters behind the scene, the lies and violence. How was this backstage audience to maintain their confidence in the empire? The easy way out was to blame the unruly natives; but then, what to make of the fact that among a quarter billion Indians, colonial authorities were not able to line up even thirty volunteers who would exhibit their crafts production, even for pay? Mathur notes that among the colonial élite there emerged

> a growing anxiety about the stability of empire. In India, as already noted, the rise of organized nationalism, symbolized by the first meeting of the Indian National Congress in 1885, had created a degree of uncertainty about the future of imperial rule, which was at its highest since the Indian rebellion in 1857 (ibid.: 501).

As the élite back home and in the colonies had demonstrated their dominance and control to the subordinate classes, i.e. the mass of spectators at home and the forcefully recruited inmates from India, they were still left with a sense of unease as far as their own role and actual control were concerned. Their unshakable outward confidence had serious internal cracks.[12] Those in the colonies knew only too well of the 'distance, isolation, and all too often, terrible adversity' (Clark 2000: 425), and not to mention frequent failures, that made colonial life often more challenging than entertaining.[13] Their trust in their 'real' success remained at least momentarily ambiguous. While many might never admit their anxieties, the latter haunt colonial histories.

Such anxieties of the colonial élite are deeply inscribed in the forever unsolved mystery of what happened in the Marabar Caves in E.M. Forster's colonial masterpiece *A Passage to India* (1992). Written in 1924, Forster's Marabar mystery hinges on the mysterious encounter between Dr Aziz, an Indian physician, and Adela, a British visitor. Aziz, educated, westernised and seemingly almost on a par with the British, takes Adela and Mrs Moore, an elderly woman, to the wonderfully located Marabar Caves. After a few twists in the story, Aziz and Adela end up climbing to the caves alone with only a guide. After a curious exchange about marriage and polygamy, they reach the caves and from here their stories diverge. Aziz returns and says Adela left to join her friends. Adela is missing, and later Aziz is accused of sexual assault (Forster 1992: 135). What had happened in the caves? Did Adela have some visions that intensified her state of confusion (which had triggered her questions about marriage earlier), or had Aziz assaulted her? In the novel, the case takes its predictable legal course, until Adela withdraws her accusations (ibid.: 206–207). What is more important for the current context, regardless of what might or could have happened, is the fact that fear and mistrust of even the most educated and europeanised colonial subject are at the centre of this encounter.[14] Whether Aziz raped Adela or not is irrelevant; the point is that he could have raped her. In the mind of the colonial élite, this is what counted; the potential, not the actual fact. The colonial legal machinery is then set in motion, almost literally to grind up Aziz because, as a colonised male, he was not totally in control of his (savage) sexuality and all his advanced modern education could not, given the worst of circumstances, keep such sexual drives in check. The witch hunt on Aziz, the potential rapist, epitomises the innermost fears of the male colonial élite. They were vulnerable through their women; and they could not even trust the most educated or westernised colonised individuals, as they all maintained an unpacified, savage corner in their being. Aspects of colonial confidence hinged on the protection of European women.

In this context the colonial club plays an important role.[15] Mrinalini Sinha (2001) argues that British colonial clubs played a central role in the negotiation of a colonial public sphere, and I would add in the construction and maintenance of colonial subjectivities. Sinha is concerned with 'clubbability,' a notion which indicates gradation of possible integration into colonial (male) élite status. She notes that colonial clubs in India were mediating spaces where newcomers would be initiated into local ways, but also where Britishness was re-enacted on a daily basis.[16] At élite clubs members did not have to encounter natives (other than possibly as servants).[17] Only a very small number of clubs allowed for élite male social mixing of the coloniser and the colonised.[18] But, what about élite colonial women? Women were not allowed into many clubs, or only admitted on special occasions and to special rooms (see e.g. Panckridge 1927). The issue of the 'clubbability' of women is a complex one. First there is the generally patriarchal nature of colonial society. More important for the current context is the question of whether women were denied admission because they would, in certain situations, be exposed to the gaze of privileged male colonised individuals.

Europeans were afraid the colonised would 'ogle' (Sinha 2001: 516) their wives.[19] Such anxieties, even with regard to (clubbable) members of the colonised élite, pervaded colonial subjectivities, which were plagued by a sense of insecurity, and the awareness of hidden dangers. The colonial élite was afraid of the small inroads into their lifeworld that might speak of larger failures of their power and control. In addition, there was the irreconcilable contradiction between the images of the colonised as on the one hand barbaric, and on the other simple-minded, benign and childlike. To combat some of their insecurities, or tensions in the colonial project at large, the colonial élite had an ongoing need for reassurance and maintenance of confidence. Some of this was done in a very subtle and mundane manner on social occasions. In order to discuss examples of these in more concrete detail, I will first introduce the context of the turn-of the-century colonial social life in Cairo.

The Cairo Season, or Having Fun in Style

Using materials from European travelogues and the Egyptian colonial daily, the *Egyptian Gazette*, I will in the following introduce types and moments of élite colonial sociability.[20] Colonial élite social life in Cairo in the early years of the twentieth-century was vibrant and lavish. It came to its annual peak in what was called the 'Cairo Season' in the winter months (Sladen 1911: 3; Fullerton 1891: 6–7). In addition to the resident colonial population, thousands of wealthy European tourists and a few American ones flocked to Egypt for its sun, antiquities, entertainment and distinguished social life. Social dynamics of the Cairo Season were watched and discussed in their minute details by everybody involved. With careful attention, they were also chronicled on the pages of the *Egyptian Gazette* (EG). Arrivals, departures, parties, concerts, sicknesses, horse races and tennis tournament were announced and commented on daily. To really be part of the upscale crowd, Cairo socialites had to make sure to dine or reside in the best hotels (if visiting), to invite the proper guests, to be invited for the most prestigious occasions, and to attend social events in appropriate attire (e.g. Nelson 1960: 1–2). The hope was that all of this would later be noted on the pages of the *Gazette*, since the Season was under continued close scrutiny, as the following note with the title 'The Cairo Season' illustrates:

> The season in Cairo may now be said to be at its height, and the gay city is thronged, all the hotels having a full complement of guests. Historic Shepheards has for many weeks past been able to show 'full house' and the sister hostelry over the water, Ghezireh Palace, … is also overcrowded. The fancy dress ball, which is to be held as usual in the magnificent ball room of the casino attached to the Ghezireh Palace on Shrove Tuesday, the 3rd March, has justly in past winters been regarded as the 'clou' of the season (EG 28.2.1908). [21]

During the Season, one event followed the other. In late January of 1908, for example, the Savoy Hotel was holding regular Saturday dances to which at times very few tickets for outsiders were available as the hotel was totally booked (EG 29.1.1908). A few days later the Gazette complained that owing 'to the great pressure upon our space we are compelled to hold over until tomorrow's issue our account of a concert being held last night at the New Khedivial Hotel' (EG 6.2.1908). On the same day a horse race, where a 'programme of music' was also going to be played in Helouan was announced (ibid.). On Sunday 16 February, a concert was given on the terrace of the Al Hayat Hotel (ibid.: 18.2.1908). Two days later on Tuesday a 'most delightful performance of "Ernani" … worthy of the company of the best' was given at the Abbas Theater (ibid.: 21.2.1908). On Friday 6 March, the Zagazig races were held. On Wednesday, 19 February, 'a party of eighty officers and their friends sat down to supper … at the Savoy after the performance of "Our Regiment" by the K.K.R. Dramatic Company at the Opera House' (ibid.: 22.2.1908). The dinner was followed by a 'small dance, which was carried on until nearly three o' clock' (ibid.).[22]

Large events such as dances were socially complicated and immensely important for social life and hierarchies. The following note describes the intricate details of such a dance at the Semiramis Hotel. The restaurant was packed with many 'dinner parties … in progress'

> chief among which was one given by Lady Oppenheimer at whose table were the Comte and Comtesse de Zogheb, the Hon. Mr. And Mrs. Idding and General and Mrs Bullock … Mrs. Brooman White had also brought her daughter from Ghezireh: she was wearing beautiful pearls and some very fine lace on her dress, the bodice draped with some transparent black chiffon upon which gleamed a large star of brilliants (ibid.: 21.3.1908).[23]

With similar style, pomp and grandeur, small balls, grand balls, fancy dress balls, confetti fetes, dinner parties, private parties, and occasional weddings were celebrated. Horse races followed tennis tournaments, cricket games, pigeon shootings, concerts, organ recitals, violin recitals, cinematograph entertainment, plays and flower shows.[24] The extent of these social events becomes all the more impressive considering that Cairo's foreign residential population at the time was just under sixty-thousand, many of whom were artisans and in similar occupations and clearly not part of the élite (Owen 1969: 337). Even including the tourist population, Cairo Season socialites numbered no more than a few thousand people.

Only rarely did the colonial social crowd engage in random and unregulated entertainment and encounters with colonised workers and entertainers. Probably the most famous site for such 'half-regulated' encounters was Shepheard's Balcony, where, from the security of the hotel's balcony, set up higher than the street level and separated from it by railings, upscale socialites became courageous and watched performances and purchased small artifacts and keepsakes. Lance Thackeray describes this curious scenery:

> Millions of piastres must have passed through its balcony railings in exchange for the various articles which the natives hawk in the street below. Shawls, beads, scarabs, flywisks, stuffed snakes and crocodiles, and many other charms and horrors, are here bargained for and bought to decorate and disfigure our western homes [*sic*].
>
> The juggler who is allowed to go through his old fashioned tricks on the balcony, the boy with the monkey who is pushed on by the 'comic' policeman, the quiet calm-faced Hindoo who will tell your fortune and take some of it, the prosperous-looking Dragomans, the picturesque Bedouin Arab, and the scarlet-skirted syrup seller – represent but a few of the types who make up this interesting crowd (1928:n.p. 'Cairo Curio; or, the Shepheard's Flock').[25]

The encounters at the Shepheard's balcony and similar ones at the steps of the Continental Hotel were perceived to be non-threatening and benign, or simply curious.[26] In this case indeed the colonised from different colonies were depicted as quaint, almost childlike characters who simply added color and ambience to one's day of leisure.[27]

Now that we have observed the scope of élite sociability of the Cairo Season, two questions arise. (1) Who did all the work of preparing, cooking, serving, cleaning and to a certain extent also entertaining? Is there any way to reconstruct at least some of their contributions, or moments of encounters between colonisers and colonised in the context of the Cairo Season? (2) In these ambitious extravaganza, characterised by material wealth and social conceit, can the critical observer detect even the most minute fissures in the socialites' subjectivities, which might necessitate repair or subtle reassurance? First, I will turn to the workers and their back stage labour.

Behind the Scene: Servants, Maids and Workers

Servants, cooks, maids, waiters and other workers silently performed the hard labour necessary to realise colonial fantasies of a glamorous social life.[28] The continuous successful realisation of grand and lavish social events attested on an everyday level to the firm control over the colonised masses. It is interesting to note, that in contrast to some of the other chapters in this volume which examine circumstances where individuals discipline themselves in order to maximise leisure, or their own recreation, the case of the colonial servants is different. Here individuals, largely against their own will are forced into bodily discipline or rigorously prescribed movements for the sake of other's leisure and recreation, while simultaneously representing of story of political success.

It needs to be mentioned here that servants in colonial homes, and waiters in hotels were not only Egyptian, but also Nubian or Sudanese (see e.g. Nelson 1960: 4).[29] Eve Powell's insightful book about the frequently overlooked multilayered relationship between Egypt and Sudan is one of the first to discuss the complicated position of such servants within Egyptian society (2003). Important for the current context is the understanding that colonised servants were not one homogeneous mass, characterised by narrowly local identities and the lack of cosmopolitanism. Instead, it was colonialism that made their complex identities and stories of migration and cultural heterogeneity invisible (see also Mathur 2001: 517). I will return to this issue below.

Reading the *Gazette* or travelogues, the reader will look in vain for mention of workers and their contributions to élite sociability. One rare exception is a lengthy article about the Mena House Hotel at large, and a Thursday ball in particular, where the author describes in great detail the physical setting of tables, lights, galleries, and beautifully decorated tables.[30] In the midst of this description, he notes that '[t]he white and red clad Arabs ran *noislessy* [*sic*] about and served an excellent dinner' (EG 19.2.1900, emphasis added).[31] This brief note about the waiters is one of the few references about the colonised doing their work that I was able to locate. It neatly illustrates servants' roles and their additional symbolic ab/-use. First, the waiters, without making a noise, without interfering into conversations, serve the guests. They do not walk, they run because not a second should be wasted in the service of the colonial crowd, lest the waiters come to think subversive thoughts, or the guests are left wanting. The waiters lost any individual subjectivities and had became generic colonised waiters, who could be treated in the same manner whether they were encountered in Egypt or India.[32]

'Clad in red and white,' these men were to give the place a touch of oriental ambience, without interfering with the fundamentally European framework of the event. Events such as a grand ball were not only conspicuous entertainment for the colonial élite, but also minutely scripted scenarios where everybody played their clearly circumscribed role. In addition to playing their internal games of social rank and hierarchy, guests reenacted the ongoing drama of cultural superiority and political dominance (see also Kuppinger 1998: 161), and boosted or simply maintained their confidence in their superior standing and mission. Underlying such events were their anxieties about the possibly incomplete nature of their control over individual natives or even just corners of the latter's existence.

Good and Bad Workers

Occasionally, the colonisers were faced with tensions or cracks in their invisible support works which in turn were indicators of fissures in the larger colonial project. Looking beyond their offices, factories, hotels, clubs, lavish gardens, and well-laid dinner tables, colonisers recognised the existence of what appeared to them as the disorderly and uncontrolled lifeworld of the colonised. What if their own workers failed, or worse, were not totally pacified and would strike back at them as an expression of residual or unconquered barbarity? These fears and the resulting helplessness could not freely be admitted, but nonetheless needed to be addressed on different levels.

In the more benign context of the coloniseds' refusal to work, when the colonisers were simply deprived of their comforts and reminded of the fragility of their position at large, Europeans were indignant, to say the least, as the tone of the following note illustrates:

> Our Samalout correspondent reports that the day before yesterday a train collision in that station blocked the line for five hours. The porters of the station were only remarkable in their absence and the passengers, beyond the inconvenience and delay occasioned by the accident, had the additional delight of effecting the porterage of their luggage from train to train themselves (EG 2.5.1908).

When the colonised workers did not properly perform their roles, 'misbehaved', somehow interfered with the smooth flow of events or, for some reason, were absent altogether, these workers instantaneously become a pressing issue.[33] To have to carry one's own suitcase for only a short distance could be done away with as a simple nuisance, and as such would certainly not deserve any mention in a newspaper. At stake, however, were not mere uncarried suitcases, but the audacity of the workers to disappear (watch the site of an accident?) and neglect their duties. If they indeed had totally internalised their roles of loyal servants, they would not have neglected their duties, even if an earthquake had struck. Their disappearance speaks of their incomplete subordination to the colonial project.

Worse still, on occasion, colonial control showed itself to be incomplete or failing altogether, and some workers stepped beyond their limits. 'To impinge on the lifeworld of the Europeans,' as Rob Shields termed it, was a very serious offence and became an instantaneous public concern (1994: 67). On March 2, 1908, the following note appeared in the *Gazette*:

> Mr. Charles Jaquilia has informed the police that Aly Saleb, his servant left his house in Kasr-el-Nil Street with a pearl brooch of the value of L 100. Mr. Frattos, of Darb el-Ahmar has also brought a complaint to the police that a gold watch and chain and other valuables belonging to him have disappeared. His servant is suspected.

The question of the morality of stealing from a colonial employer is not the issue here. Instead, it is important to note that such short announcements of petty crimes frequently appeared in the *Gazette*. Similarly, notes informing readers about arrests of vagabonds or escapees from prisons were often published.[34] Complaints about the absences of workers, newspaper articles about the occasional theft or petty crime committed by servants or the colonised population at large disclose the colonial élite's sense of unease. Such notes serve the purpose of keeping readers alert, and reminding them to never let their guards down.[35] Any servant could be a thief and therefore deserved close supervision. To steal from one's employers was not only a material crime, but a profound challenge of colonial control.[36]

The everyday awareness of the incomplete nature of colonial control made the issues of asserting authority and maintaining confidence all the more urgent. Newspaper notes, everyday talk, gossip and rumours about servants and workers were aspects of the daily confrontation with colonised misbehaviour and transgression. Aware of the precarious situation in which they conducted their everyday lives, it was deemed necessary by the colonial élite to stage occasional demonstrations of total control over individual native lives and movements. This purpose was best achieved by completely, that is from head to toe, and inside out, remaking colonial subjects and controlling the movement of every millimetre of their bodies. Such performances of carefully orchestrated movements, were occasionally staged on narrowly circumscribed platforms within highly controlled colonial spaces. I will turn to two examples of such 'stage plays' next.

Staging Control: The Colonised in Uniform and Formation

In addition to the daily performances of 'noiseless' servants and workers, more complete and poignant examples of absolute control were occasionally staged. One of the most interesting and complex examples of such stage plays were the performances of the 'Giza Boys' Band,' a music band consisting exclusively of inmates of the Giza Juvenile Reformatory. Their highlights were bagpipes which were in constant demand for 'playing out' (Coles 1918: 117–18). For years, one of their playing out commitments was at the Giza Zoo where the boys regularly played on Friday afternoons.[37]

By the turn of the century, the Giza Zoo was one of the fashionable hang-outs where the colonial crowd spent leisurely afternoons observing exotic animals and sipping tea in the lavish green of a beautiful park.[38] However, relaxing, seeing and being seen, and turning one's back to the noise and crowd of downtown Cairo, were not the only reasons to visit the Zoo. Here, in the middle of nicely caged, contained and controlled wildlife, neatly planted and ordered trees and plants, a show of dominance over colonised humans added perfection to a leisurely afternoon. The young inmates of the Reformatory served this purpose in a complex manner: not only did they wear uniforms and march in straight lines while playing music, much more significantly they were living proofs of the colonisers' ability to transform young Egyptian criminals into useful members of modern society (see also Tolen 1991).

The boys' playing – what I suppose to be European music and marches – illustrated the whole scope and merit of colonial occupation: (1) to reform native individuals who were prone to petty criminality; (2) to order and organise them as a group/nation into rational and controllable formations and (3) to rescript their lives into a socially useful trajectory.[39] These achievements of reform and order needed to be presented within the clear and strict framework of colonial society – here represented by the order of the Zoo (see also Kuppinger 1998: 158, 163). This show of the successful remaking of former youthful criminals was not staged in a random location, but behind the high walls of the Zoo, which itself is one of the products of modern ordering, classification and categorisation. Access to the Zoo was limited to those who could pay the fees, and was physically restricted by high walls and entry gates. One cannot but notice that the juvenile inmates, while not caged like the animals, were narrowly circumscribed by the Zoo's wall. Like the animals they were on display and were prevented from leaving.

If such routine examples of daily reenacted dominance over the colonised – all displayed at leisurely occasions – still left uneasy feelings or doubts among the colonial élite, occasional performances of control of native lives and movements, only for the sake of this display, were being staged. In all the above examples, the ordered and controlled movements of the colonised produced tangible services, such as food being cooked and served, music being played, or luggage being carried. The next 'challenge' (or humiliation) was to make the colonised march in formations at social events only for the sake of having them march in formation and thus demonstrate their subordination.[40] The boys of the Reformatory once more seemed to be perfect actors for such a stage play. Because they were young and deprived of any rights as prison inmates, living under the strictest of control and supervision, being part of a harsh system of punishments and rewards and removed from their lives and families, little resistance could be expected from these boys. Like the Indian prisoners on display in London in 1886, they were marginalised in colonial society, and therefore were unlikely to become the focus of much nationalist attention or critique (see Mathur 2001: 507).

It needs to be noted here that the Reformatory was the pet project of Coles Pasha, who served as Inspector General for Prisons in Egypt in the early years of the twentieth century ('this Reformatory for Juveniles has been my hobby for years' noted Coles 1918: 113). As such it not only reflected larger colonial discourses and policies, but also the private ambitions of its planner and supervisor. Coles ran 'his' institution with absolute power and considered it almost a piece of private property. His Reformatory, to use Foucault's terms, was a colonial '*heterotopia*', a space to penetrate, order and normalise individuals and society (Foucault 1986: 24; see also Foucault 1979). It was a perfect place to stage performances of absolute control over colonised subjects, as the following note illustrates:

> A very pleasant garden party was given by Mrs. Coles Pasha at the Reformatory in Ghizeh, yesterday afternoon. The Reformatory boys gave a fine display of club swinging, physical drill, and gymnastics to the music of the reformatory band, which played capitally. Visits were paid to the workshops and the afternoon proved most enjoyable to the 150 odd who were present, among them were Lord and Lady Cromer (EG 8.3.1906).

Here the boys played the 'club swinging' extras for the colonial administrational élite such as Lord Cromer and Coles Pasha. Instead of withdrawing to their villas and gardens with their everyday shows of 'noiseless' servants, this élite crowd spent their Wednesday afternoon in a juvenile prison. (Why did they not need to work in the first place? Or was this indeed the hard labor of confidence construction?). The party crowd had itself symbolically locked up with young petty criminals in order to partake in a show of their power over these inmates. Even inside the den of the lion, or among the 'worst' of the colonised, the colonisers remained victorious and proved to themselves that they were neither afraid nor vulnerable. At this 'pleasant garden party', the boys moved in front of officials' and their wives' eyes as examples of successfully controlled and orchestrated native movement. Their purpose for moving was entertainment, but clearly also confidence-maintenance for their spectators. Their reenactment of the illusion of total control and dominance made the boys' performance so important and necessary (see also Kuppinger 1998: 166).

A note on the gendered nature of such performances is necessary here. It is not coincidental that males are being paraded here as examples of successful pacification. As noted above in the discussion of colonial clubs, males, and possibly their sexuality, were seen as a threat to colonisers and the colonial project. Labouring within the confines of a European nineteenth century patriarchal discourse, it was easy for the colonisers to assume that once they had pacified the males, their female kin would simply follow the male lead. As such women were neither much of a threat nor were they in need of direct pacification.

Such periodic performances of neatly coordinated native movement point not simply to the control yielded by the colonisers, but much more to their persistent unacknowledged sentiments of fear and insecurity. These sentiments needed to be repeatedly exorcised in ritualistic encounters with groups of 'pacified' people in very specific (perfectly controlled and secluded) locations such as hotels, prisons, sports clubs or the Zoo, which were fortresses of colonial design and physical control.[41] Forster's cave encounter clearly underlines this point. Danger lurks in the literally 'dark recesses' of colonised society. What happened, or could have happened in the cave would certainly have never occurred in the colonial club or European hotel. Only in such places which had been built and organised along the colonisers' own lines, and were tightly controlled in their everyday workings, did the colonial élite feel safe enough to stage these shows of superiority and control. Beyond those highly regulated and closely monitored spaces, the lifeworld of the colonised dominated everyday lives and movements in the colony and as such continued to be perceived as unpredictable or even threatening. In city streets and villages lanes, colonisers felt largely uneasy. They preferred to simply avoid these places, lest they be confronted with their failure, and even more so their injustice to the colonised.[42]

Conclusion

When members of the colonial élite gathered to party and celebrate, they did so – without doubt – to have a good time. Having a good time, being served and entertained, was one of the fundamental privileges that colonisers claimed as their reward for the hard labour of civilising the colonised. I have also shown, however, that colonial élite social life, served additional 'serious' purposes. First, I argued that an important aspect of colonial social events was the everyday demonstration of accomplishments in reforming and ordering the natives; and the successful transformation of the rather 'useless' colonised masses into productive members of modern society. Second, I maintained that the neat orchestration of native services and movements, and especially inserted performances, were necessary elements of the everyday making or maintenance of colonial subjectivities and confidence. As much as the colonisers had 'conscripted' the colonised, to use Talal Asad's term, into the colonial universe, the awareness remained that this conscription was far from complete (1992). Open or subtle adversity against the colonial project continued. Despite the colonial élite's proclaimed self-confidence in their mission and work, their everyday staged shows of control and dominance attest to the recognition of this lingering adversity, and bear witness to their unacknowledged anxieties and insecurities. Colonial subjectivities thus were never perfectly confident and free of fear and as such needed occasional maintenance procedures. Without speaking their anxieties, the colonial élite unconsciously displayed such ambiguous sentiments by their repeated staging of different public performances of well-functioning pacified colonised individuals or groups. The colonial élite thus exorcised their subtle anxieties in leisurely contexts which in turn became therapeutic exercises for the collective colonial soul.

An analysis of the work performed for the maintenance of colonial subjectivities displays additional tensions and ambiguities, as much as it clearly illustrates global/trans-imperial dynamics in the making and remaking of both colonial and colonised subjectivities. Reviewing the literature, one notes that comparatively little has been said about colonial spectacles and colonial subjectivities for the case of Egypt. Taking a look at the writing and everyday lives and politics of some colonial administrators, it becomes clear that there is an interesting link between Indian colonial services and Egyptian colonial services. High-ranking officials such a Lord Cromer or Coles Pasha (or Sir Auckland Colvin) had done their colonial apprenticeship in India before they reached the peak of their careers in Egypt. They brought to Egypt anxieties and concerns that they had acquired in India. Moreover, they brought with them images of just how the world worked, drawn from the self-referential discourse of Orientalist writing, practices and fantasies (Said 1979; Alloula 1986). Exhibitions and similar events reinforced such ideas. Mitchell notes that emerging from such a world back home, some individuals never realised that they had actually left the world of images and exhibitions, when they settled in the colonies (1989: 13).

Consequently, the construction of colonial subjectivities includes at least three localities: England, India and Egypt (and possibly other colonies). Residual fears originating in the Indian Great Mutiny were as much an aspect of their practices as the memories of the Egyptian Urabi Revolt. These in turn were supplemented by the everyday talk of crime in the colonial newspapers and dining rooms. The sum total of such trans-imperial sentiments, that transcend specific times and localities, needed to be dealt with in the localised context of Cairene parties and events. It is here that the Mr von Muller's party for his fellow Germans in Cairo becomes interesting. With regard to colonial élite social life, while nationality certainly played a role, by the turn of the century, this was not the most decisive element. More important was the articulation of European/white with élite status within one's own community. Mr von Muller's German guests were part of the same larger dynamics, they played the same game based on a rigidly racialised and elitist worldview as their fellow British, French or Italian élite party-goers at the Continental, Shepheard's or Savoy Hotel.

From the colonised perspective, servants and waiters, whether in India or Egypt, were largely treated the same. The colonisers perceived of all these people as subordinate to white superiority. In order not to deal with their possible difference, they were put in uniforms that obliterated their origins and catered to the colonial stereotypes of the 'Indian' or the 'Egyptian.' Thus they became the almost generic colonial servant, whose task it was to noiselessly serve his/her superior and attest to the latter's civilisational efforts. This in turn disguised the complexity, and sometimes trans-imperial nature, of their subjectivities. As noted above, many servants and waiters in Egypt were of Nubian or Sudanese origin. The Sudanese, in particular, had their own complicated relationship with Egypt. While being British colonial subjects by the turn of the twentieth century, they had also been under Egyptian rule for much of the nineteenth century. While the colonisers saw themselves as cosmopolitan, the colonised, regardless of their experiences were denied this status. Beyond the geographical context of Egypt and the Sudan, there are indications that, albeit in small numbers, the colonised were mobile across the empire. Lance Thackeray, in his description of the Shepheard's Balcony, had described the 'quiet calm-faced Hindoo who will tell your fortune' (1928). While we have no report of how this Indian/Hindu had come to Cairo, his presence speaks to the trans-imperial or cosmopolitan experience of at least some of the colonised.

The servant/waiter/entertainer and pleasure-seeker encounter in the context of colonial élite sociability is not a simple meeting between the server and the served but instead is a complicated relationship fraught with multiple tensions, and displaying multiple agendas. Originating in two dramatically different lifeworlds, servants and members of the colonial élite meet very closely, it seems almost uncomfortably closely, at parties, dances and dinners. Remaining symbols of their largely uncontained lifeworlds, the colonial servants/waiters/entertainers are given particularly disciplined roles to perform at such occasions to both underline and demonstrate their perfect subordination to the superior lifeworld of the colonial élite. The endless repetition of these very same standardised stage plays in multiple imperial contexts, including multiple colonial and colonised subjectivities discloses the ritualistic nature of these acts of servitude and their importance for the everyday maintenance of colonial subjectivities. Jean and John Comaroff were right when they noted that 'hegemony is indeed homemade' (referring to contexts of domesticity, 1992: 68). I would add that hegemony is re/-made in leisurely and sociable events.

Notes

1. I want to thank Tamara Kohn, Simon Coleman, Farhat Haq and Simon Cordery for their helpful comments on this paper.
2. Egyptian Gazette, 3 January 1900. (From now on EG).
3. Efforts to demonstrate control, which led to the tight control and uniforming of the subordinate classes are, of course, not unique to the colonial context, but are equally present in, for example, nineteenth century encounters with working classes. One example would be uniforms worn by domestic servants.
4. About the role of certainty, for example, in the context of colonial exhibitions, see Mitchell (1989: 7 and 13).
5. Among colonisers there existed the belief, which Coles Pasha, the long time inspector general of prisons in Egypt in the late nineteenth and early twentieth century, so aptly expresses in his memoirs, that 'eastern officials do not understand power unless associated with ceremony' (1918: 35).
6. Some of the fear of the savage nature of the colonised peoples was fostered in the popular contexts by exhibits of 'wild savages.' Corbey notes that individuals from particular cultures sometimes were 'more closely associated with living nature than with civilization, [and] were exhibited in local zoos behind bars or wire fences' (1993: 345).
7. In the following I concentrate on only one such example, yet there are many others. David Trotter (1990), for instance, discusses 'Wild West' shows both in the U.S. and in Europe, and the case of South African captives being exhibited at the Greater British Exhibit in 1899. More crude and hideous, Mitra (1996) relates the case of two people from the Andaman and Nicobar Islands who were paid for being on display in the Calcutta Zoo in 1876, in the midst of displayed animals.
8. For an excellent discussion on very different events and exhibitions that included humans, see Corbey (1993).
9. Colonial exhibitions were not the only ones to include the display of humans. Humans of different backgrounds were unfortunately made objects of the spectators' gaze in very different contexts in the nineteenth century. See for example Corbey (1993); Bogdan (1988); Jirousek (2002); Reiss (2001).
10. Mathur notes in this context: The inmates 'could be forced to cooperate, … to perform a repetitive task day after day. Further, as men already marginalized in colonial society, they were unlikely to generate the kind of nationalist public attention that occurred with the earlier troupe of performers for Liberty's' (2001: 507). Liberty's the department store had brought in 'real' artisans a few months prior to this event, and their exhibit ended in a disaster (ibid).
11. Colonial postcards are, of course, another important avenue for spreading sentiments of colonial control and dominance. Malek Alloula (1986) provides an excellent discussion of

the production and dissemination of such cards that depict human models in colonial Algeria. Using socially marginal people (often prostitutes), photographers reproduced their sexual fantasies of exotic, mysterious and docile Eastern women. Mass produced, these cards were the poor man's reassurance of successful colonial discipline and dominance, while simultaneously the cards catered to their buyers and recipients' orientalist fantasies.

12. For a short description of how colonial 'assurance was temporarily interrupted', for example during the Mutiny of 1857 see Pearson (1933: 219). While this is certainly a very early and rather dramatic example, there are many others.

13. Examples of failures to remake colonised lifeworlds are plenty. See, for example, Comaroff (1985) and Comaroff and Comaroff (1992).

14. I am aware that I am privileging a colonial over a feminist reading of the story. I do maintain that the colonial aspects of the story supersede the feminist issues. For an excellent analysis, along similar lines, of the Aziz/Adela encounter and its broader implications see Sharpe (1993: 118).

15. Just how central colonial clubs were, can be inferred from Pearson's note that by the 1880s there was a 'definite "Clubland" in Calcutta' (1933: 225). See also Clark (2000: 422).

16. The Bengal Club is one of the oldest such élite male clubs in India. Away from any subordinates such as women, natives and children, powerful males created an exclusive space for themselves. It is curious to note that the original rules of the club (1827) make no mention of any of these subordinate groups. Their absence is taken for granted. In contrast, rule 8 point 9, explicitly stipulates that dogs cannot be brought to the club (Panckridge 1927: 64).

17. In more detail, Sinha explains: 'It was, then, precisely under the conditions of nineteenth-century British imperialism and colonialism that the private gentleman's club in Britain, a cultural site for the distribution and mediation of élite power, articulated a concept of clubbability that was itself mediated by its imperial location. The model of the concept of clubbability that was entrenched in such self-governing institutions as the clubs was always the "manly independent individual" whose social identity in the nineteenth century, as Catherine Hull has demonstrated, was always defined in relation to the dependent and the subjected – women, children, servants, employees, slaves, and the colonized' (2001: 496–97).

18. The exclusive nature of colonial clubs hints at the multiple divisions in colonial society. There was, of course, the class line as large numbers of the European populations in the colonies were 'poor whites' and as such excluded from clubs (ibid.: 505).

19. In the Calcutta Club which had been established in 1907, a rule stipulated that 'no man whose wife was in purdah was to be permitted access to the [ladies'] annex' (Sinha 2001: 516). Here, it was the incompletely modernised colonial individual who kept his wife in purdah who was seen as a (staring) threat to the vulnerable colonial wife.

20. One author noted in such a context: '... and with the polo, the balls, the races, and the riding, Cairo begins to impress itself upon you as an English town in which any quantity of novel Oriental sights are kept for the aesthetic satisfaction of the inhabitants, much as the proprietor of a country place keeps a game reserve or deer park for his own amusement and that of those who are so fortunate as to share his hospitality' (Fullerton 1891: 6–7). See also Wright (1909: 332 and 338); Kelly (1923: 11); Kaufmann (1926: 106).

21. For the role of the colonial/imperial press in the making/maintenance of élite sociability see also Clark (2000: 427).

22. See Clark (2000: 423) for a short, but very similar list of fashionable entertainment in Calcutta, albeit one hundred years earlier.

23. It is interesting to point out the striking difference between the uniformed workers and the individualised expressions of wealth and fashion.

24. Egyptian Gazette 18.2./22.2./25.2./5.3./13.4./23.4./16.5./19.5./25.5.1908; see also Lamplough (1909: 27). With regard to the variety of available sports' facilities at the Ghezireh Club alone, see the following information provided by Coles Pasha (see also below): 'But what a unique place Ghizireh [*sic*] is: three polo grounds, two race courses, golf course, squash racket courts, and tennis and croquet lawns ad lib. All in a fence ring.' (1918: 158)

25. For a similar scenery at the Continental Hotel, see Sladen (1911: 45). Another odd, to say the least, encounter with colonised helpers was to have Egyptians literally push tourists up the Pyramids, as Sladen noted, 'with one Arab in front to pull, and the other behind to push …' (ibid.: 44–45). In some cases it took three people to manoeuver lazy tourists up the Pyramids: 'A number of Arabs had accompanied Mr. Freeland; one was pushing him from behind, two others in front dragging him up by the arms' (Chennells 1893: 20).

26. Sladen (1911: 49); Nelson includes some photographs of the balcony/terrace (1960: 49–50).

27. See also the description of markets by Sladen (1911: 138).

28. A quick look at the 1913 Baedeker travel guide to Egypt shows just how ubiquitous and available servants were in the Egyptian winter season. Squeezed between information about cars/carriages and postal services, is an entry called 'Lohndiener,' which roughly translates into salaried servants. The notes explains how to get the latter (by way of the hotels) and how much to pay them per day (1913: 8).

29. See e.g. (Farag 1999: 45) for the cosmopolitan nature of the staff at one late colonial élite household.

30. Another exception is a short paragraph in Coles Pasha's reflection about his time in Egypt as the inspector-general of prisons (1918). His narrative is fairly predictable with regard to how the British enlightened Egypt and how he was very successful with his prison reforms. Only once he briefly deviated from his discourse and notes: 'I cannot close this chapter on hospitality without a reference to the Arab domestics who so largely contribute to our comfort in Egypt … But in order to really appreciate Arab domestics I think one must return to England and be dependent on the females who have taken the place of the old-fashioned domestic servant of the past. It is then that one misses Ali and Ibrahim, but I suppose that in time we shall success in spoiling the Arabs as we have spoilt our own English strain of domestic servants' (ibid.: 154). Embedded in ethnocentric and snobbish reasoning, the reader can detect a serious appreciation for the Egyptian domestics servants' valuable work. Nonetheless, such statements are rare.

31. Nina Nelson notes about the 'safragis' (waiters) at the Shepheard's Hotel that they were 'dressed in crimson and gold embroidered jackets and white pantaloons – as if they had stepped out of the pages of Ali Baba' (1960: 3–4). As Mitchell had noted, visitors in such contexts never left orientalist exhibitions/fantasies (1989).

32. The obsession with uniforms to obliterate subjectivities, of course, goes beyond the colonised. Civil servants both at home and in the colonies were subject to minutely designed uniforms that in fine details disclosed their rank. See, for example, *Uniforms to be Worn by Her Majesty's Civil Servants at Home and in the Colonies*, 1866.

33. There is also plenty of the predictably arrogant lure of the simplemindedness of local servants, which served to justify their position of servitude, see for example Nelson (1960: 56).

34. See e.g. 2.5.1908; 20.8.1908.

35. The 'talk of crime' is a complicated issue. It is beyond the scope of this paper to weigh the actual crime rate against concerns about crime, or to establish in how far 'talk of crime' was mere hysteria. Caldeira (2000) provides a very interesting discussion for contemporary Sao Paulo in this context.

36. Issues of control, resistance and rebellion are, or course, very complex. It is beyond the scope of this paper to critically engage with these themes. Whether an act is simply petty crime, an act of resistance or in any other manner a political act/statement needs more detailed analysis (see Scott 1985; 1990).

37. See e.g. EG 24.7.1906; 9.12.1907; 25.5.1908.

38. A contemporary voice noted about the Zoo: 'Here are to be found the wonderful Zoological Gardens, under the competent and enthusiastic direction of Captain Flower. The large grounds are kept in splendid order and teem with bright-hued flowers of every conceivable kind, and lakes, rockeries, rustic bridges, bowers and seats. There is no place in Egypt where one can spend a day more pleasantly and with more entertainment than here. It is a veritable oasis for the jaded Cairo resident in the hot dry summer, and in addition to seeing the large and fine collection of animals of all kinds, representatives of the fauna of Egypt and the Soudan, a visit to the exquisitely laid-out grounds is a pleasure indeed after the oppressive heat of the day in the dusty city. A native military band plays regularly, and teas are provided under the shade of the trees for those who desire them' (Cunningham 1912: 31–32).

39. Once more, this type of reform programme is not unique to the colonial context. Indeed Coles Pasha who was central in the design of the institutions and its program was deeply influenced by similar institutions in Europe. He had even taken a tour of some before realizing his 'own' (1918).

40. To demonstrate subordination, or march in formation in front of superiors has parallels in other contexts. Army or other parades in front of military or political leaders would be other examples.

41. It goes without saying that such performances set up by the powerful for self-assurance and to demonstrate the subordination of the powerless were not limited to the colonial context, but are a recurrent element in contexts of political and social domination. The beginning scene in Ralph Ellison's Invisible Man (1980 [1947]), where African American youths in a southern town are made to fight a crowd boxing match and later are made to battle over electrified coins, is an interesting literary example for this. I am grateful to Erika Solberg for bringing this scene to my attention.

42. See for example a short newspaper note that reports about an incident where village children threw stones at a group of Europeans who refused to give them 'baksheesh.' In the aftermath of the incident the entire village was surrounded by police (EG 6.4.1904).

References

Alloula, M. 1986. *The Colonial Harem*, Minneapolis: University of Minnesota Press.

Asad, T. 1992. 'Conscripts to Western Civilization', in *Dialectical Anthropology: Essays in Honor of Stanley Diamond*, ed C. Gailey, Gainesville: University Press of Florida, pp. 333–51.

Baedeker, K. 1913. *Aegypten und der Sudan*, Leipzig:Verlag von Karl Baedeker.

Bogdan, R. 1988. *Freak Show*, Chicago: University of Chicago Press.

Breckenridge, C.A. 1989. 'The Aesthetics and Politics of Colonial Collecting: India at World Fairs', *Comparative Studies in Society and History*, 31, no. 2: 195–216.

Caldeira, T.P.R. 2000. *City of Walls*, Berkeley: University of California Press.

Chennells, E. 1893. *Recollections of an Egyptian Princess by her English Governess* (2 vols.), Edinburgh and London: William Blackwood and Sons.

Clark, P. 2000. *British Clubs and Societies 1580–1800*, Oxford: Oxford University Press.

Cohn, B. 1983. 'Representing Authority in Victorian India,' in *The Invention of Tradition*, (eds) E. Hobsbawm and T. Ranger, Cambridge: Cambridge University Press, pp. 165–210.

Coles Pasha, C. 1918. *Recollections and Reflections*, London: Saint Catherine Press.

Comaroff, J. 1985. *Body of Power, Spirit of Resistance: The Culture and History of a South African People*, Chicago: University of Chicago Press.

Comaroff, J. and J. 1992. 'Home-Made Hegemony: Modernity, Domesticity, and Colonialism in South Africa' in *African Encounters with Domesticity*, (ed.) K.T. Hansen, New Brunswick NJ: Rutgers University Press.

Comaroff, J. 1997. 'Images of Empire, Contests of Conscience' in *Tensions of Empire*, (eds) F. Cooper and A.L. Stoler, Berkeley: University of California Press, pp. 163–97.

Cooper, F. and A.L. Stoler (eds), 1997. *Tensions of Empire*, Berkeley: University of California Press.

Corbey, R. 1993. 'Ethnographic Showcases, 1870–1930', *Cultural Anthropology*, 8 no. 3: 338–69.

Cunningham, A. 1912. *To-Day in Egypt*, London: Hurst and Blackett Ltd.

Ellison, R. 1980 [1947]. *Invisible Man*, New York: Vintage.

Farag, M. 1999. *The Palace*, Cairo: Max Group.

Forster, E.M. 1992 [1924]. *A Passage to India*, New York: Random House.

Foucault, M. 1979. *Discipline and Punish*, New York: Vintage.

———— 1986 [1967]. 'Of Other Spaces', *Diacritics*, 16 no. 1:22–27.

Fullerton, W.M.M. 1891. *In Cairo*, London: MacMillan and Co.

Hansen, K.T. 1992. *African Encounters with Domesticity*, New Brunswick NJ: Rutgers University Press.

Hobsbawm, E. and T. Ranger (eds) 1983. *The Invention of Tradition*, Cambridge: Cambridge University Press.

Jirousek, L. 2002. 'Spectacle Ethnography and Immigrant Resistance: Sui Sin Far and Anzia Yezierska,' *MELUS* 27 no. 1: 25–52.

Kaufmann, A. 1926. *Ewiges Stromland. Land und Mensch in Aegypten*, Stuttgart: Verlag von Strecker und Schroeder.

Kelly, R.T. 1923. *Egypt*, London: A. and C. Black Ltd.

Kincaid, D. 1973 [1938]. *British Social Life in India, 1608–1937*, London and Boston: Routledge and Kegan Paul.

Kuppinger, P. 1998. 'The Giza Pyramids: Accommodating Tourism, Leisure and Consumption', *City and Society*, Annual Review: 105–19.

———— 2000. 'Giza: Enframed and Lived Spatialities', unpublished Ph.D. Dissertation. New School for Social Research.

Lamplough, A.O. 1909. *Egypt and How to See It*, London: Ballantine and Co. Ltd.

Mathur, S. 2001. 'Living Ethnological Exhibits: The Case of 1886', *Cultural Anthropology*, 15 no. 40: 492–523.

Mitchell, T. 1989. *Colonising Egypt*, Cairo: The American University in Cairo Press.

Mitra, D.K. 1996. 'Ram Bramha Sanyal and the Establishment of the Calcutta Zoological Gardens', in *New Worlds, New Animals*, (eds) R.J. Hoage and W. Deiss, Baltimore: Johns Hopkins University Press, pp. 86–93.

Nelson, N. 1960. *Shepheard's Hotel*, Bath: Chivers.

Owen, R. 1969. 'The Cairo Building Industry and the Building Boom of 1897 to 1907', in *Colloque International sur L'Histoire du Caire*, (ed.) Ministry of Culture of the Arab Republic of Egypt, Cairo, pp. 337–50.

Panckridge, H.R. 1927. *A Short History of the Bengal Club*, Calcutta: H.R. Panckridge..

Pearson, R, 1933. *Eastern Interlude. A Social History of the European Community in Calcutta*, Calcutta: Thacker, Spink.

Powell, E.M. Troutt. 2003. *A Different Shade of Colonialism*, Berkeley: University of California Press.

Raafat, S.W. 1994. *Maadi 1904–1962. Society and History in a Cairo Suburb*, Cairo: The Palm Press.

Ranger, T. 1983. 'The Invention of Tradition in Colonial Africa', in *The Invention of Tradition*, (eds) E. Hobsbawm and T. Ranger, Cambridge: Cambridge University Press, pp. 211–62.

Reiss, B. 2001. *The Showman and the Slave*, Cambridge, Mass: Harvard University Press.

Said, E. 1979. *Orientalism*, New York: Vintage.

Scott, J.C. 1985. *Weapons of the Weak. Everyday Forms of Peasant Resistance*, New Haven: Yale University Press.

———— 1990. *Domination and the Arts of Resistance*, New Haven: Yale University Press.

Sharpe, J. 1993. *Allegories of Empire: The Figure of Woman in the Colonial Text*, Minneapolis: University of Minnesota Press.

Shields, R. 1994. 'Fancy Footwork: Walter Benjamin's Notes on Flanerie', in *The Flaneur*, (ed.) K.Tester, London and New York: Routledge, pp. 61–80.

Sinha, M. 2001. 'Britishness, Clubbability, and the Colonial Pubic Sphere: The Genealogy of an Imperial Institution in Colonial India', *Journal of British Studies*, 4 (October): 489–521.

Sladen, D. 1911. *Oriental Cairo. The City of the 'Arabian Night'*, London: Hurst and Blackett.

Thackeray, L. 1928. *The Light Side of Egypt*, London: A. and C. Black Ltd.

Tolen, R. 1991. 'Colonizing and Transforming the Criminal Tribesman: The Salvation Army in British India', *American Ethnologist*, 18 no. 1: 106–25.

Trotter, D. 1990. 'Colonial Subjects', *The Critical Quarterly*, 32 no. 4: 3–20. *Uniforms to Be Worn by Her Majesty's Civil Servants at Home and in the Colonies*, 1866. London (Harrison, Bookseller to the Queen), (no author).

Wright, A. (ed.) 1909. *Twentieth Century Impressions of Egypt*, London: Lloyds Greater Britain Publishing Company.

Newspapers:
The Egyptian Gazette (EG)

10

BOWING ONTO THE MAT: DISCOURSES OF CHANGE THROUGH MARTIAL ARTS PRACTICE[1]

Tamara Kohn

I currently practice and teach a Japanese martial art called aikido. I also practise and teach anthropology. These practices are often inseparable. For a start, when I sit at my office desk or stand in front of a class full of students, the frequent aching in my body, as well as momentary reflections I have on aikido practice and body movement, permeates my work, informs my thought, and refigures my identity. It does this both in terms of the social world I engage in as well as in a sense of personal growth that I feel and inwardly discuss with myself. The time that society around me would class as 'free time' that cushions the scheduled necessities of work and family – my 'leisure time' – for me this is far from free. I am firmly committed to structured, disciplined work on my body and 'self' at those times. And, I am not alone. Not only are there tens of thousands of martial artists who would claim similar things, but there are millions of sports enthusiasts (players and spectators) of infinite variety, train-spotters, travellers, pet keepers, theatre and opera buffs, star-gazers, body builders, palm readers, fox-hunters, feng-shui enthusiasts etc. who by their behaviours, attitudes and experiences challenge loaded dichotomies such as 'work' and 'leisure'.

In this chapter I attempt to reveal the fuzziness of these categories that are so liberally used to classify human experience. I would like to look at various social constructions of work and leisure alongside associated constructions of time, space and locality. To deal with these themes, I will introduce you to aikido so that you know something about its practice as well as the thoughts and experiences of its practitioners in 'the West'. Since the type of activity I have been studying involves a working of the body, then individual practitioners' expressions of ideas about how the body shapes and is shaped by society will clearly be a valuable resource. I draw my material from my own experience of training in the art as well as from fieldwork conducted in various aikido dojos[2] in the U.K., France, and California. In order to orient the discussion, I will introduce 'the mat' as a space that is both confined to a particular location (e.g. to a 'dojo' in a particular town) as well as being part of a trans-nationally inhabited imaginary space. It is a space where one's body is simultaneously away from its workaday life and engaged in rigorous work.

By examining the disciplined in-body practice of aikido in such a space I intend to join my colleagues in this volume to challenge some popular notions of the meaning of leisure. Turner writes that '"Leisure" … presupposes "work": it is a non-work, even an anti-work phase in the life of a person who also works' (1982: 36). In other words, this formulation prescribes leisure as an antidote to work, and everything associated with work in terms of its discipline, productivity and use for identification in a larger social world is hence thought to be absent from leisure practice. Interestingly, it implies that if you don't 'work', then 'leisure' ceases to exist. Dumazedier defined leisure as 'activity – apart from the obligations of work, family and society – to which the individual turns at will for either relaxation, diversion or broadening his knowledge and his spontaneous social participation, the free exercise of his creative capacity' (1967, cited in Rojek 1989: 1). We will find that aikido practice is sometimes some of these things and sometimes none of them – it is non-work and it is work (although usually unpaid); it is chosen but committed; it is a pleasurable diversion while it is also a painful hardship; it leaves work and family behind while it also brings them onto the training mat; it is 'free time' in which people feel fully committed while often feeling trapped. It is leisure and it is non-leisure.

Sociologists have challenged the 'leisure/work' dichotomy for some time and anthropologists have more recently joined the fray. Some of them have noted that leisure pursuits have work-like elements, just as work time can be punctuated by leisure (e.g. coffee breaks, computer games). The tendency in many of their critiques, however, has been to peer on the surface at etic relationships of activity, structure, economy, and time, with little attention to emic reflections on bodily experience and transformations of identity.

For example, Clarke and Critcher, in *The Devil Makes Work*, show us how leisure has been defined by capitalism as 'time in relation to the processes of production, reproduction and consumption' (1985: 208) and how our use of this supposedly 'free' leisure is shaped by many hidden political and social constraints (ibid.: 205). Chapters in Rojek's edited collection, Leisure for Leisure, reject assumptions that leisure relations are simply about self-determination and freedom by examining leisure policy, economic trends, and bourgeois thought (1989). But telling us how leisure pursuits are constrained by extant social, political and historical structures does not in itself tell us much of anything about what a particular 'leisure pursuit' means to the individuals who pursue it and how it is positioned in their lives. Informing us, as Turner (1982) and many others have, that leisure has been 'sharply demarcated from work … in all societies which have been shaped by the Industrial Revolution' (ibid.: 29) doesn't help us describe and attribute meaning to sentiments and spaces of current practice that surely dull the sharpness of that line. In 1961, Anderson wrote a small book section about 'the discipline of leisure', but his examples came from showing how leisure pursuits such as miniature boat sailing on ponds follows specific rules and shared moralities, that social dancing can be so institutionalised that 'it becomes a painful duty' (1961: 211–12). Discipline thus carries over from work into leisure, but we don't hear about how such disciplined work is experienced in the boating, dancing bodies that must move in and out of a myriad of different social and personal contexts. Adorno persuasively takes issue with the whole notion of 'free' time that appears to trivialise the importance of activities that take place outside the bounds of a recognised profession (e.g. music making, reading etc.) (1991: 188–89). In many of these critiques, extant stringencies of definition that exist around 'work', 'leisure', 'free time' etc. are challenged and the multi-vocality of their dictionary meanings are sometimes analysed (e.g. Turner 1982: 30), but the ways these categories shift and glide in individual experience is not.

In an analysis of voluntary risk taking in 'dangerous sporting' contexts and others, Lyng suggests (following Aronowitz 1973) that 'people find in some leisure pursuits a requirement for the type of skills that have been systematically purged from the labor process under capitalist ownership and experience what they cannot in work – an opportunity for action that is conscious, purposive, concentrated, physically and mentally flexible, and skillful' (1990: 871). Such a sociological assessment of what motivates people's choices (such as a desire for controlling 'the seemingly uncontrollable' (ibid.: 872)) we will find to be applicable to the 'work' of aikido as 'leisure practice' in the West, but it could benefit by ethnographic grounding that reveals often ambiguous understandings of practitioners' experiences and desires.

Aikido

Aikido was founded by Morihei Ueshiba (1883–1969), also known as 'O-Sensei' (Great Teacher) to his students. The art developed out of Ueshiba's spiritual and martial informal and formal training in the early 1900s, integrating judo, sword, spear, and hard jujutsu practice with principles of Shinto and Zen Buddhism. Aikido is generally practiced 'empty hand' (as a body art without weapons), but as its techniques and movements are derived from the art of Japanese swordsmanship, students also practice with wooden swords and spears (*bokken* and *jo*). As a 'modern manifestation of the Japanese martial arts (*budo*)' (K. Ueshiba 1984: 14), aikido is a defensive practice in which one learns to 'blend' with and then neutralize or redirect the energy of an attack to throw or pin the attacker. Aikido has been translated to mean the way (*do*) of harmony (*ai*) of spirit (*ki*). In 1948 an 'Aiki Foundation' was established in Tokyo to promote aikido, the first public demonstration of the art was held in 1956, and around that time foreigners, many of whom learned of aikido through their military experience, began practicing. Some travelled to Japan to train, but the real spread occurred when a number of O Sensei's disciples left Japan to establish aikido abroad. Some of these included Yoshimitsu Yamada Sensei, Akira Tohei Sensei, T.K. Chiba Sensei, Mitsunari Kanai Sensei, Seiichi Sugano Sensei, Yutaka Kurita Sensei (all settled in North America) and Nobuyoshi Tamura Sensei (in France). From their work and future generations of teachers from Japan and elsewhere in the world, there are now thousands of aikido dojos around the globe. Much of my material comes from several months training with and working with Chiba Sensei and his students in San Diego California as well as at camps in England and France. I have also, however, trained with other masters and their students and it is clear that there are distinct variations in style and emphasis that guide practice in these different 'schools' or 'organisations'. I will return to look at how some of these differences are perceived by practitioners in a later section.

When practised today in dojos in Japan, Australia, Europe, or in the sunny beach towns of California, there are many who would consume the whole cultural package and suggest that the spiritual practice of the founder is so intrinsic to the practice itself that one cannot begin to understand the creative power of aikido without at least a firm awareness of those cultural and spiritual roots. 'It's like tending a tree's branches after cutting off its roots', one teacher commented. And yet many other teachers (in Japan and elsewhere) have contributed to the secularisation of the art and their students often remain fairly unaware of the deep spiritual foundation of the practice. Some focus their attention on how the techniques embody an exceptionally powerful and skillful method of self-defense. Take the following U.K. aikido club website introduction as an example: "We emphasise the practical aspects of Aikido ... Our Sensei (instructor) believes very strongly that Aikido should enable you to defend yourself in real-life situations" (www.dur.ac.uk/aikido.club/what_is_aikido.php).

The 'Japaneseness' of the art can be more or less important to practitioners as well (see Kohn 2001). The art has grown out of a rich and involved development in the Arts of War in Japan, and traditions of dress, etiquette and style of transmission continue to be impressed to different degree by the art's cultural background, particularly while Japanese *shihan* (masters) are still at the helm of the art's organisational structures. Americans and Europeans, for example, may initially be drawn to Japanese arts because of the enchantment and allure of the 'oriental', the power and the mystique of various Asian in-body disciplines and fighting arts (encouraged by a popular culture full of Teenage Mutant Ninja Turtles and Bruce Lee wannabes) (Donohue 1994). They may as likely be drawn to aikido practice by accident or as a suggested means of physical training or even therapy, unconcerned and sometimes even unimpressed by the culturally grounded ritual and etiquette that occurs within the space of the dojo. Others will observe the rituals of training without any reference to the cultural roots of the practice but with a clear sense of respect and commitment. It is significant here to note that by observing a Japanese art's globalised practice outside Japan, the 'creative ambiguity of self and place' (Chapman 2005) one may observe extends dramatically beyond the possibilities available in a Japanese *dojo* where the focus is most firmly on the local and national. Here, the main focus has to be on the practice itself as experienced by all, and the common denominator amongst aikidoists who have trained for any length of time is how they come to understand their practice in terms of a number of key principles of movement that are very commonly related to analogous reactions and events in their everyday social worlds. It is this capacity to intertwine growing awareness of movement in the physical activity with strategies and understandings in social interactions with others that gives it centrality in the minds of those who practice – that ensures it is not internally classified as a peripheral leisure pursuit.

Aikido practice is centred on learning a series of forms/movements (*kata*) in which the student must participate as the executor of the technique (*tori*) and the receiver (*uke*) in paired exercises. Circular or spiralling movements are key in the understanding of how to absorb and redirect the energy of an attack to execute aikido techniques. There are many different styles of aikido practice, both 'soft' and 'hard'. 'Hard' styles are generally more dynamic and 'martial' in their application, but all styles are based on the same principles. A sense of familiarity or foreignness/difference is triggered by sensations and qualities of contact and movement between uke and tori – at a large course one might expect a 'stranger' to embody the art in an entirely different way if he/she has come from another teacher and style of training.

Despite many variations in style and form, these basic principles are clarified and taken into the body only through repetitive and reflexive practice on 'the mat' over many years, but they are also simultaneously understood through a consciousness of their general applicability in the process of living from day to day. I will illustrate some of these applications of aikido practice principles off the mat, but first wish to describe what happens around and upon the mat.

Mat 'Work', Mat Ritual

Most dojos I have visited in California and France have been permanent (rented) spaces with a 'fixed' mat (*tatami*) area and beautifully fitted '*kamiza*' area (a focal shrine in the dojo involving a raised platform or table decorated with a picture of the founder and other items like calligraphy, weapons, floral arrangements, that are all treated with respect). By contrast, in the U.K. most *dojos* are rather drab rooms in sports facilities where, for each practice, mats are laid on the floor in a large square or rectangle, and a picture of O Sensei is placed at the front of the room as a makeshift '*kamiza*'. There are very clear rules of etiquette for how one should behave on the mat, regardless of its permanence, that are taught by example. These, on the surface, have remained largely intact from the art's Japanese etiquette-rich cultural roots, despite the variable extent to which the international community of practitioners understands the Japanese historical associations attributed to the traditions. It usually falls to the higher ranked members of the dojo (*sempai*) to ensure that rules of etiquette are understood and followed by all members. One's feet should be clean, and *zori* (flipflop sandals) should be left neatly outside the edge of the mat. Notions of purity and pollution, hierarchy, 'tradition', as well as the important concepts of inside and outside (*uchi* and *soto*) in Japanese discourse and thought, may be usefully summoned to understand such patterns of behaviour in relation to Japanese culture and locality. For instance, Hendry's descriptions of the place of shoes in the Japanese home (1987) introduce these analytical concepts very effectively. It becomes challenging, however, to apply such analyses to an aikidoist from the north of England preparing to enter a training mat in France or Wales who has never spoken to anyone Japanese before. To study the cultural roots of any behavioural tradition is not always appropriate when one is attentive to the experiences and meanings of a body practice in the global ecumene. One needs to begin with a much larger playing field of meanings and associations, even if they often might take you right back to a real or imagined Japan.

Hans, a German working in the North East of England, kept arriving at our local dojo in army boots with no socks on. He would slip them off before bowing and entering the mat, as feet are always bare in aikido training. This action was not even remotely stimulated with reference to Japanese tradition, but from a combination of mimicry and common sense. His feet, however, stank terribly. The horrific foot odour became a topic of worry and humour and disgust, and dojo members would gossip after class about the nauseous sensation of training with or near him and having their heads pinned within inches of his toes. The dojo chief instructor was urged to broach the subject with Hans as sensitively as possible in the changing room one day. He did this, gently suggesting remedies such as regular washing, foot powders, and the use of socks. The rationale offered for raising the problem was the communal local discomfort and a generalised notion of appropriate personal hygiene during contact activity. The smell didn't change, but gradually people avoided training with Hans and eventually he disappeared with his smelly feet. His Germanness, and aikido's Japaneseness were beside the point. Ideas of conformity and appropriate behaviour may be situationally specific long before they acquire cultural associations in local consciousness. Months later, the memory of Hans and his feet was evoked, and someone said, 'I've met several smelly Germans in my day, but he took the cake!' Another added, 'Can you imagine what a Japanese teacher would have made of his disgusting feet on the mat?!' Here, cultural specificity becomes reflexively layered on top of the post-cultural order and meanings attributed to the events at the time when Hans was present.

If we return now to a general recounting of the behaviours expected on an aikido mat, after removing one's footwear, one should kneel and 'bow on' to the mat, well before the class begins. After some quiet stretching, the teacher arrives, someone claps and everyone swiftly 'lines up' kneeling in neat rows, with the most senior ranked students and teachers on the right side of the mat, facing the front. The teacher, or '*Sensei*' walks from the edge to centre in front of the *kamiza*. She or he kneels facing the students, and then turns around to face the *kamiza*. All bow to the picture of O Sensei as a sign of respect to the founder of the art. Sensei then turns and bows to students who simultaneously bow back, and both say *onegaishimasu* ('please teach me'). The teacher leads the class in a gentle stretching warm-up that involves a number of exercises designed to complement the training. Then the teacher will clap and demonstrate a technique a few times on a partner he or she selects from the group. Others will sit in a circle around the demonstration and watch. Then they pair off and practice until the instructor demonstrates again.

There is technically no talking on the mat – communication is primarily through the body (see Kohn 2001) – however, different teachers create different atmospheres, and while the class taught by some masters (particularly Japanese instructors) may be silent, other teachers augment their demonstration with words about how to move. O Sensei was often said to be in trance once he was on the mat. When a senior teacher (*Shihan*) such as Chiba Sensei teaches, people speak of how the mat is 'injected with energy', how the 'atmosphere changes'. The people at large courses come from all over the world – from the U.K., France, Germany, Switzerland, U.S., Japan, Eastern Europe, Greece, Kazakhstan, etc. – and you get to know the majority by name and become very familiar over many years of shared body practice with each other's movements and level of training. I call the space of such a mat 'transnational', a term that was once just used to describe the social worlds of ethnically identified migrants, but can now (following Jackson et al. 2004) realistically accommodate a much larger range of experience. People voluntarily participate in transnational space 'irrespective of their own migrant histories or "ethnic" identities'. (ibid.: 2).

At the end of the class the students again line up in rank, the teacher and students bow to the *kamiza*, and then to each other saying '*domo arigato gozaimasu*' ('thank you very much for training with me'), the teacher will leave the mat, bowing a final time before stepping off it, and the students bow to the dojo and then to each other, repeating their thanks to those they trained with. When it's the last class of the day, senior students carefully fold their *hakama* – the long divided skirts traditionally worn by Samurai.

One could quite happily call such rituals 'rites of practice', playing, of course, on Van Gennep's famous cross-cultural study of ritual process entitled 'rites of passage' (1960). The rituals on the aikido mat all mark time, space, attitude, and behaviour. These, as we see in the next section, pull together a range of communities within and without the ritually-bound context of the mat.

Off the Mat and in the Pub

Dojos are small activity-generated communities (with shared identities based on shared activity and practice rather than idealised shared markers of blood, land, ethnicity, nationality, etc.), and they tend to have a solid core of long term members as well as some newcomers who may or may not continue training in the *dojo* for long. Large courses bring together people from *dojos* around the world, and after a number of years these teachers and students come to feel part of a larger aikido community, joined at the helm by their organisation's head and a master of the art. At these events the 'locals' are not the people who live in that geographical region, but they are the known members of the hosting aikido community who can come from anywhere in the world. The incomers are those who visit from other organisations and train in a different style. Locals are felt to be local by the way they interact and move on the mat. So they can come from far away. People who live around the corner can be strangers. Locality becomes deterritorialised and resituated in the body.

Those incoming bodies move differently and come from different aikido traditions trained through different masters who in turn have absorbed different elements of the art they have directly and indirectly inherited from the founder and developed in diverse ways. Some of them are aware of themselves as respectful visitors who make every effort to follow what they see and feel on the host's mat and put their own habits aside while they are there. If they do this well, their 'foreignness' is not always readily observable, but it is generally something a more advanced 'local' can feel. Some visitors are simply not cognizant and believe their bodies to be doing what is demonstrated when in fact they unselfconsciously slip into moving in the same way they do back on their 'home' mat. This can be easily witnessed in their movements and felt in their responses, and is often discussed by 'locals' reflecting on their experiences of practice at a given class. Julian[3] (*sandan* and *fukushidoin*[4]) distinguishes these two types in the following discussion we had one day after class at a summercamp:

> Did you practice with those two *yudansha* [black belts] over there? I wonder who they train with – do you know them? The tall one isn't so bad, actually – he was really trying hard, I think, although his *ukemi* is weird – reminds me of Tamura's students … but the other one's a stiff bugger to handle and kept trying to correct *my* technique! I don't think he even saw what sensei was doing. I find that so annoying!

The last comment is interesting in that while there is a basic principle of ranking in which a junior student always follows the lead of a senior, there is also a sense of rank inherent in the notions of home and away – a highly graded 'visitor' or incomer forfeits his right to exercise his seniority if he is away from his 'home' in the embodied sense described above. Julian felt aggrieved because the visitor he trained with was pulling rank that wasn't earned in the 'local' style of training.

Ironically, the master who was teaching that class and was Julian's sensei had written the following missive about the attitude that one should have about other organisations in the notes accompanying the *fukushidoin* declaration that Julian will have signed as a junior instructor:

> It should be remembered that whatever kinds of organizations exist, the distinction between them is not one of substance, but lies only in the degree of their understanding of Aikido. The Truth can be expressed through various channels and in

different degrees, corresponding to different human characteristics and personal circumstances.

Therefore one ought not criticize people in other organizations. Whether we are right or wrong cannot be proved by criticizing others, and whether others are right or wrong cannot be judged and assessed by our standards …

Here is a clear idea of cultural relativity that should be applied in one's contact with various forms of aikido practice. And yet this ideal missive also acknowledges that: 'Despite the fact that the nature of organizations is material and relative, it is human hearts that control them.' Hence, the reality of practice and the investment of time and energy people give to training in a particular style with particular *senseis* means that such human hearts do judge others. For our purposes, what is significant is how that embodied notion of 'self' (in community, in 'organization') and 'other' is, in the context of on-the-mat training, detached from locale – deterritorialised – located in movement and somatic experience.

Off the mat and in the pub, the first question that tends to be asked is: Where and with whom do you train? People become placed in histories and genealogies of aikido that are likewise separate from locale, even though the pub space itself isn't. One hardly ever overhears discussions in the pubs during summer camp about what people do for a living. One tends to learn about people's various occupations through the gossip of others or through the direct reportage of aikido's relevance to individuals' jobs.

Back in the home *dojo* this blending of diversity is remarked upon frequently in comments about the character of the aikido social world, because it often contrasts with people's social experience in other social realms. If one doesn't share much information about career and family at national courses, one does in one's home *dojo* over years of shared pints. The *dojo* becomes a labour resource (like other voluntary organisations) a small organic society – you go to someone in your dojo before you call the yellow pages, and services are shared and supported. In my years in the Durham *dojo* we had a hairdresser, electrician, carpenter, painter, computer systems manager, taxi driver, pediatrician, prison guard, special needs teacher, and a number of students and anthropologists (who needless to say tended to be the least 'useful'!).

Aikidoists often comment on the way they can travel the world and almost always find, through the aikido network, a bed for the night and place to train. They can feel at home anywhere in the world where they find others who hold the same principles in their trained bodies (shared even when the styles and ideas about 'proper' technique or *ukemi* may differ significantly). This experience serves as a useful example to support Appadurai's notion that 'locality is relational and contextual rather than … spatial' (1996: 178). Appadurai asks 'what is the nature of locality as a lived experience in a global deterritorialized world?' He suggests that the answer lies in the role of the imagination in social life (ibid.: 52). This point will become clear from the examples that follow.

Taking Things Away from the Mat

Once 'off the mat' and back home from the local *dojo* and the pub, the 'work' (in the applied and productive sense of the word, unlike 'activity') of aikido is not finished. The principles of movement practiced on the ritual space of the mat are reflected upon, refined 'in theory', and then metaphorically and sometimes physically applied to many other aspects of an individual's life.

These understandings of aikido principles are shared and passed on to others in social interaction. They are also frequently expressed in essays submitted for dan grade (black belt) tests and in contributions to aikido and other martial arts publications. In a bar near the *dojo* in Encinitas (a beach town north of San Diego), Marcus told me how he often applies aikido principles on his verbally abusive boss by 'meeting at the point of attack' … entering and then blending with his aggressive energy and redirecting it to his weak point with a calm and centred response. The way that Marcus controls this difficult social interaction is by consciously framing the movement of exchanged words in a language of aikido bodily movement and control.

In an article for Sancho, the aikido journal of the United States Aikido Federation's Western region (produced in San Diego), an aikidoist wrote an article called, '*Ukemi* in Relationships'. It begins by saying that there are several 'principles that are critical to ongoing growth and understanding of both Aikido and interpersonal relationships' (La Cerva 1994: 12). The first is 'commitment' (cf. Kohn 2001) to go to practise (to enter the 'mat') 'regardless how we "feel"'. La Cerva suggests there are no rules that enforce this – in aikido 'discipline is not a set of have to's, oughts or shoulds imposed from outside'.[5] Rather it is a commitment to develop 'inner strength, which one can draw upon in times of difficulty' (La Cerva 1994: 12). This commitment brings the student onto the 'mat'. Once there he must also show 'commitment' to every attack (giving *nage* enough energy to work with). But then he goes off the mat to express and act upon a perceived and related 'commitment' to treating family and strangers 'with respect and compassion'. La Cerva writes: 'Similar to the strike in Aikido … we must summon all our energies to be present to what is happening … to deal with … conflicts …' (ibid.: 13).

These embodied revelations connecting activities and sentiments on and off the mat are expressed by people from many occupational and cultural backgrounds (not just Veblen's 'leisure classes', nor 'psychobabbling' Californians). Aikidoists call the off mat consciousness of principles 'the big aikido' (vs the 'small aikido' which takes place on the mat alone) (see Kohn 2003: 151). In such reflection, the 'small aikido' on the mat is metonymic of the world at large. Aikido big and small, alongside other martial ways, is considered to be a life practice that is perpetually enacted, applied, remembered and developed in all moments in the serious practitioners' life.

This type of connection is abstractly, but nonetheless usefully described by the psychologist, Eugene Gendlin. In *Experiencing and the Creation of Meaning*, he purports that any action can be seen and then described with symbols (including language), but any such description lacks the 'feel' of the action (1962). These 'felt' meanings exist in the body even before they can be externally observed (ibid.: 68–9). If we apply this to aikido, the mat becomes a place where this sort of meaning is generated and felt through bodily practice. Gendlin goes on to suggest that metaphorical experience joins together old and new, using 'old' felt meanings and applying them to a new area of experience, hence generating new meaning (ibid.: 113). So we see how the pub, the home, the office and many other places off the mat may become locations where this sort of new meaning is generated. The memory of the felt experience appears to be consciously as well as subconsciously re-enlivened on the street, at work, in the train. I have stretched my wrists while deep in some non-aikido-related thought in front of my computer screen, and stories of wrist stretches in strange places abound amongst aikidoists (particularly relatively new practitioners who seem to be constantly amazed at the way their practice 'never seems to end'). I once approached a stranger on a train who was obviously deep in thought and who was making *kokyu* extension movements with his hands. Sure enough, he was an aikidoist on his way to work. Here is a habitus of a different colour – a body encoded with aikido 'culture' that tells us less about class and social-structural prerequisite, and more about how the meaning of aikido principles evolve and transform everyday consciousness.

So having found these various locations where new meaning is generated – through body, through memory, through metaphor – I would suggest that the aikidoist may then return to the mat with a new vigour because she has understood how entwined her practice has become in every facet of her life. If leisure is about experience, then we see how the vision of leisure as being spatially and temporally bounded is not very useful. The experience expands itself through metaphor – 'leisure' becomes freed into other spaces and times (including 'work' and 'family') through experience-generated meaning.

This framing of leisure is not just a postmodern abstract orientation that does away with the order and clocked precision of modernism. Nor is it just a convenient way to describe the hodgepodge of heady experiences that some tripping Californians string together in their never-ending self-analysis – in the New Age consumptive aestheticisation of their everyday lives. Instead, it suggests a central reframing and production of the self through body and experience that happens in many different contexts and permeates many different types of lived space. The problem in this chapter is not to prove how, when and why this happens but rather to show how it challenges the Cartesian dualism or binarism inherent in our linguistic framing of leisure time.

Bringing Things Back to the Mat

So we have seen how principles developed on the mat become exported into other realms and spaces and times. We can look further at how the outside world may permeate the space of the mat in aikidoists' reflections about their practice. These are nicely illustrated by comments shared during a focus group discussion held in the San Diego Aikikai *dojo* with the '*kenshusei*' (the students who come from all over the world to enroll in a special intensive teacher training programme with Chiba Sensei that can last for years). Two senior students kicked off the discussion around how they first got involved in aikido training.

> I think Aikido shows so much of yourself, you know ... you're almost seeing yourself practising, you are seeing whether you are being superficial or being connected. And when you are having troubles in your life, I really feel that you confront them on the mat, and they become very evident. They almost like smack you right in the face, you can't run away from them and maybe that's what kinda drew me subconsciously in the beginning, was this purity, this honesty that you really gain from the training ... (Alfonzo – a male computer programmer)
>
> I was working with violent kids where I was dealing with life threatening situations every day and I wanted to find a better way to handle that and handle myself ... And I got hooked on the physical part of aikido right away and the first year I thought, this is fantastic and I just loved it, and when I came here I realised it was much more of a serious study. The fun went away – not completely but ... But it was good, it was like progressing ... like love. You fall in love and the first few years you think wow this is wonderful, and then you realise that you need to make a commitment and it's different. (Brenda – a female social worker)

So Brenda's work with violent kids, or Alfonzo's life troubles are carried within them and then confronted on the mat. They are not finding an escape from life on the mat, but rather finding a progression in the self that allows for a new framing of that life – a new way to 'handle' it all. The mat becomes a place of confrontation – physical and mental and metaphorical. The mat becomes a place of work, not play. It is like love that starts with 'fun' and moves to 'hard' 'commitment'. In these words we see how such training, while initially 'chosen' by free will to fill free time, becomes committed and laborious ... and sometimes quite painful.

Most *kenshusei* work at least part time to support their training (for which they pay an annual fee that helps keep the *dojo* running). Most are at a crossroad in their lives and are looking to eventually leave the programme to start their own '*dojos*'. Most dream of being able to make aikido their vocation, but realise that few can afford to do this as a full time job (in the U.K. there are only a handful who would call themselves 'professional' aikido teachers, while in the U.S. there are a fair number). They all train under Chiba Sensei who is a 'professional' – a 'master'. His practice and teaching is his lifework, or as Mark says, 'he is on a one-way path' (thus totally eclipsing the work/leisure opposition!). In emulating, respecting, and, in a bodily way, mimicking his work, his students 'work' alongside him on the mat. They also attempt to tread a 'path' (the '*do*' in 'aikido') rather than pop on and off it in their training.

Part of their training is to work inside the dojo and around it – keeping it clean and tidy and well maintained – washing the mat, cleaning the windows, sweeping the leaves outside. The world outside of this busy workspace is simultaneously present and absent. We have just heard Alfonzo and Brenda tell us that their lives are confronted on the mat, and that new stressors (presumably imposed by Sensei's intensity) are present there. In one class I told a student to relax her shoulders, arms and face during her *bokken* (wooden sword) cuts in *suburi* or 'cutting' practice, and she replied, 'but you don't know who I'm cutting!' Sometimes it is not just through power of imagination that the outside world comes in. In a special issue of *Sancho* magazine dedicated to 'Aikido and Family – exploring how different people try to balance their commitment to both – there is a picture of a senior instructor training with a student using one arm while holding his baby with the other.

However, many students have expressed how they love aikido practice because they can leave home and work and any associated problems off the mat because the concentration required for practice leaves no space in their minds for anything else. Whatever they make their livings from feels so far away from the space and intention on the mat that it disappears. Ultimately, for all these people – for those who bring things on the mat as well as for those who think they leave everything behind, the seriousness of mat 'work' becomes the glue that holds the society of practitioners together. 'YOU DON'T TAKE THIS SERIOUSLY ENOUGH!' barked Sensei during a *kenshusei* class with weapons. 'Each moment is LIFE / DEATH and you must show this in your training!'. Familiarity with this 'one cut, one life' philosophy in popular literature on Samurai culture may make an observer chuckle at such a comment, but facing the power and sense of potential danger in advanced practice with Chiba Sensei on the mat makes it very real indeed!

In fact, sometimes the intensity of practice on the mat is likened to the war front. In San Diego, Lucy said: 'Sometimes I'll spend a lot of time in the *dojo* … training really intensely and … sometimes you feel like you're at war. And then I go home and there's Peter, like trying to cuddle or something, and it's almost like I've come off the front – it's really, really hard to just go home and relate …', to which Kevin added, 'That's why we like to socialize after we practice – go to the pub and have a chat, and then go home … Transition.' In other words, some relaxation, unwinding, 'free time', is required to ease the movement from one serious commitment to another, and if there is no 'time' for this, then some social or personal conflict can arise. Last year, when Jim, a senior student in the British Aikikai (BA), didn't appear at the annual BA summer camp and was missed, his dojo-mates said that he felt he needed a holiday from his aikido. They explained that his 'free' time from work was very limited and for years he used that time for attending aikido seminars, but that he and his girlfriend needed a break from that

– in other words, he needed a holiday from the hard work of his primary leisure interest.

Urry, in his critique of Veblen's famous discussion of leisure as a privilege of the higher 'leisure class', suggests that everyone in Western society today 'has at least some rights to leisure' (1995: 130). However, the amount of 'days off' that one can take will vary tremendously, and attitudes around taking that time can vary immensely too, within and also between societies. In an interview with Chiba Sensei about the differences he has observed in his students who come from different countries, he volunteered some thoughts on 'time'. He said, 'Americans have lots of time if they want to have time … and still keep going on. Elsewhere, I know, it's very difficult to have time on your own … In Europe you steal time. In Japan it's the extreme other case (from America) … If you use time … you're treated like a criminal. Everybody's watching you.' I asked, 'But if you use it for martial practice, isn't that OK?', to which he answered, 'Yes, that's more creative … Any discipline that affects individual groups … we shut our eyes'. So from this we learn of Sensei's perceptions about national difference in the value of leisure time. His take on Japanese notions of time and training supports Cox's discussion of the modern conflation of leisure and play in Japan, as well as a lack of distinction between creativity and order, that allows the most serious ritual pursuits to be viewed as constructive use of 'play' time (2002: 169–170). But we can also see in Chiba Sensei's words how the trans-national space of the mat is occupied during time that is made available for training against very different values of how such non-occupationally occupied time may be spent.

We have seen how the mat is demarcated as ritual space in ritual time that is far from free. You pay with commitment, sweat and cash, and you work until your body aches and your mind is bursting, you share a sense of communitas with other *aikidoka* – in your *dojo* and beyond, you avoid being late to the mat and would not contemplate leaving early. You do all this because of your commitment to others, your understanding of your practice in terms of your own personal development, and also because of the ritual formalities that envelop the space and time of your bodily practice. The mat is both real and fluid/conceptual/imagined; both local and trans-national or global. The body that is worked there generates meaning through physical practice and intersubjective experience that in turn generates new meaning through reflection.

Several theorists draw attention to the 'consumption' of leisure. Urry, for instance, usefully discusses not only how 'places' may be consumed, but how time (through leisure) may too. As he writes: '"I need a holiday" is a particularly clear reflection of such a modern view of the need to consume time away from work' (1995: 130). But the example I gave about the aikidoist who needed a holiday from his aikido training in his leisure time surely complicates the picture. Appadurai has alerted us to the intrinsic complexity of leisure-oriented 'translocalities' (1995) where local subjectivity is commoditised for a circulating leisure class, but here we have an example that witnesses the consumption of a foreign/other practice against the production of a growing new sense of self in a non-local ritual space that, like a church or Mosque, is home to all who know how to treat it properly. The ritual space of the mat peripheralises allegiance to locality and searches out far more sensual, embodied, transnational, and post-local senses of self /community and other.

To conclude, contemporary leisure may be as much a site of production as it is of consumption. It is a place where selves as well as social relations are discovered and reformulated as illustrated in my small aikido example through individual voices and with reference to activities and principles of movement practiced and imagined, on the mat and off. The mat itself is a real space and an imagined one. It is a global village that situates a transnational community of practitioners. Work and leisure take place on the mat and off it. Work and leisure are hence not about fixed times and places, but about attitudes – about frames of mind (cf. Rapport, this volume).

Notes

1. I would like to thank Simon Coleman and the late Allan Kaprow for their helpful comments on this chapter. I am also grateful to The British Academy for a travel grant to support my attendance at the 2001 American Anthropological Association meetings where a portion of this paper was first presented and where the idea for this volume was born.

2. Note that the term '*dojo*' (literally translated from Japanese as 'place' (*jo*) for practicing 'the Way' (*do*)) is related to the Sanskrit word *bodhimanda*, a place where Buddha achieves enlightenment (Davis 1980: 1). In contemporary usage in Japan and abroad, '*dojo*' refers to a place for various forms of disciplined training of the body, mind and spirit, including Zen meditation and martial arts practice.

3. Note that many personal names have been changed to preserve anonymity.

4. *Sandan* is the Japanese term for third *dan* (third degree black belt), and *fukushidoin* is a teaching qualification recognised by the Aikido World Headquarters.

5. For further critical discussion on 'discipline', see Kohn's chapter 'Creatively Sculpting the Self through the Discipline of Martial Arts Training' in Dyck (forthcoming).

References

Adorno, T. 1991. *The Culture Industry*. London: Routledge.

Anderson, N. 1961. *Work and Leisure*. London: Routledge and Kegan Paul.

Appadurai, A. 1995. 'The Production of Locality', in R. Farden (ed.) *Counterworks*, London: Routledge.

Appadurai, A. 1996. *Modernity at Large: Cultural Dimensions of Globalization*, Minneapolois and London: University of Minnesota Press.

Aronowitz, S. 1973 *False Promises: The Shaping of American Working Class Consciousness*, New York: McGraw-Hill.

Chapman, K. 2005. *Inside the Dojo: Participation and Performance in the Japanese Martial Arts*, Unpublished Ph.D. Thesis, London: SOAS.

Clarke, J. and C. Critcher 1985. *The Devil Makes Work: Leisure in Capitalist Britain*, London: Macmillan Press.

Cox, R. 2002. 'Is there a Japanese Way of Playing?', in Hendry, J. and M. Raveri (eds), *Japan at Play: The Ludic and the Logic of Power*, London: Routledge.

Davis, W. 1980. *Dojo: Magic and Exorcism in Modern Japan*, Stanford, California: Stanford University Press.

Donohue, J.J. 1994. *Warrior Dreams: the Martial Arts and the American Imagination*, Westport, CT: Bergin and Garvey.

Dyck, N. (ed.) (forthcoming) *Exploring Regimes of Discipline: Ethnographic and Analytic Inquiries*, Oxford: Berghahn.

Gendlin, E. 1997 (1962). *Experiencing and the Creation of Meaning: A Philosophical and Psychological Approach to the Subjective*, Evanston, Illinois: Northwestern University Press.

Hendry, J. 1987 (1995). *Understanding Japanese Society (2nd edition)*, London: Routledge.

Kohn, T. 2001. 'Don't Talk – Blend: Ideas about Body and Communication in Aikido Practice', in J. Hendry and C.W. Watson (eds.), *An Anthropology of Indirect Communication*, London: Routledge.

———— 2003 'The Aikido Body: Expressions of Group Identities and Self-Discovery in Martial Arts Training', in N. Dyck and E.P. Archetti (eds) *Sport, Dance and Embodied Identities*, Oxford: Berg Press.

La Cerva, V. 1994 'Ukemi in Relationships', *Sancho: Aikido Newsletter of the San Diego Aikikai*, San Diego, California, pp. 12–16.

Lyng, S. 1990 'Edgework: A Social Psychological Analysis of Voluntary Risk Taking', *The American Journal of Sociology*, Vol 95(4): 851–86.

Rapport, N. 2003. *I am Dynamite: An Alternative Anthropology of Power*, London: Routledge.

Rojek, C. (ed.) 1989 *Leisure for Leisure*, London: Macmillan Press.

Turner, V. 1982. *From Ritual to Theatre: The Human Seriousness of Play*, NYC: Performing Arts Journal Publications.

Ueshiba, K. 1984. *The Spirit of Aikido* [trans. Taitetsu Unno], Tokyo: Kodansha International.

Urry, J. 1995 *Consuming Places*, London: Routledge.

Van Gennep, A.1960. *The Rites of Passage*, Chicago: The University of Chicago Press.

NOTES ON CONTRIBUTORS

Thomas Carter is an anthropologist and Senior Lecturer at the Chelsea School of Sport, University of Brighton. He has written about a variety of issues surrounding the politics of sport and leisure based on his ethnographic fieldwork in Havana and Belfast. Recent work includes an edited section of *City & Society* entitled 'The Sport of Cities: Spectacle and the Economy of Appearances', 18(2), 2007; and his ethnography on Cuban baseball, *The Quality of Homeruns* (Duke University Press, 2008).

Simon Coleman is Professor of Anthropology at the University of Sussex. Previously he was Reader in Anthropology and Deputy Dean of Social Sciences and Health at the University of Durham. Publications include *The Globalisation of Charismatic Christianity: Spreading the Gospel of Prosperity* (2000, CUP), *Tourism: Between Place and Performance* (ed. with M. Crang, Berghahn, 2002) and *Pilgrim Voices: Narrative and Authorship in Christian Pilgrimage* (ed. with J. Elsner, Berghahn, 2003).

Noel Dyck is Professor of Social Anthropology at Simon Fraser University in Canada. The author of several works on relations between Aboriginal peoples and governments, he has also written about community sports for children and youth. His recent research has focused upon immigration, integration and sport in Canada as well on programs of youth mobility.

Maurice Kane has worked as an adventure guide and outdoor educator in New Zealand, Nepal, India and North America. He is presently completing a PhD with the Tourism Department at the University of Otago, New Zealand. His research interests are focused on the concept of adventure, the understandings of adventure in social space and its personal practice.

Tamara Kohn is Senior Lecturer in Anthropology at the University of Melbourne. Previously she was Lecturer in Anthropology and Human Sciences at the University of Durham. Her research interests and publications range from the studies of identity, body, ethnicity, gender, and kinship in small scale rural communities (e.g. in the Scottish Hebrides and the hills of East Nepal) to the study of transnational communities of practice (e.g. in leisure and arts, tourism, caring practice).

Petra Kuppinger is an Associate Professor of Anthropology at Monmouth College in monmouth Illinois. She works on the Middle East, Egypt and Cairo. Topical interests include cities, space and power, colonialism, globalization, and the emergence of a new Muslim consumerism. Her recent publications include 'Pyramids and Alleys: Global Dynamics and Local Strategies in Giza' in *Cairo Cosmopolitan: Urban Structure, Spaces and Identities in the New Middle East*, D. Singerman and P. Amar (eds), 2006, and 'Globalization and Exterritoriality in metropolitan Cairo' *The Geographical Review* 95(3), 2006. She is currently conducting ethnographic research on 'Space, Culture and Islam in Stuttgart, Germany.

Garry Marvin is Reader in Social Anthropology at Roehampton University, U.K. He has a particular interest in human/animal relationships – early research projects included ethnographic studies of the Spanish bullfight, cockfighting and zoos. His interest in foxhunting is now being developed into a wider research project on big game hunting. Associated with this is a study of animal trophies and taxidermy.

Nigel Rapport holds a Canada Research Chair in Globalization, Citizenship and Justice at Concordia University of Montreal where he is founding Director of the Centre for Cosmopolitan Studies; he also has positions at the Norwegian University of Science and Technology, Trondheim, and at the University of St. Andrews. His most recent books are *I Am Dynamite: An Alternative Anthropology of Power* (2003, Routledge) – a study of the 'existential power' to pursue life-projects – and the edited collection *Science, Democracy and The Open Society: A European Legacy?* (2005, Lit Verlag). He is working on the monograph *Hospital Porter: An Ethnographic Study of Hierarchy and Transcendence*.

Hazel Tucker is Senior Lecturer in Tourism at the University of Otago, New Zealand. She received her Ph.D. from the University of Durham in Social Anthropology in 1999. Her major research interests include tourism representation and experience, host-guest relationships and social change. As well as publishing in tourism journals, she is author of *Living With Tourism: Negotiating Identity in a Turkish Village* (Routledge 2003) and co-editor of *Tourism and Postcolonialism* (Routledge 2004).

Jacqueline Waldren, BS (UCLA), MA, D.Phil (Oxon) is a Social Anthropologist, Director of Deia Archaeological Museum and Research Centre DAMARC), Research Associate at International Gender Studies (IGS) Queen Elizabeth House, Part-Time Lecturer at Oxford University, and Series Editor for *New Directions in Anthropology* with Berghahn Books.

INDEX

Note: Page numbers in bold type, e.g. **57–71**, indicate detailed discussion of the topic.

Abram, S., 87n1
activity
    aikido, 171–73, 175–77, 180, 185
    Canadian sport, 109, 123
    colonial societies, 5
    Cuban leisure, 129–33, 142
    ethnographic focus, 2
    foxhunting, 91–93, 96, 103–4, 107n17
    kayaking, 58, 60–61, 64, 66, 69–70
    muscular Christianity, 6, 41–43, 45, 47–48, 50
    philosophical views, 12, 17nn3–4
Adair, D., 113
Adorno, Theodor, 173
adventure, 3, 8, 58–59, 64, 66–70
    See also kayaking
adventure tourism, 8, **57–71**
aesthetics
    colonial societies, 166n20
    foxhunting, 95–96, 101
    muscular Christianity, 45, 50
    New Age, 181
    sport, 15
African Americans, 168n41
Afro-Cubans, 137–38
agency, **15–16**, 50, 97
aikido (Japanese martial art), 2, 5, 15–16, 33, 51n4, **171–86**
alcohol. *See* drinking alcohol
Algeria, colonial, 165n11
Alloula, Malek, 163, 165n11
Alter, J.F., 13, 15, 116
alternative therapies, 73, 79, 85–87, 87n1

Althusser, Louis, 11–12
Anderson, N., 172–73
Anderson, S., 113
Andrews, D.L., 113, 120
animals
    colonial displays, 160, 165n7, 168n38
    foxhunting, 4, 8, 14, 16, **91–107**, 171
Appadurai, Arjun, 13–14, 81, 179, 184
Archetti, E., 15, 50
Ardener, Shirley, 24
Aristotle, 17n3
Aronowitz, S., 173
arts, 2, 4, 10, 16, 74–85, 88n7
Asad, Talal, 163
asceticism, 13, 41, 51
Åsell, Kenneth, 50
Asian immigrants in Canada, 110, 112, 117–23
Asian martial arts. *See* martial arts
assimilation. *See* integration
athletes
    Canada, 109–10, 114, 117
    Cuba, 140, 142
    muscular Christianity, 41, 43–44, 47
Augé, M., 8
Australia
    aikido, 174
    expatriates in Mallorca, 78
    soccer in, 120

Baedeker travel guide: Egypt (1913), 167n28
Bairner, A., 113
Bale, J., 7–8, 12
Bammer, A., 33
Baptists, 42

baseball
  Canada, 120
  Cuba, 5, 8, 127–28, **139–43**
  muscular Christianity, 43–44
  United States, 5, 118, 140
basketball, 43, 117, 119–20
Bauman, Z., 58
Beaufort, Duke of, 106n13
Benítez-Rojo, A., 136
Billig, M., 12
bodies
  agents of temptation, 40, 42, 44, 47
  aikido, 171–73, 176–78, 181, 185n2
  civilisation of, 10
  colonized, 150, 152, 157–62, 164,
    167n15, 167n32
  Cuba, 137–19
  discipline, 3, 5, 16
  docile (*See* docile bodies)
  Foucault, 6–7, 9
  foxhunting, **91–107**
  functions, 46, 138
  healthy, 31, 40, 44, 46, 52n16, 114, 138
  immigrants, 4
  of Jesus, 41, 44–48, 52n15
  leisure and, 4
  Mallorca, 77
  muscular Christianity, 40–43, 45–47,
    49–51, 51n11, 52n16
  objectification of, 2, 78
  politics, 132
  Scottish hospital bodybuilder, 27, 29,
    30–32, 33–34
  sport, 2, 13, 114
  transformation, 2, 79
  wrestling, 15
  See also embodiment; identity; movement
body culture, 12–13
body-trading, 8
bodybuilding, 7, 12, 171
  muscular Christianity, 3, 42, 45–46, 50
  Scottish hospital porter, 2–3, 6, 16,
    23–37
Bogdan, R., 165n9
Botswana, 14
Bourdieu, Pierre, 13, 16, 58, 60–61, 69,
  87n4, 124, 131
Braswell, M., 41
Brazil, 11, 168n35

Breckenridge, C.A., 151
Britain. *See* United Kingdom
Brownell, S., 13, 132
Bunck, J.M., 133
Burawoy, M., 133–34
Butler, Brett, 44

Caillois, Roger, 92
Cairo colonial social life, 3, 5, 9, **149–70**
'Cairo Season', 155–57
Caldeira, T.P.R., 168n35
Calvinism, 41–42
Canada
  Minister's Task Force on Federal Sport
    Policy (1992), 109, 115
  sport and immigrant identities, 4–5,
    8–9, **109–25**
Canard, H., 59
capital, 60, 65, 67–68
  cultural, 16
  personal development, 24, 34
  specific, 61, 63, 69
  symbolic, 63, 67
capitalism
  Cuba and, **128–36**, 140–43
  leisure and, 5, 10–11, 172–73
  religion and, 40
  sport and, 11
  See also production
Caplan, P., 84
Carneval (Cuba), 132
Carrier, Roche, 111
Carter, Thomas F., 139, 142
  chapter by, 5, 8, 11, **127–45**
  note on, 187
Cartmill, Matt, 106n1, 107n18
Cashmore, E., 17n6
Castro, Fidel, 132, 137, 140
Catholics, 7, 41, 50
Celsi, R.L., 60, 63–64
ceremonial. *See* ritual
Chalip, L., 60
challenge
  Canadian sport, 114
  foxhunting, 4, 91–95, 98–100, 102–3,
    105
  kayaking, 58–59, 61–62, 64–66, 68, 70
  muscular Christianity, 43, 51
  Scottish hospital bodybuilder, 3, 7

Chapman, K., 174
charismatic Christians, 7, 41, 44, 47–51
Chaucer, Geoffrey, 106n11
Chennells, E., 167n25
Chiba, T.K., 174, 177, 182–84
children
  recreation, 11
  sport, 117–18, 120, 123
Chile, 67
Chinese
  Canadian immigrants, 121–23
  Mallorca expatriates, 78, 86, 87n6
  sport, 13, 132
  values, 85, 87n6
choice. *See* optionality
choreography, 5, 10
Christian Science, 43
Christianity
  Catholics, 7, 41, 50
  globalisation, 12
  leisure and, 41–42
  muscular, 3, 6, 14, **39–53**
  Scottish hospital bodybuilder, 34
  sporting metaphors, 3, 11, 41, 43–44,
    46–47, 49–50, 51n10
Christmas, 132
Clark, P., 153, 166n15, 166n21, 167n22
Clarke, J., 11, 13, 130, 172
class
  aikido practice, 181
  colonial societies, 153, 165n3, 166n18
  Cuba, 138, 141
  kayaking, 60, 68
  leisure, 10–11, 180, 184
  muscular Christianity, 42, 46
  Scottish hospital bodybuilder, 26
  sport and, 10, 13, 17n8
clubs, colonial, 154–55, 162,
  166nn15–19, 167n24
Cohen, A.P., 119
Cohn, B., 151–52
Cold War, 129, 139, 143
  See also socialism
Coleman, Simon, 27, 34, 43, 45–46,
  52n12, 85
  chapter by, 3, 6–7, 12, 14, **39–53**
  introduction by, 1–19
  note on, 187

Coles Pasha, C., 160–61, 163, 165n5,
  167n24, 167n30, 168n39
colonial clubs, 154–55, 162, 166nn15–19,
  167n24
colonial society, 5, **149–70**
colonial spectacles & exhibitions, 151–53,
  160–63, 165n4, 165nn6–9
colonial subjectivities, 150, **151–55**,
  157–58, 163–65, 167n32
colonialism
  British, 51n6
  British in Egypt, 9, **149–70**
  British in India, 13–14, 152–54, 158,
    161, 163–64, 165n7, 166n12,
    166nn15–17, 166n19, 166n22
  Cuba, 129, 135–36, 138, **139–40**, 143
  sport and, 12, 16, 113, 119
colonized bodies, 150, 152, 157–62, 164,
  167n25, 167n32
Colvin, Sir Auckland, 163
Comaroff, Jean, 14, 165, 166n13
Comaroff, John, 165, 166n13
commitment
  aikido practice, 172, 180, 182–84
  Cuba, 133, 140
  kayaking, 60, 63, 67
commodification (Cuba), 130, 138, 140,
  143
communicative events, 24
communism. *See* socialism
communitas, 81, 85, 87n3, 88n8, 184
consciousness
  aikido, 175–76, 180–81
  Canadian sport, 117
  Cuba, 133
consumption
  aikido, 181, 184
  conspicuous, 5, 10, 132
  Cuba, 129, **131–39**, 141–43
  leisure as site of, 2, 172
  Mallorca, 74, 80, 86
contact
  aikido, 175–76, 179
  Cuba, 137
  foxhunting, 98, 100, 103
  Mallorca, 79
  sport, 48
control, 2, 8

adventure tourism, 67–66
colonial societies, 150, 155, **157–64**,
    165n3, 165n11, 168n36
Cuba, 130, 133–34
extreme sports, 17n4
foxhunting, 94–95, 97–99, 104
leisure practices, 173
Scottish hospital bodybuilder, 28, 33
self-control, 2, 40, 68, 104, 139
sports, 11–13, 114
Corbey, Raymond, 151–52, 165n6,
    165nn89
Corrigan, P., 131
corruption (Cuba), 142
Costa Rica, 65
countryside. *See* landscape
Cox, R., 184
Crick, M., 136
cricket, 10–11, 13–14, 17n7, 52n14, 156
Critcher, C., 11, 13, 130, 172
Cromer, Lord, 161, 163
Cronje, Hansie, 52n14
Csordas, Thomas, 6–7, 50
Cuba, 5, 8, **127–45**
Cubanness, 138, 142
cultural capital, 16
cultural intimacy, 74, 110, 128, 135
Cummins, J., 106n11
Cunningham, A., 168n38
curling, 121–22

danger
    aikido practice, 183
    colonial societies, 150
    extreme sports, 17n4, 173
    foxhunting, 99, 103
    kayaking, 8, 15, 58, 63–66, 68–70
Dann, G., 62
Davis, W., 185n2
Dawson, A., 33, 35
Debord, G., 128
Deia. *See* Mallorca
Descartes, R., 77, 181
deterritorialisation, 7, 178–79
dinner parties. *See* social life
discipline, **9–17**
    adventure tourism, 4
    aikido practice, 5, 171–73, 180, 185n2,
        185n5

body, 3, 5, 16
Catholic charismatics, 6–7
colonial societies, 14, **149–70**
Cuba, 128, 130, 142–43
Foucault, 9
foxhunting, 4, 7, **94–101**
kayaking, **64–67**
of leisure, 9, 15–16, 73
Mallorca, 77
muscular Christianity, 40–41, 44
political & cultural dislocation, 9
Scottish hospital bodybuilder, 35
sport, 2, 12, 14, 109, 114–15
work & leisure, 6
discourse, 6, 12, 34
    change through martial arts practice,
        171–86
displays. *See* colonial spectacles &
    exhibitions; performance
docile bodies
    colonial societies, 150, 153, 166n11
    foxhunting, 94, 97, 99
Dodds, Gil, 43
domestication
    animals, 94, 99
    class and, 46
    games, 10
domesticity, 165
Donnelly, P., 60, 63
Donohue, J.J., 174
Douglas, M., 35
drinking alcohol
    pub, as refuge, 2, 6, **177–79**, 180–81, 183
    Scottish hospital bodybuilder, 26–28,
        32, 34–35
    students, 39
drugs, 28–32
Dumazedier, J., 10, 172
Dunning, E., 10, 15, 17n6
Dyck, Noel, 11, 15, 50, 114, 118, 185n5
    chapter by, 4–5, 8–9, 11, **109–25**
    note on, 187

Eastern Europe, 129, 131, 140
Eco, U., 128
Eddy, Mary Baker, 43
Egypt. *See* Cairo
Egyptian Gazette (newspaper), 155–56,
    158–59, 161, 167n24, 168n37, 168n42

Egyptians, in colonial Cairo, 9, 149–50, 157–58, 167n25

Eisen, G., 113

Ekman, Ulf, 47, 52n19

Elias, N., 10, 17n6

Ellison, Ralph: *The Invisible Man,* 168n41

Elsner, John, 34

embodiment, 6–7
  Canadian sport, 110
  of discipline, 5
  foxhunting, 95–96, 105
  muscular Christianity, 6
  Scottish hospital bodybuilder, 33
  sport, 15

emotion, 15, 17n7, 141–43

enactment, 2
  aikido, 180
  colonialism, 152, 154, 158, 161–62
  Cuba, 137–38, 142
  foxhunting, 4, 102, 105

England
  alienation from, 32
  foxhunting, 4, 7, **91–107**
  muscular Christianity, 42
  sportsmanship, 13–14
  See also United Kingdom

English language, in Mallorca, 79, 82

Englishness, 4, 8, 32, 99

entertainment, in colonial Cairo, **149–70**

ethnicity
  aikido, 177
  Cuba, 128–29, 137–38
  sport and, 113, 119, 121, 124
  See also immigration

etiquette, 2
  aikido, 174–77
  foxhunting, 7–8, 93, 103, 106n7
  sport, 12

Europe
  aikido, 174, 177, 184
  body culture, 12
  leisure, 184
  sex tourism, 138
  trade, 136

European imperialism. *See* colonialism

European models, in colonial societies, 149, 151, 154–55, 158–60, 162, 164, 166n18, 168n39, 168n42

evangelicalism. *See* muscular Christianity

Ewert, A.W., 60

excitement
  Cuban baseball, 139
  foxhunting, 93, 95–96, 100, 103–4
  kayaking, 58, 68–70
  quest for, 10

exhibitions. *See* colonial spectacles & exhibitions

expatriates
  Mallorca, 4, **73–87**
  See also colonial society

experience
  adventure tourism, 15, **57–71**
  aikido practice, 171–73, 176, 181
  Canadian sport, 114, 119–21
  Cuba, 128–29
  Mallorca expatriates, 4, **73–88**
  stories, 66, **67–69**, 70

extreme sports. *See* danger

'fair play,' 40

Faith Movement ('Health and Wealth' ideologies), 3, 43, **44–51**, 52n20

Fanon, F., 135

fans. *See* sport spectatorship

Farag, M., 167n29

'feel for the game.' *See* habitus

Fees, C., 78

feminism. *See* gender

Fernández, N., 138

'field'
  immigration & sport, 110, 113, 118
  kayaking, 58–64, 66–70
  play, 17
  sporting practices, 13

Finnish ice hockey players in Canada, 112

Fissell, M., 106n11

Fleming, S., 113

football, American, 41, 43

football, Canadian, 110, 114, 117, 120, 123

football (soccer), 10, 13, 16, 17n7, 34–35, 118, 120–21

foreignness (aikido), 175, 178

Forster, E.M.: *A Passage to India,* 154, 162, 166n14

Forstorp, P.A., 47

Foster, G.M., 62
Foucault, Michel, 6–7, 9, 12, 14, 33, 44, 97, 161
fox-hunting, 4, 8, 14, 16, **91–107**, 171
fox-killing, 92, 94–95, 101, 103, 106n5, 106n12
France, aikido in, 171, 174–77
freedom
    adventure tourism, 59
    aikido practice, 171–73, 183–84
    Cuba, 130–33
    foxhunting, 98, 100, 103–4
    leisure, 10–11
    Mallorca, 76–77
    sport, 2, 14
    tourism, 4, 11
    See also optionality
French Canadians, 111
Frykman, J., 46
Fulder, S., 85, 87n1
Fullerton, W.M.M., 155, 166n20

games, 92, 128
    See also play; sport
gaze, 8, 11, 13, 127, 155, 165n9
gender
    colonial societies, 154–55, 162, 166n14, 166n17, 166n19
    Cuba, 138
    muscular Christianity, 40, 42, 44–45, 51n2, 51n8
    Scottish hospital bodybuilder, 26, 35
    sport, 12, 14
Gendlin, Eugene, 180–81
Germans
    aikido, 176–77
    colonial Cairo, 149–50, 164
    Mallorca, 78, 82
Giza Zoo, Cairo, 160–62, 168n38
globalisation
    aikido, 5, 7, 171–79, 182, 185
    Canadian sport, 115
    Christianity, 12
    colonial societies, 163
    kayaking, 59, 64
    Mallorca, 81–83, 85
    sport, 8, 16
    See also transnational identities

Goffman, Erving, 32–33
Graham, Billy, 43
Gramsci, A., 17n8
Graves, Robert, 74–77
Green, D.C., 60
Griffith, R., 42–44, 51n11
Grossberg, L., 141
Guevara, E., 129
Guyana, 11
gym. *See* bodybuilding; Young Men's Christian Association (YMCA)

habitus ('feel for the game')
    aikido, 181
    Bourdieu, 13, 58, 60–61, 69, 87n4
    kayaking, 58–61, 63, 66–67, 69
    sport, 13–14
Hargreaves, J., 11–13, 17n8
Harré, Rom, 6, 35
health, 43, 48, 52n16
'Health and Wealth' ideologies (Faith Movement), 3, 43, **44–51**, 52n20
Heidegger, Martin, 87n4
Hemingway, Ernest, 136
Hendry, J., 176
Herzog: *Aguirre,* 85
Hewison, D., 74
hexis, 14
hierarchy
    aikido, 176
    colonial societies, 156, 158
    Cuba, 138
    foxhunting, 97
    hospital, 24, 35
Higgs, R., 41
Hobsbawm, E.J., 10
Hodgkinson, Tom, 1
horse riding (fox-hunting), 4, 8, 14, 16, **91–107**, 171
hospital bodybuilder, 3, 6–7, **23–37**
hounds (fox-hunting), 4, 8, 14, 16, **91–107**, 171
Hufford, M., 106n11
Hughes, Thomas, 40, 51n2
Hull, Catherine, 166n17
Hunt countries, 7, 101–2, 107n17
hunting, 11, 91, 104–5, 120–21
    as sport (fox-hunting), 4, 8, 14, 16, **91–107**, 171

ice hockey, 111–13, 116–18, 121
identity
    aikido practice, 171–72, 179
    Canadian, **109–25**
    colonial societies, 150
    Cuba, **127–45**
    cultural, 78
    enacting & contesting, 2
    formation, 2, 60, 62–63, 69
    foxhunting, 92, 105
    immigrant, 4
    national, 4
    personal, 15, 48, 50, 77, 86
    Scottish hospital bodybuilder, 27, 33–35
    social, **75–77**
    transnational (*See* transnational identities)
    work and, 2
ideologies, 1–5, 11–14, 77
    Canada, 109, 123
    Cuba, 129–32, 136–37, 140, 142
    muscular Christianity, 40, 45–46
The Idler, 1
Igali, Daniel, 123
immigration, 16, 177
    Canada, 4, 8–9, **109–25**
    colonial societies, 158
    United States, 42
imperialism. *See* colonialism
India
    British rule, 13–14, 152–54, 158, 161,
        163–64, 165n7, 166n12, 166n19,
        166nn15–17, 167n22
    cricket, 13–14
    kabaddi (game), 116–18, 123
    kayaking, 58
    martial art *(kalarippayatu)*, 5, 7, 14
    wrestling, 13
Indians
    colonial Cairo, 157, 164
    immigrants in Canada, 115–20, 122–23
individuals
    aikido, 171–73, 179–80, 184–85
    Canadian sport, 110, 113, 115, 119, 123
    colonial societies, 9, 151–52
    Cuba, 128, 130–31, 133, 135–36,
        139–42
    foxhunting, 98–99, 104
    kayaking, 60, 63–64

leisure as possessive of agency, 15–16
    leisure as release, 11–14
    Mallorca, 76, 78, 80, 82, 86
Industrial Revolution, 172
institutions, 6–7, 16
    British leisure, 11
    colonial societies, 161, 168n39
    foxhunting, 97
    Scottish hospital bodybuilder, 24, 30–34
instrumentality, 2, **115–19**
integration
    Canada, 4, 109–11, 115, 122
    civic, 110, 115
    colonial societies, 150
    cultural, 109–11, 113
    social, 8–9, 109, 113
integrity, 3, 24, 33–34
interactions
    aikido, 175, 178, 180
    Canadian sport, 115
    colonial societies, 5
    Cuba, 128, 130, 141
    foxhunting, 92, 105
    kayaking, 60–62
    Mallorca, 81
    muscular Christianity, 7
    Scottish hospital bodybuilder, 25, 36n1
    See also work and leisure
Iranian immigrants in Canada, 121–22
irony
    academic studies, 16, 119
    colonial societies, 153
    Cuba, 135, 137, 140
    Scottish hospital bodybuilder, 6, **32–34**

Jackson, M., 15
James, A., 114
Japan
    leisure, 184
    martial art (aikido), 2, 5, 15–16, 33,
        51n4, **171–86**
    objectification of U.S. through baseball, 5
Japaneseness, 174–77, 184, 185n4
Jatar-Hausmann, A.J., 134
Jenson, J., 141
Jesus, 41, 44–48, 52n15
Jewish immigrants, in United States, 118
jineterismo, 129, **135–39**

Jirousek, L., 165n9
John Paul II (Pope), 132

kabaddi (Indian game), 116–18, 123
kalarippayatu (Indian martial art), 5, 7, 14
Kanai, Mitsunari, 174
Kane, Maurice J., 58
  chapter by, 3, 8, 15–16, **57–71**, 143n1
  note on, 187
Kaufmann, A., 166n20
Kay, J., 60, 63–64
kayaking, 3–4, 8, 15–16, **57–71**
Kelly, R.T., 166n20
killing foxes, 92, 94–95, 101, 103, 106n5,
  106n12
Kingsley, Charles, 40, 51n2
Klarwein, Mati, 85
Knight, John, 106n1
Kohn, Tamara, 24, 174, 177, 180, 185n5
  chapter by, 2, 5–7, 15–16, 33, 51n4,
    171–86
  introduction by, **1–19**
  note on, 187
Krizek, B., 141
Kuppinger, Petra, 158, 160, 162
  chapter by, 3, 5, 9, 12, 14, 129, **149–70**
  note on, 188
Kurita, Yutaka, 174
Kutzinski, V., 138

La Cerva, V., 180
Laberge, S., 60, 63–64
labour. *See* work
Ladd, T., 10, 43–44, 51n2
Lamplough, A.O., 167n24
landscape
  Bale, 7–8
  foxhunting, 4, 7, **91–107**
  idyllic ('Paradise'), 4, 16, 73–74, 78,
    79–85, 86, 88n7
  Mallorca, 4, **73–86**, 88n7
Larkin, Philip, 32
Lefebvre, H., 140
Leigh, T.W., 60, 63–64
leisure
  agency, **15–16**, 50, 97
  discipline of, 9, 15–16, 73
  ethnographic research, 1–3, 9, 15,
    16–17, 173

  genres of, 10
  as release, 9, **10–14**
  serious (*See* serious leisure)
  work and (*See* work and leisure)
leisure class, 10, 180, 184
leisure from leisure, 6, 183–84
Lewis, Gilbert, 106n10
Lewis, Sinclair: *Elmer Gantry*, 51n10
life-project, 27
Lindquist, G., 2, 17n3
linguistic habits. *See* metaphors; rhetoric
Lithman, Y., 11–12
locality
  aikido practice, 171–72, 174, 176,
    178–79, 185
  colonial subjectivities, 164
  leisure and, 2, 7
  Mallorca, 77–79
  work and, 2
Löfgren, O., 11, 46, 75
Lukács, J., 133–34
Lutz, C., 142
Lyng, S., 17n4, 173

McBurney, Robert J., 42
McCauley, Ray, 45, 52n14
MacClancy, J., 16, 113
McGinn, B., 12
MacLeod, D., 87n1
Mallorca, 4–5, 7, 16, **73–88**
Mangan, J.A., 10, 40, 113
Mansfield, A., 12
mapping (foxhunting), 7, 101–2, 107n17
Markus, T., 11
martial arts, 114, 117, 174
  See also aikido; *kalarippayatu*
Martínez-Alier, V., 138
Marvin, Garry, 106n12, 107n16
  chapter by, 4, 6–7, 14–16, **91–107**
  note on, 188
Marxism, 12, 131–32
masculinity. *See* gender
mat. *See* aikido (Japanese martial art)
materialism
  Cuba, 129
  Mallorca, 78, 82, 86
Mathison, J., 10, 43–44, 51n2
Mathur, S., 151, 158, 161, 165n10

memory
    aikido, 176, 181
    Cuba, 137
    kayaking, 62, 64, 69
    Mallorca, 77
    muscular Christianity, 48
    See also nostalgia
Mena House Hotel, Cairo, 158
Mentore, G., 11
Messenger, T., 51n7
metaphors, sporting, 3, 11, 41, 43–44,
    46–47, 49–50, 51n10
Methodism, 42, 51n7
migration. *See* immigration
Miller, D., 87–79
Mintz, S., 136
Mitchell, Timothy, 151, 163, 165n4,
    167n31
Mitra, D.K., 151, 165n7
modernity
    aikido practice, 181, 184
    colonial societies, 150
    Cuba, 5, **130–31**, 132, 136, 139
    evangelicalism, 40
    foxhunting, 4
    leisure, 3, 7, 10–11, 46
    Mallorca, 78, 82
    sport, 2, 7–8, 12–13, 16, 40
    Weber, 17n5
Moody, Dwight, 43
Moore, P., 120
Moore, R., 42
morality
    colonial societies, 159
    cricket, 14
    Cuba, 128–29, 135, 139, 141–43
    leisure, 173
    muscular Christianity, 3, 42, 51n2
    Scottish hospital bodybuilder, 27
movement
    aikido, 171, 175, 180, 185
    colonial societies, 162
    Mallorca, 77
muscular Christianity, 3, 6, 14, **39–53**
myths
    Cuba, 140
    Mallorca, 74, 76–77, 79–80, 84

nation building, 10, 119
    See also state
nationalism
    colonial societies, 150, 153, 161, 165n10
    sport and, 12, 14, 113, 115, 119, 142
nationality
    aikido, 174, 184
    Canada, 4, **109–25**
    colonial societies, 164
    Cubanness, 138, 142
    Englishness, 4, 8, 32, 99
    Japaneseness, 174–77, 184, 185n4
Negro, Del, 85
Nelson, Nina, 149, 155, 157, 167n26,
    167n31, 168n33
neocolonialism. *See* colonialism
Nepal, 67
New Age, 181
    See also alternative therapies
'New Man' (Cuba), 129, **130–31**, 133
New Thought Movement, 43–44, 51n11
New Zealand, adventure tourism in, 3–4,
    57–71
Nietzsche, Friedrich, 17n3
Nigerian immigrants in Canada, 123
non-places, 8
non-Western contexts, 9
North Americans, 3, 136, 138, 174
    See also Canada; United States
nostalgia, 129, 136–38, **139–40**, 142
    See also memory
Nubians, in colonial Cairo, 149, 157, 164

Olympic Games
    ice hockey, 111–13
    kayaking, 59, 62
    wrestling, 123
optionality
    aikido, 172–73, 179
    choice, 2, 15, 119
    leisure, 73, 130
    obligation and, 6, 10
    sport, 12, 17n4, 110, 119
    See also freedom
Orientalism, 14, 158, 163, 166n11,
    166n20, 167n31, 174
Other
    aikido practice, 179

colonial societies, 12, 152
Cuba, 137–38, 143
Scottish hospital bodybuilder, 27
Owen, R., 156

Panckridge, H.R., 154, 166n16
Paradise. *See* landscape, idyllic
participation in sport, 11, 13, 110, 118,
    123
A Passage To India (E.M. Forster), 154,
    162, 166n14
Passeron, J., 124
patriotism, 3, 40, 51n2
Pearce, P.L., 62
Pearson, R., 166n12, 166n15
Pentecostal Christianity, 44
Pérez, L., 137
Pérez-López, J.F., 134
performance, 7, 10
    Canadian immigrants, 116
    colonial societies, 150–53, 156–58,
        160–63, 165, 168nn40–41
    Cuba, 128, 137
    foxhunting, 95, **101–5**
    Mallorca, 81
    See also spectacle
personal development, 3, 5
Peters, P., 134
Prieto González, A., 137
place
    aikido practice, 5, 174, 181, 184
    Mallorca expatriates, 4, **74**, 78, 84
    See also globalisation; space
placelessness, 8
Plato, 17n3, 51n5
play
    adventure tourism, 4, 59
    aikido, 182, 184
    Canada, 4, 8, **109–25**
    foxhunting, 7
    Indian cricket, 14
    muscular Christianity, 40–42
    philosophical views, 17n3
    See also sport
playing for real, 1–2
pleasure, 1, 11, 17n4, 110, 130
politics
    Canada, 9, 114

China, 13
colonial societies, 9, 150, 157–58, 163,
    168n36, 168n39–41
Cuba, 132–34, 143
foxhunting, 7
leisure practice, 15, 172
Mallorca, 76, 84
muscular Christianity, 41, 46
sports and, 16, 119
porters, hospital, 3, 6–7, **23–37**
positive thinking
Powell, Eve, 157–58
practices, 1–4, 9, 12–15, 17n4, 17n8, 60
    aikido, 2, 5, 15–16, 33, 51n4, **171–86**
    baseball, 5
    Canadian sport, 109, 114, 120, 123
    colonial & Orientalist, 151, 163–64
    Cuban leisure, 128, 130–31, 133, 138,
        142
    fox-killing & fox-hunting, 91–92, 94,
        97, 103, 105, 106n5, 106n8
    kayaking, 8, 58, 60–61, 63, **64–67**
    Mallorca, 4, 73, 77–79, 85–86
    muscular Christianity, 40–41, 45–51
    Scottish hospital bodybuilder, 24, 27,
        34–35
pre-Socratic philosophy, 17n3
Prieto González, A., 137
Prince, R., 87n3
prisoners, 6, 32, 34, 153, 159–62, 165n5,
    165n10, 167n30
production
    aikido practice, 172–73, 181, 184–85
    colonial, 153
    Cuba, 5, 130, **131–35**, 136
    leisure as site of, 2
    Mallorca, 74, 80
Protestant Ethic, 40, 51n1
Protestantism, 3, **39–53**
    See also muscular Christianity
pub, as refuge, 2, 6, **177–79**, 180–81, 183
Putney, T., 42, 51n5

Quimby, Phineas P., 43, 46

Ranger, T., 151
Rapport, Nigel, 32–35
    chapter by, 2–3, 6–7, 12, 16, **23–37**, 185

note on, 188
rebellion. *See* revolution
recreation
  children's, 11
  Christianity and, 41, 44
  colonial societies, 157
  rational, 10
  Scottish hospital bodybuilder, 32
  of the self, 2
  See also tourism
Reiss, B., 165n9
relationships
  aikido practice, 180, 185
  Canadian sport, 109, 119
  colonial societies, 164
  Cuba, 141
  foxhunting, 92, 96–99, 101, 103–4
  muscular Christianity, 45
  Scottish hospital bodybuilder, **30–32**
release, leisure as, 9, **10–14**
religion, 10–12
  Mallorca, 76
  See also Catholics; muscular Christianity
revolution
  colonial societies, 164, 166n12, 168n36
  Cuba, 129, 132–33, 137, 140
rhetoric
  Canadian sport, 114, 116, 122, 124
  Cuba, 129
  muscular Christianity, 41, 43, 49–50
  See also metaphors
Rhodes, Arthur, 88n7
Riches, D., 87n3
Riding, Laura, 75
riding (foxhunting), 4, 8, 14, 16, **91–107**,
  171
Rising, Brad, 76
risk. *See* danger
ritual
  aikido, 174, **175–77**, 180, 184–85
  Catholic charismatics, 7
  colonial societies, 162, 165, 165n5
  foxhunting, 4, 93, 106n10
  muscular Christianity, 50, 67
Roberts, Robert, 42
Rojek, Chris, 7, 10, 15, 129–30, 172
romanticism, 129
Rosaldo, R., 136

Rose, L.R., 60, 63–64
Rozek 1989, 172
rugby, 39–41
Rumar, Svante, 49
Rusinol, S., 73, 87n5
Rwanda, 12
Ryan, C., 62

Sabater, Gaspar, 74, 80
Sage, G., 132
Sahlins, M., 136
Said, E., 163
Sanders, Deion, 41
Sandiford, K.A., 11, 17n7, 40, 51n3, 51n8
Sayer, D., 131
Scarpaci, J., 134
Schmidt, C.J., 58, 62
Schopenhauer, 17n3
Schwartz, R., 137
Scott, J.C., 168n36
Scottish hospital bodybuilder, 3, 6–7,
  23–37
self
  aikido practice, 171, 174, 179, 181–82,
    184–85
  Cuba, 135, **141–43**
  muscular Christianity, 39–42, 46, 50
  remaking, 2
  Scottish hospital bodybuilder, 27, 33
self-control, 2, 40, 68, 104, 139
self-determination, 17n4, 172
self-direction, 114
self-discipline, 14, 73, 78, 104, 110, 157
self-help, 46
self-identity. *See* identity
self-improvement, 42, 73, 79
self-mastery, 17n5, 44
self-objectification, 7, 12
self-realisation, 3, 77
self-revelation, **75–77**
self-surveillance, 3, 11–12, 41
self-understanding, 6, 47
Selwyn, T., 62, 80
serious leisure
  Cuba, 130
  kayaking, 3, 58–59, **60–61**, 62, 67, 69
serious study of leisure, 15–16

servants & waiters, 149–50, 154, **156–60**,
     162, 164, 165n3, 166n17, 167nn28–31,
     168n33
sexuality
     colonial societies, 154–55, 162, 166n11
     Cuba, 8, 127, 129, 135, 137–39, 143
     Mallorca expatriates, 4, 76, 84, 88n8
Sharpe, J., 166n14
Shepheard's Hotel, Cairo, 149, 155–57,
     164, 167n26, 167n31
Sheppard, P., 77
Shields, Rob, 159
Shilling, C., 8
Shinto, 173
Sikh immigrants in Canada, 116–18
Simmel, Georg, 10
Sinha, Mrinalini, 154–55, 166n17
skill
     aikido, 15, 173
     colonial Cairo, 149
     extreme sports, 17n4
     foxhunting, 100–101
     kayaking, 58, 60–61, 63–70
Sladen, D., 155, 167n25–167n27
soccer (football), 10, 13, 16, 17n7, 34–35,
     118, 120–21
social Darwinism, 51n3
social life, in colonial Cairo, **149–70**
socialism
     China, 13
     Christian, 40
     Cuba, 5, 128–29, **130–35**, 136–38,
          142–43
     Eastern Europe, 129, 131, 140
     See also Cold War
Solberg, Erika, 168n41
South Africa, 14, 45, 52n14, 165n7
Soviet bloc, 129, 131, 140
Soviet Union, 111
space
     aikido practice, 171–72, 177, 179–85
     Cuba, 5, 129
     foxhunting, 103
     leisure and, 3
     Mallorca, 7, 76–78, 84
     work and, 2
     See also place

spectacle
     colonial, 151–53, 160–63, 165n4,
          165nn6–9
     Cuba, 128
     foxhunting, 101
     See also performance; sport spectatorship
Spencer, Herbert, 40, 51n3
sport, 10–14
     amateur, 13, 115
     Bale, 7
     Canada, 4, 9, **109–25**
     children's, 117–18, 120, 123
     colonial Cairo, 149, 167n24
     Cuba, 132–33, 140
     ethnographic focus, 2–3, 5, 13–16, 40,
          115, 117–18
     foxhunting as, 7, 91–94, 99, **101–5**,
          106n4, 107n18
     Mallorca, 79
     muscular Christianity, 6, **39–51**, 51n10,
          52n14
     participation, 11, 13, 110, 118, 123
     professional, 13, 120
     rules, 8, 12, 17n6, 91–93, 101, 103
     spectators (See sport spectatorship)
     state and, 4–5, 110–12, 114–15
     United Kingdom, 10–11, 51n8
     work and, 117, 120, 171
     See also baseball; basketball; cricket;
          curling; football; ice hockey;
          kayaking; rugby; soccer; tennis;
          volleyball; wrestling
sport spectatorship, 11, 13, 171
     Cuba, 5, 8, 127, 132, **141–43**
     India, 14
     muscular Christianity, 42
     United States & Canada, 120
sportization, 17n6
Springwood, C., 5
Stål, Rolf, 47–48
state
     Canadian sport and, 110–12, 114–15
     Cuban leisure and, **128–39**, 142–43
     leisure and, 4, 10–13, 46
     sport and, 4–5, 11
Stebbins, R.A., 60, 62
stereotyping
     colonial societies, 51n6, 164

Cuba, 137–38
Scottish hospital bodybuilder, 35
steroids, 28–32
Stoler, A.L., 138
stories of experience, 66, **67–69**, 70
style
aikido, 175
colonial Cairo, 155–57
foxhunting, 99
sub-culture, 60
Sudanese, in colonial Cairo, 149, 157–58, 164
Sugano, Seiichi, 174
Sunday, Billy, 43
The Sweater (film), 111
Sweden
leisure, 11
muscular Christianity, 3, 40, 42n19, **45–51**, 51n9, 52n17
Swedenborgianism, 43, 51n9
symbolic capital, 63, 67

Taiwan, curling in, 122
Tamura, Nobuyoshi, 174
team games. *See* sport
teams
Canadian sports, 109, 111–12, 116, 118–19, 121–22
Cuba, 127–28, 140, 142
television
Mallorca, 77
spectator sport, 8, 116, 120, 141
tennis, 8
Terry, P., 106n11
Thackeray, Lance, 157, 164
theatre, 10, 48, 171
Thompson, E., 130
thrill. *See* excitement
time
aikido practice, 171–73, 177, 181–84
Cuba, 5, **131–35**, 143n1
foxhunting, 103
leisure and, 2–3
Mallorca expatriates, 4, 7, **74**, 76–78, 84
muscular Christianity, 40
work and, 2–3
Tohei, Akira, 174
Tolen, R., 160

Tom Brown's Schooldays (Thomas Hughes), 40, 51n2
Tomas, T., 77
tourism
adventure, 8, **57–71**
colonial Cairo, 155–56, 167n25
Cuba, 5, **127–45**
industry, 11
Mallorca, 4, 73–75, 78, 81–82, 85, 87n1
package (guided), 3–4, 65–67, 69–70
tradition, 2
aikido, 174–78
Canada, 111
Cuba, 136, 138
Mallorca, 4, 78–79, 81, 83–84, 86–87
training
aikido, 6, 171, 173–79, 182–83, 185n2
foxhunting, 97, 99
leisure and, 10
Scottish hospital bodybuilder, 28, 31
sport, 14, 114
See also bodybuilding
transnational identities
aikido, 5–7, 177, 185
Canadian sport, 124
colonial Cairo, 5
Mallorca, 4, 74, 79
muscular Christianity, 6, 44, 48
See also globalisation
Trotter, David, 151, 165n7
Trujillo, N., 141
Tshidi people, 14
Tucker, Hazel
chapter by, 3, 8, 15–16, **57–71**, 143n1
note on, 188
Turner, Terence, 6
Turner, Victor, 10, 51n1, 73, 81, 84, 87n3, 88n8, 172–73

Ueshiba, K., 173
Ueshiba, Morihei (O-Sensei), 173, 175–77
United Kingdom
aikido practice, 171, 174–77, 179, 182–83
aristocrats, 51n6
colonial Cairo, 149–50, 160–61, 163–64, 166n20, 167n24, 167n30, 168n39

expatriates in Mallorca, 78, 82–83, 88n7
Indian Empire, 13–14, 152–54, 158,
    161, 164, 166n12, 166n19,
    166nn15–17, 167n22
leisure practices, 1, 11, 13
muscular Christianity, 3, 39–42
Scottish hospital bodybuilder, 3, 6–7,
    23–37
sports, 10–11, 51n8
tennis, 8
See also England
United States
    aikido, 171, 174–75, 177, 180–84
    Canadian diplomat in, 112
    Catholic charismatics, 7
    colonial Cairo, 155
    expatriates in Mallorca, 75, 78, 85
    Japanese objectification through baseball,
        5
    Jewish immigrants, 118
    kayakers, **57–71**
    muscular Christianity, 3, 40–46, 50,
        51n7, 51n11
    soccer in, 120–21
    sport, 132
    tourists in Cuba, 127–30, 135–41, 143
    'Wild West' shows, 165n7
Urry, J., 129, 184

van der Veer, P., 12
Van Gennep, A., 177
Veblen, Thorstein, 10, 131, 180, 184
Verdery, Katherine, 129, 131, 133
Victorian attitudes, 45, 152
Victorian capitalism, 11
Victorian cricket, 11, 14, 17n7
Victorian nation state, 10
Villaverde, C., 138
volleyball, 43
voluntary character. *See* optionality

waiters. *See* servants & waiters
Waiwai people, 11
Waldren, Jacqueline, 81, 87n1
    chapter by, 4–5, 7, 15, **73–88**, 143n
    note on, 188
Waldren, W., 75

Walter, R., 77
Waugh, Thomas, 11, 17n7
Weber, Max, 17n5, 40
weightlifting. *See* bodybuilding
Werbner, P., 113
Western capitalism. *See* capitalism
Western practitioners of aikido, 171, 173
Western values & attitudes, 9–11, 40, 78,
    80, 86, 109, 136, 154, 173, 184
Wheaton, B., 60, 63
White, Hayden V., 34
White, P., 137
Wiggins, D.K., 113
Willis, P.E., 124
Wimbledon Tennis Club, 8
Wolf, Eric, 133
Word of Life ('Health and Wealth'
    congregations), 3, 43, **44–51**, 52n20
work and leisure, 1–3, 5–7, 9–12, 16
    aikido practice, 171–73, 175–77, 179–85
    colonial societies, 149–50, 156, **157–62**,
        163–64, 166n17, 167n22
    Cuba, 130–33, 138, 142
    fox-killing & fox-hunting, 92, 95, 99, 102
    kayaking, 63
    Mallorca, 79, 81, 84
    muscular Christianity, 40–41, 51n1
    Scottish hospital bodybuilder, 24–25,
        28, 31–35
    sport, 117, 120, 171
Workers' Educational Associations, 13
Working Men's Clubs, 13
World War II, 75–76
wrestling, 13, 15, 123
Wright, A., 166n20

Yamada, Yoshimitsu, 174
Yampolsky, M., 131
Young, K., 60, 63
Young Men's Christian Association
    (YMCA), 42–43

Zarrilli, P., 5, 7, 14
Zen Buddhism, 173, 185n2

Date Due

AUG 2 7 2008		
OCT 0 6 2008		